REVELATION
for
EVERYONE

NEW TESTAMENT FOR EVERYONE

N. T. Wright

REVELATION
for
EVERYONE

N. T.
WRIGHT

WJK WESTMINSTER
JOHN KNOX PRESS
LOUISVILLE · KENTUCKY

© 2011 Nicholas Thomas Wright

First published in 2011 in Great Britain by the
Society for Promoting Christian Knowledge
36 Causton Street
London SW1P 4ST
www.spckpublishing.co.uk

and in the United States of America by
Westminster John Knox Press,
100 Witherspoon Street
Louisville, KY 40202

13 14 15 16 17 18 19 20—10 9 8 7 6 5 4 3 2

Map by Pantek Arts Ltd, Maidstone, Kent, UK
Typeset by Graphicraft Ltd, Hong Kong
Cover design by Lisa Buckley
Cover art: © istockphoto.com

British Library Cataloguing-in-Publication Data
A catalogue record for this book is available from the British Library.

ISBN: 978-0-281-06463-2 (U.K. edition)
eBook ISBN: 978-0-281-06464-9

Library of Congress Cataloging-in-Publication Data

Wright, N. T. (Nicholas Thomas)
 Revelation for everyone / Tom Wright.
  p. cm.—(New Testament for everyone series)
 ISBN 978-0-664-22797-5 (alk. paper)
1. Bible. N.T. Revelation—Commentaries. I. Title.
BS2825.53.W75 2011
228'.077—dc23

2011028912

⊗ The paper used in this publication meets the minimum requirements
of the American National Standard for Information Sciences—Permanence
of Paper for Printed Library Materials, ANSI Z39.48-1992.

Most Westminster John Knox Press books are available at special quantity
discounts when purchased in bulk by corporations, organizations, and special-
interest groups. For more information, please e-mail SpecialSales@wjkbooks.com.

For
Oliver and Rebecca
Celebrating God's new creation

CONTENTS

Contents

INTRODUCTION

On the very first occasion when someone stood up in public to tell people about Jesus, he made it very clear: this message is for everyone.

It was a great day – sometimes called the birthday of the church. The great wind of God's spirit had swept through Jesus' followers and filled them with a new joy and a sense of God's presence and power. Their leader, Peter, who only a few weeks before had been crying like a baby because he'd lied and cursed and denied even knowing Jesus, found himself on his feet explaining to a huge crowd that something had happened which had changed the world for ever. What God had done for him, Peter, he was beginning to do for the whole world: new life, forgiveness, new hope and power were opening up like spring flowers after a long winter. A new age had begun in which the living God was going to do new things in the world – beginning then and there with the individuals who were listening to him. 'This promise is for *you*', he said, 'and for your children, and for everyone who is far away' (Acts 2.39). It wasn't just for the person standing next to you. It was for everyone.

Within a remarkably short time this came true to such an extent that the young movement spread throughout much of the known world. And one way in which the *everyone* promise worked out was through the writings of the early Christian leaders. These short works – mostly letters and stories about Jesus – were widely circulated and eagerly read. They were never intended for either a religious or intellectual elite. From the very beginning they were meant for everyone.

That is as true today as it was then. Of course, it matters that some people give time and care to the historical evidence, the meaning of the original words (the early Christians wrote in Greek), and the exact and particular force of what different writers were saying about God, Jesus, the world and themselves. This series is based quite closely on that sort of work. But the point of it all is that the message can get out to everyone, especially to people who wouldn't normally read a book with footnotes and Greek words in it. That's the sort of person for whom these books are written. And that's why there's a glossary, in the back, of the key words that you can't really get along without, with a simple description of what they mean. Whenever you see a word in bold type in the text, you can go to the back and remind yourself what's going on.

There are of course many translations of the New Testament available today. The one I offer here is designed for the same kind of reader: one who mightn't necessarily understand the more formal, sometimes even ponderous, tones of some of the standard ones. I have of course tried to keep as close to the original as I can. But my main aim has been to be sure that the words can speak not just to some people, but to everyone.

Many people today regard Revelation as the hardest book in the New Testament. (Many, if it comes to that, can't even get its name right: it's Revelation, singular, not 'Revelations', plural!) It is full of strange, lurid and sometimes bizarre and violent imagery. You might have thought that in a world of clever movies and DVDs, stuffed full of complex imaginative imagery, we would take to Revelation like ducks to water; but it doesn't always seem to work that way. As a result, many people who are quite at home in the gospels, Acts and Paul find themselves tiptoeing around Revelation with a sense that they don't really belong there. But they do! This book in fact offers one of the clearest and sharpest visions of God's ultimate purpose for the whole creation, and of the way in which the powerful forces of evil, at work in a thousand ways but not least in idolatrous and tyrannous political systems, can be and are being overthrown through the victory of Jesus the Messiah and the consequent costly victory of his followers. The world we live in today is no less complex and dangerous than the world of the late first century when this book was written, and we owe it to ourselves to get our heads and our hearts around John's glorious pictures as we attempt to be faithful witnesses to God's love in a world of violence, hatred and suspicion. So here it is: Revelation for everyone!

The Seven Churches of Asia

REVELATION 1.1–8

Look! He Is Coming!

[1]Revelation of Jesus the Messiah! God gave it to him to show his servants what must soon take place. He signified it by sending a message through his angel to his servant John, [2]who, by reporting all he saw, bore witness to the word of God and to the testimony of Jesus the Messiah. [3]God's blessing on the one who reads the words of this prophecy, and on those who hear them and keep what is written in it. The time, you see, is near!

[4]John, to the seven churches in Asia: grace to you and peace from He Who Is and Who Was and Who Is To Come, and from the seven spirits that are before his throne, [5]and from Jesus the Messiah, the faithful witness, the firstborn from the dead, and the ruler of the kings of the earth. Glory to the one who loved us, and freed us from our sins by his blood, [6]and made us a kingdom, priests to his God and father – glory and power be to him for ever and ever. Amen.

[7]Look! He is coming with the clouds, and every eye shall see him; yes, even those who pierced him. All the tribes of the earth shall mourn because of him. Yes! Amen.

[8]'I am the Alpha and the Omega,' says the Lord God, Who Is and Who Was and Who Is To Come, the Almighty.

The house lights went down, and the excited buzz of audience chatter quickly subsided as well. Soon it was quite dark in the theatre. Then music began, softly and mysteriously at first, but soon building up, swelling and rising. Just as it reached its climax, the curtain was drawn up in an instant, and we all gasped not only at the blaze of sudden light but at what we saw.

The stage was brilliantly set so as to give the impression that we, the audience, were ourselves in a large room, one end of which was on display. Almost at once actors began to emerge from hiding-places in the auditorium, so that their voices were coming from among us as they made their way up to the stage. And the stage itself, designed as a great room in a castle, was

1

already half full of people, and animals too. There was an air of anticipation: clearly something important was about to happen . . .

I will leave you to guess what play it was. But the point for us now, at the start of Revelation, this most wonderful and puzzling of biblical books, is to get our heads round the idea of *revelation* itself. That's the word that has come to be used as the title for the book (not 'revelations', plural, please note). This is partly because the original word, 'Apocalypse', wasn't well known at the time of earlier translations into English. Now, of course, 'apocalypse', and its cousin 'apocalyptic', have become well known in English. Perhaps too well known: they have come to refer, not so much to the sudden unveiling of previously hidden truth, but to 'apocalyptic' *events*, violent and disturbing events such as natural disasters (earthquakes, volcanoes, tsunamis) or major and horrific human actions. In that sense, September 11, 2001 was an 'apocalyptic' event.

But that isn't quite the sense that 'revelation' or 'apocalypse' has in this book. John, its author – sometimes called 'John the Seer' or 'John the Divine', sometimes (probably wrongly) identified with the John who wrote the gospel and epistles – is picking up a way of writing well known in the Jewish world of the time. This way of writing was designed to correspond to, and make available, the visions and 'revelations' seen by holy, prayerful people who were wrestling with the question of the divine purpose. Like the theatre audience, they and the rest of God's people felt themselves in the dark. As they studied their ancient scriptures and said their prayers, they believed that the music was building up to something, but nobody was quite sure what. But then, like someone all by themselves in the theatre for the first performance, the 'seer' – the word reflects the reality, 'one who sees' something that other people do not – finds that the curtain is suddenly pulled up. Suddenly the 'seer' is witnessing a scene, is in fact invited to be part of a scene, within God's ongoing drama.

'Revelation' – the idea, and this book – are based on the ancient Jewish belief that God's sphere of being and operation ('**heaven**') and our sphere ('earth') are not after all separated by a great gulf. They meet and merge and meld into one another in all kinds of ways. For ancient Jews, the place where this happened supremely was the **Temple** in Jerusalem; this is not unimportant as the action proceeds. Most humans seem blind to this, only seeing the earthly side of the story. Some are aware that there is more to **life**, but are not quite sure what it's all about. Ancient Jews struggled to see both sides of the story, though it was often too much of an effort.

The early Christians believed that Jesus of Nazareth had become, in person, the place where heaven and earth met. Looking at him, and contemplating his death and **resurrection** in particular, they believed they could see right into God's own world. They could then understand things about his purpose which nobody had imagined before.

But it didn't stop there. As the early Christian movement grew, and developed momentum, further questions emerged. What was God doing now? What were his plans for the little churches dotted around the Mediterranean world? Where was it all going?

In particular, why was God allowing followers of Jesus to suffer persecution? What line should they take when faced with the fastest growing 'religion' of the time, namely the worship of Caesar, the Roman emperor? Should they resist?

There may have been several groups of Christians in ancient Turkey, where John seems to have been based. They would have been mostly poor, meeting in one another's homes. By contrast, people were building grand and expensive temples for Caesar and his family in various cities, eager to show Rome how loyal they were. What would Jesus himself say about this? Did it mean that, after all, the Christians were wasting their time, following a crucified Jew rather than the one who was rather obviously the 'lord of the world'?

Revelation is written to say 'no' to that question – and to say much more besides. At its centre is a fresh 'revelation of Jesus the **Messiah**' (verse 1). John, with his head and his heart full of Israel's scriptures, discovered on one particular occasion, as he was praying, that the curtain was pulled back. He found himself face to face with Jesus himself.

We will come to that in the next passage. But in this passage, the introduction-to-the-introduction of his book, we already learn five important things about what sort of book this is and how we ought to read it. (It goes without saying that we ought to read it with careful prayer and thought, being ready for God to lift the curtain so that we, too, can glimpse more than we had imagined.)

First, this book is a four-stage *revelation*. It is about something God has revealed to Jesus himself (verse 1), and which Jesus is then passing on, via an angel, to 'his servants', through one particular servant, John. God – Jesus – angel – John – churches. These lines get blurred as the book goes on, but the framework remains basic.

Second, the book takes the form of an extended *letter*. There are particular letters in chapters 2 and 3 to the seven churches in western Turkey, but the book as a whole is a letter from John to all the churches, telling them what he has seen.

Third, the book is a *prophecy* (verse 3). Like many prophets in ancient Israel, John draws freely on earlier biblical traditions. These were in themselves revelations of God and his purposes. Again and again, they come up fresh, in new forms.

Fourth, the book functions as *witness* (verse 2). Here we meet a familiar problem. The words for 'witness' and 'testimony' are basically the same, but it's hard to settle on one of these English words to the exclusion of the other, and I have used both. We should, though, remember two things whenever we see either word.

4

(a) They regularly carry a sense that God is ultimately conducting a great heavenly lawcourt. In that lawcourt, the 'witness' borne by Jesus and his followers is a key to the ultimate judgment and verdict.

(b) They regularly carry the sense which the Greek original word, 'martyr', has given to the English language. Those who bear this 'testimony' may well be called to suffer, or even to die, for what they have said.

Fifth, and far and away the most important: everything that is to come flows from the central figure, Jesus himself, and ultimately from God the father, 'He Who Is and Who Was and Who Is To Come' (verses 4, 8). Even in this short opening John manages to unveil a good deal of what he believes about God and Jesus, and about the divine plan. God is the Almighty, the beginning and the end (verse 8: Alpha and Omega are the first and last letters of the Greek alphabet, and this title occurs at the beginning and the end of John's book (see 22.13)). Other 'lords' and rulers will claim similar titles, but there is only one God to whom they belong.

And Jesus is the one who, through his death and resurrection, has accomplished God's purpose. His love for his people, his liberation of them by his self-sacrifice, his purpose for them (not just to rescue them, but to put them to important work in his service) – all these are stated here briefly in verse 6. And, not least, Jesus is the one who will soon return to complete the task, to set up his rule on earth as in heaven.

Nobody in the first century knew exactly when Jesus would return. We still await that moment today. But Christian living, and indeed belief in this one God, only makes sense on the assumption that he will indeed come to set everything right at last.

We settle in our seats, put other concerns out of our minds, and wait for the curtain to rise.

REVELATION 1.9–20

Jesus Revealed

[9]I, John, your brother and your partner in the suffering, the kingdom, and the patient endurance in Jesus, was on the island called Patmos because of the word of God and the testimony of Jesus. [10]I was in the spirit on the Lord's day, and I heard behind me a loud voice like a trumpet. [11]'Write down what you see in a book,' it said, 'and send it to the seven churches: to Ephesus, Smyrna, Pergamum, Thyatira, Sardis, Philadelphia and Laodicea.'

[12]So I turned to see the voice that was speaking with me. As I turned, I saw seven golden lampstands, [13]and in the middle of the lampstands 'one like a son of man', wearing a full-length robe and with a golden belt across his chest. [14]His head and his hair were white, white like wool, white like snow. His eyes were like a flame of fire, [15]his feet were like exquisite brass, refined in a furnace, and his voice was like the sound of many waters. [16]He was holding seven stars in his right hand, and a sharp two-edged sword was coming out of his mouth. The sight of him was like the sun when it shines with full power. [17]When I saw him, I fell at his feet as though I was dead.

He touched me with his right hand. 'Don't be afraid,' he said. 'I am the first and the last [18]and the living one. I was dead, and look! I am alive for ever and ever. I have the keys of death and Hades. [19]Now write what you see, both the things that already are, and also the things that are going to happen afterwards. [20]The secret meaning of the seven stars which you saw in my right hand, by the way, and the seven golden lampstands, is this. The seven stars are the angels of the seven churches, and the seven lampstands are the seven churches themselves.'

Some years ago there was an eclipse of the sun. These things happen rarely enough, and to witness it is a great experience. But staring at the sun, as it slips behind the moon and then emerges the other side, is dangerous. If you look through binoculars, or a telescope, the sun's power on your eye can do permanent damage. It can even cause blindness.

On this particular occasion, there were public warnings broadcast on radio and television, and printed in the newspapers, to the effect that people should be careful. Only look, they said, through special dark glasses. Eventually one person, who obviously had very little understanding of natural phenomena, got cross about all this. Surely, they thought, this was a 'health and safety' issue. A letter was sent to the London *Times*: if this event was so dangerous, why were the government allowing it in the first place?

Fortunately, even the most totalitarian of governments has not yet been able to control what the sun and the moon get up to. But the danger of full-power sunlight is worth contemplating as we hear John speaking about his vision of Jesus. As I write this, the sun has just emerged through watery clouds; even so, I can't look at it for more than a second before having to turn away. So when John, with the brightness of a Mediterranean sky in his mind, speaks of Jesus in this way (verse 16), we should learn to think of this Jesus with a new kind of reverence.

For some, Jesus is just a faraway figure of first-century fantasy. For others, including some of today's enthusiastic Christians, Jesus is the one with whom we can establish a personal relationship of loving intimacy. John would agree with the second of these, but he would warn against imagining that Jesus is therefore a cosy figure, one who merely makes us feel happy inside. To see Jesus as he is would drive us not to snuggle up to him, but to fall at his feet as though we were dead.

This vision of Jesus (verses 12–16) introduces us to several things about the way John writes. Like someone reporting a strange dream, the things he says are hard to imagine all together. It's more like looking at a surrealist painting, or a set of shifting computer-generated images. It's not a simple sketch. For a start, when John hears a voice like a trumpet (verse 10), he tells us that 'I turned to see the voice'. There is a sense in which this is just right: the Jesus whom he then sees is indeed

7

The Voice, the living **Word** of the father, the one through whom God spoke and still speaks. And the words which Jesus himself speaks turn into a visible sword coming out of his mouth (verse 16), echoing Isaiah's prophecy both about the coming king (11.4) and about the suffering servant (49.2). A great deal of this book is about ideas-made-visible, on the one hand, and scripture-made-real on the other. It is, in fact, the sort of thing someone soaked in scripture might see in a dream, after pondering and praying for many days.

In particular, this vision of Jesus draws together the vision of two characters in one of the most famous biblical visions, that of Daniel 7. (Along with the books of **Exodus**, Isaiah, Ezekiel and Zechariah, Daniel is one of John's favourites.) There, as the suffering of God's people reaches its height, 'the Ancient of Days' takes his seat in **heaven**, and 'one like a **son of man**' (in other words, a human figure, representing God's people and, in a measure, all the human race) is presented before him, and enthroned alongside him. Now, in John's vision, these two pictures seem to have merged. When we are looking at Jesus, he is saying, we are looking straight through him at the father himself.

Hold the picture in your mind, detail by detail. Let those eyes of flame search you in and out. Imagine standing beside a huge waterfall, its noise like sustained thunder, and imagine that noise as a human voice, echoing round the hills and round your head. And then imagine his hand reaching out to touch you . . .

Yes, fear is the natural reaction. But here, as so often, Jesus says, 'Don't be afraid.' It's all right. Yes, you are suffering, and your people are suffering (verse 9). Yes, the times are strange and hard, with harsh and severe rulers running the world and imposing their will on city after city. But the seven churches – seven is the number of perfection, and the churches listed in verse 11 thus stand for all churches in the world, all places and all times – need to know that Jesus himself is standing in their midst, and that the 'angels' who represent and look after each of them are held in his right hand.

And the Jesus in question has, as his credentials, the fact that he 'was dead', and is 'alive for ever' (verse 18). Like someone whispering to us that they know the secret way out of the dungeon where we have been imprisoned, he says, 'I've got the keys! The keys of death and Hades – I have them right here! There's nothing more you need worry about.'

To grasp all this requires faith. To live by it will take courage. But it is that faith, and that courage, which this book is written to evoke.

Already we are learning quite a bit about the way John writes, and the way he means his readers to understand what he says. Like anyone describing a dream or a vision, he must know that what he says is impressionistic. It appeals not to logic, but to the imagination – which has been starved rotten in some parts of our culture, and over-stimulated in others. Now we are being asked to imagine: what would it look like if the curtain between heaven and earth were suddenly pulled up, revealing the Jesus who had been there all along but whom we had managed either to ignore or to cut down to our own size? This is the answer: a Jesus who is mind-blowing, dramatically powerful but also gentle and caring; a Jesus in and through whom we see his father, God the creator; a Jesus who has spoken, and still speaks, words which explain what is going on in the present, and warn of what will happen in the future (verse 19).

John, we discover here (verse 9), is on the island called Patmos, about 35 miles off the coast of south-western Turkey. He is there 'because of the word of God and the testimony of Jesus'; this probably means that the authorities have put him there, in exile, as a punishment for his fearless teaching, and to try to stop his work having any further effect. The result has been the exact opposite. Exile has given him time to pray, to reflect, and now to receive the most explosive vision of

God's power and love. He is still, he says, a partner with the churches 'in the suffering, the **kingdom**, and the patient endurance in Jesus': an odd combination, we might think. How can the 'kingdom' – which means the sovereign rule – sit together with suffering and patient endurance? That is part of the whole point of the book. Jesus himself won the victory through his suffering, and so must his people.

REVELATION 2.1–7

The Letter to Ephesus

[1]"Write this to the angel of the church in Ephesus. "These are the words of the one who holds the seven stars in his right hand, and who walks in among the seven golden lampstands. [2]I know what you have done, your hard labour and patience. I know that you cannot tolerate evil people, and that you have tested those who pass themselves off as apostles, but are not, and you have demonstrated them to be frauds. [3]You have patience, and you have put up with a great deal because of my name, and you haven't grown weary. [4]I do, however, have one thing against you: you have abandoned the love you showed at the beginning. [5]So remember the place from which you have fallen. Repent, and do the works you did at the beginning. If not – if you don't repent – I will come and remove your lampstand out of its place. [6]You do, though, have this in your favour: you hate what the Nicolaitans are doing, and I hate it too. [7]Let anyone who has an ear listen to what the spirit is saying to the churches. The tree of life stands in God's paradise, and I will give to anyone who conquers the right to eat from it."'

The first time I visited Ephesus, I was overwhelmed with the size and scale of the place. Massive buildings still stand, dating back to the first century and beyond. The amphitheatre alone takes your breath away. Streets, houses, shops: it's possible to get a very good picture there of what life was like. There is a gladiators' graveyard, indicating how some of the population spent their free time. The Temple of Artemis (the Greek name for the Roman goddess Diana) was one of the wonders of the world, and the Romans, when they established temples to the city of Rome and to the emperor, did so carefully within the massive precincts of Artemis herself. The population of the city in the first century has been estimated at around a quarter of a million. It was the local capital, the most important city in the whole of western Turkey.

The one thing you don't see today in Ephesus, or in the surrounding modern towns and villages, is an active church. To begin with this may not seem odd. But Ephesus had been one of the major centres of early Christianity. By the early second century, Christian writers were holding up Ephesus as a great example of Christian **faith, life** and witness. For several centuries it held a position of pre-eminence, and one of the great fifth-century church councils was held there (AD 431). Archaeologists have found a church building in the city, which may be where that council took place. But there are, to repeat, no active churches there today. If there are any Christians there, they are in hiding.

That would have been almost as unthinkable to John's audience as it would be for us to imagine our great churches empty and in ruins, with no new Christian **fellowships** rising up to take their place. But this sense of devastation, of a place where there once was a thriving Christian witness but where there is no more, is precisely what Jesus warned the Ephesian church about in verse 5: 'If you don't repent, I will come and remove your lampstand out of its place.' Like much in these letters, that is a severe warning.

The seven letters, of which this is the first, are sharp and pointed messages to the churches in question, and, through them, to the many other Christian groups already in the area – and to all others, then and now, who can listen in to what the risen Lord is saying. The letters all follow the same pattern.

They begin with a reminder of some aspect of the description of Jesus in chapter 1. They continue by congratulating the church on what has been going well (only in Laodicea is there nothing to praise), and then warning about what has been going badly (only in Smyrna and Philadelphia is there no fault to be found). The letters then end with a solemn warning and promise: the **spirit** is speaking to the churches, calling Christians to 'conquer', and promising them some aspect of the glorious future which God has in store. We should not imagine that Christians in Ephesus are *only* promised the right to eat of the tree of life, or that those in Smyrna are *only* promised that they will escape the second death, and so on. All the promises, and all the warnings, are for all the churches.

But, at the same time, John is well aware of the specific differences. The local colour of the letters is quite remarkable, and in the case of Ephesus one point stands out in particular. The great temple of Artemis had within its extensive grounds a wonderful garden focused on a particular tree which was used, not only as a sacred shrine, but as the focal point of a system of asylum. This tree even featured on some of the local coins. Criminals who came within a certain distance of it would be free from capture and punishment. It is no accident, then, that this letter finishes with the promise that God, too, has a 'Paradise', a beautiful garden, with 'the tree of life' at its heart.

But God's 'Paradise' is no refuge for unrepentant criminals. It is the place where 'those who repent' (verse 5) and 'those who conquer' (verse 7) will have the right to eat from the tree, and so to obtain 'life' of a sort which God always intended his human creatures to possess but which, until now, they have forfeited by their sin. 'The tree of life', after all, was there in the original garden (Genesis 2.9; 3.22), and will be there, planted many times over, in the 'garden city', the new Jerusalem (Revelation 22.2).

But this is to run ahead of the letter itself. It opens by reminding the church in Ephesus, the most obvious centre of imperial

12

power in the region, that Jesus is the sovereign one who holds the seven stars in his right hand. And when Jesus looks at the Ephesian Christians he is delighted: they have worked hard, they have been patient even under threat and persecution (verse 3), and they have drawn a clear line between those who are really following Jesus and those who are not (verse 2). Indeed, when some people have arrived trying to pass themselves off as 'apostles', they have seen through them. We don't know who these people were, but the early Christians seem to have travelled a lot, and it's quite likely that others, seeing what was happening, would show up and try to claim hospitality, and even a hearing for new teaching. And the Ephesians would have none of it.

All well and good: but, as all church workers know, there is often a delicate balance, and a group who are rightly concerned for the truth of the gospel may forget that the very heart of that gospel is love. The Ephesians had fallen into that trap: 'you have abandoned the love you showed at the beginning' (verse 4). This may refer to their love for Jesus himself, and certainly that must always be kept firm and central. But here it's clearly a matter of things people actually do: 'Repent,' says Jesus, 'and do the works you did at the beginning.' 'Love', in the early Christian sense, is something you *do*, giving hospitality and practical help to those in need, particularly to other Christians who are poor, sick or hungry. That was the chief mark of the early church. No other non-ethnic group had ever behaved like this. 'Love' of this kind, reflecting (they would have said) God's own self-giving love for them, was both the best expression of, and the best advertisement for, faith in this God.

It's easy to let this slip. It's easy to settle down into a vaguely comfortable existence which puts its own needs first and, sometimes, last as well. The Ephesian church needs to wake up, to remember how things used to be, to repent and get back on track.

At this point the letter passes another positive comment, but it is hard for us to understand: the church in Ephesus refuses to tolerate 'the Nicolaitans'. These people crop up again in the letter to Pergamum (verse 15), where again nothing more is said to identify who they were or what they were teaching (that's the point in the Pergamum letter) and doing (that's the point in the present one). Various attempts have been made, in the ancient church and in modern scholarship, to figure this out, with hardly any success. The main point we can gain from this mention of the 'Nicolaitans' is that the church must always be on the lookout for individuals or groups who try to teach strange new ideas or to introduce strange new practices. This doesn't mean that God never has new things for the church to learn; far from it. But these new things will come from prayerful, spirit-filled study of scripture, not through mere innovation.

Why do the letters emphasize the importance of 'conquering' (verse 7)? Putting together all the references in the book, we get a clear answer. The main challenge the young churches face is the threat of pagan persecution. Indeed, these seven letters seem to be written as part of the Lord's preparation of these churches for worse to come. They are to 'conquer', not by fighting back, but by following Jesus himself, who won the victory through his own patient suffering. Some in these churches will suffer. Some will die. All must bear patient witness to Jesus, thereby 'conquering' the evil forces that surround and threaten them.

REVELATION 2.8–11

The Letter to Smyrna

[8]"Write this to the angel of the church in Smyrna. "These are the words of the First and the Last, the one who was dead and came to life. [9]I know your suffering and poverty (but you are rich!). I know the blasphemy of those self-styled Jews. They

are nothing of the kind. They are a satan-synagogue. [10]Don't be afraid of what you are going to suffer. Look: the devil is going to throw some of you into prison, so that you may be put to the test. You will have ten days of affliction. Be faithful all the way to death, and I will give you the crown of life. [11]Let anyone who has an ear listen to what the spirit is saying to the churches. The second death will not harm the one who conquers."'

I was involved some years ago in making a series of radio programmes where people from quite different backgrounds came together for an hour to discuss complex and challenging topics of the day. Since this was being made by the British Broadcasting Corporation (BBC), there were some in-house guidelines. We were not supposed, for instance, to recommend particular brand-name products on air, since the publicly funded BBC does not advertise.

But I had not expected to be pulled up short simply for answering one of the questions. A listener had written in, asking the panel, 'If you could choose your religious **faith**, what would it be, and why?' Since I was the only obvious 'religious' representative on the panel, the person chairing the discussion asked me to speak first (each panellist was given about fifty seconds for an opening statement, and then we discussed it together). In my opening fifty seconds, I tried to make three points. First, I said that Christianity isn't exactly a 'religion' in the sense people mean today; it's much bigger than that, much more all-embracing. Then I pointed out that hardly anyone actually 'chooses' a faith, like someone in a supermarket picking out a particular brand of soup. Then I began to say why, granted all that, I would argue for the truth of the Christian faith and for the positive, healing, **life**-giving effect it has.

I was only a few words into that third section, which was after all answering the question, when I was interrupted by the chair. 'Oh Tom,' she said, 'we can't say that sort of thing on air. That's proselytizing.' Fortunately, the rest of the panel – all of them, I think, atheists or at least agnostics – came to my defence. Of course I had to be able to say it, they said. I'd been asked a question and I had to be able to answer it! So, despite the knee-jerk reaction of a lifelong BBC let's-be-neutral-about-everything organizer, I was able to continue.

I tell that story because our world today, in the West at least, has become like that BBC employee: paranoid about any actual claims, not only that we might have the truth but that someone else might not. Only today I heard a snatch of a radio programme bending over backwards to explain the predicament of Muslim children in British schools during the Ramadan fast, and the second-order predicament of local communities and newspapers commenting on the policies the schools were adopting. We are hypersensitive about all such matters, in the way that someone with badly bruised toes will be hypersensitive about anyone walking anywhere near their feet.

And then we read the New Testament . . . and we find passages like this. 'I know the blasphemy of those self-styled Jews.' We recoil. How can anyone say such things? But in fact, in the real world (as opposed to the fantasy-world of the relativist), there are hard edges, hard questions, tough challenges. And in the early church, Jewish to the core, some of the hardest questions came straight out, as we see already in Paul. Who are the children of Abraham? Are they all his physical family (in which case, what about the descendants of Ishmael and Esau?), or the larger, worldwide family which God promised to Abraham? It was not least the scandal of a community which gave the second answer (Abraham's family are now multi-national) which led Saul of Tarsus to persecute the early Christians violently, and which then got him into the same trouble when he changed sides. But, as we see when we look at other Jewish renewal movements of the period, like the one at Qumran, we see that this was essentially a struggle *within* Judaism, not *against* Judaism. The early church firmly clung to the ancient Jewish hope, and the ancient Jewish scriptures, and they claimed that they were all fulfilled in Jesus the Jewish **Messiah**.

In western Turkey, by the time this book was written, it is likely that the church contained a fair mixture of Jews and non-Jews. But there was a large and lively synagogue community as well, whose members did not believe that Jesus was God's Messiah, sent to Israel to announce God's **kingdom**, and raised from the dead to prove the point. Since the nub of the Christian faith was not that this was a new 'religion', invented out of nothing, but rather that it was the fulfilment of the ancient promises to, and hopes of, the people of Israel, this immediately caused a problem. This was especially so when members of the synagogue, not content with their own rejection of Jesus, actively blasphemed him, perhaps calling down curses upon him.

In our politically correct age it would be much more convenient if these real-life challenges did not happen. But they did, and they do. It is impossible simultaneously to say that Jesus was raised from the dead and so is God's true Messiah, Israel's king and the world's true lord, and that he wasn't and isn't. Who, therefore, is the true Jew? Paul already gave the answer in Romans 2.25–29: the one who is the 'Jew' in the heart. John would agree – and so, according to this letter, would Jesus himself. This means that, like it or not, the Jewish synagogue in Smyrna has become a '**satan**-synagogue' – not just in a vague, general, abusive sense, but in the rather sharply defined sense that, as 'the satan' is, literally, 'the **accuser**', the synagogue in town has been 'accusing' the Christians of all kinds of wickedness. In particular, in a city where Roman imperial presence and influence was everything, the Jews would have been exempt from taking part in the festivities of the imperial cult . . . and they may well have been accusing, to the authorities, the Christians who were claiming that exemption as well. Perhaps it was accusations like that, with social and political consequences, that had given Smyrna's Christians a taste of poverty in an otherwise rich city (verse 9).

All this is at the heart of the message to Smyrna. In this church the Lord finds nothing to criticize. His main task is to warn that fierce persecution is on the way; and he does so as the one who is First and Last, who was dead and came to life. (There may be a local allusion here, because Smyrna, as a city, had once been destroyed and then rebuilt.) Whatever happens, the times and the fates of the Christians in Smyrna are safe in his hands. The **devil** may well imprison and 'test' some of them. The 'ten days' here is likely to be figurative, since a 'day', in writing like John's, sometimes means a year or a more general period of time.

The warning is again surrounded with promises that are immediately relevant to a church under this threat. Those who are 'faithful all the way to death', as Jesus himself had been (Philippians 2.7–8), will receive 'the crown of life', meaning perhaps 'life as a crown': that is, the true, renewed life of God's new age, whose possessors will be marked out by it as royalty is marked out by crowns. Again, Smyrna itself was thought of as a city with a crown, due to the way its splendid architecture used the natural advantages of a steep hill to good effect.

The final promise points in the same direction. Anyone who is, quite naturally, afraid that they may face death for their beliefs is introduced to an idea to which John will return near the end of the book. There are, it seems, two forms of death. The first is the bodily death to which all will come except the generation still alive when the Lord returns. Jesus has already passed that way, and those who belong to him can know that he will first welcome them on the other side and then, at the end, raise them to new life in his final new world. But the 'second death' is the ultimate fate of those who steadfastly and deliberately refuse to follow Jesus, to worship the one God who is revealed in him. This 'second death' will, it seems, do for the entire personality what the 'first death' will do for the physical body.

This is a terrifying prospect, to which John will return in chapter 20. But his point at the moment is this: do not be afraid to face the first death. Some of you will have to do that. To 'conquer' – to face that martyrdom in faithful patience – will mean that you will have nothing to fear from the 'second death'. Be content to go with Jesus through the first death. He was dead, and came to life; and so will you.

REVELATION 2.12–17

The Letter to Pergamum

[12]'Write this to the angel of the church in Pergamum. "These are the words of the one who has the sharp two-edged sword. [13]I know where you live – right there where the satan has his throne! You have clung on to my name, and have not denied my faith, even in the days of Antipas, my faithful witness, who was killed in your midst, in the dwelling-place of the satan. [14]But I do have a few things against you: you have some people there who hold the teaching of Balaam, who instructed Balak to cause the children of Israel to stumble, making them eat idol-food and indulge in sexual immorality. [15]So, too, you have some among you who hold the teaching of the Nicolaitans. [16]So: repent! If you don't, I will come to you quickly and will fight against them with the sword of my mouth. [17]Let anyone who has an ear listen to what the spirit is saying to the churches. To anyone who conquers I will give secret manna, and a white stone, with a new name written on that stone which nobody knows except the one who receives it."'

From the train, many miles away, you can see the skyscrapers. You come up through New Jersey, from the direction of Philadelphia, past the lovely town of Princeton, and on through somewhat less lovely townships; and then, if you're looking in the right direction, suddenly there they are. The ground they are standing on – the quite small island of Manhattan – is more or less at sea level. But the tops of the buildings stretch up towards the sky, and indeed on many cloudy days they disappear into that cloud. Even after the terrible destruction

19

of the Twin Towers, the buildings that remain are stupendous: the highest, the Empire State Building, rises to 1,454 feet. They can be seen from far and wide.

One English city has the same effect, for a different reason: Lincoln. Surrounded by flat fenland country, Lincoln itself is built on the top of a tall mound which rises up quite suddenly and, like New York's skyscrapers, can be seen from miles around. Lincoln, of course, has an enormous cathedral, which adds to the striking power of the view from up to 20 miles away.

Something like that effect was created in the city of Pergamum, both by the natural geography, which gave it a high acropolis in the middle of the city, and by the majestic set of temples which sat there, dominating the view not only from the rest of the city but from much of the surrounding countryside. Many local inhabitants in the first century must have been proud of all this. But for the little Christian community it represented a threat – and a threat with which, it seemed, the Christians were not coping particularly well.

The letter to Pergamum refers to the city as the place 'where the **satan** has his throne'. Since 'the satan' – 'the **accuser**', or 'the **devil**' – is referred to elsewhere in Revelation as 'the ancient serpent' (20.2), we may find the clue to this description in Pergamum's famous local religions. For a start, there was the shrine of the healing-god Asclepius, whose symbol was a serpent. But, in addition, Pergamum was another city with a major centre of the imperial cult of Rome and its emperors. John does not identify Rome with the devil. But, as we shall see, he believes that the devil has been using Rome for his own ends, not least to attack the church. And Pergamum was the seat of the Roman governor of the whole region.

How then should a Christian live in a city like Pergamum? What could one do, and what should one not do? We can only guess at the many anxious discussions, and varied teachings, that might have attempted to address these questions. Should one take part in the normal civic life – which included festivals

20

of the gods, not least Rome and the emperor? Was there a way in which one might do enough to get by while drawing back from full involvement? Paul had addressed these issues in two letters (1 Corinthians 8—10; Romans 14), and had given careful and nuanced advice: no compromise with pagan temples and cult, but flexibility on food that had been offered to idols, and indeed on meat and drink in general.

At this point, some in the church at Pergamum seem to have taken that permitted flexibility all the way into cultural assimilation. There's no point standing out; we are part of this society, let's go with the flow. Some people, faced with the challenge to deny Jesus, have refused to do so. One in particular, Antipas, has died as a result (verse 13). But there are others – perhaps in reaction – who are keen not to stand out. They have gone along with the prevailing culture.

For these people Jesus has stern words. This is, more or less, the same mistake that the Israelites committed when King Balak of Moab hired the prophet Balaam to curse Israel (verse 14). Balaam found he couldn't curse them; he was, to that extent, a true prophet. But he still wanted Balak's promised reward, and so he encouraged the king to use a different tactic. Where direct spiritual attack (the curse) had failed, more subtle temptation might work; and, as often, the best temptation would be sexual. In an ancient version of the 'honey-trap' beloved of spy novels (and, for all I know, actual spying), Moabite women were sent to entice the Israelite men – who, presumably, already had Israelite wives. Through this means, they were drawn into idolatry, worshipping gods other than YHWH. Job done.

The same tactic still works remarkably well today. Sexual morality isn't, as it is so often portrayed, a matter of a few ancient rules clung to by some rather conservative persons when the rest of society has moved on. It is, rather, a matter of the call of the creator God to faithful man-plus-woman marriage, reflecting the complementarity of **heaven** and earth

21

themselves. That is the theme which finally emerges in the great scene at the end of the present book. Married love is a signpost to the faithfulness of the creator to his creation. The reason sexual immorality is so often coupled with idolatry, as here, is because such behaviour points to different gods – the gods of blood and soil, of race and power. It's a toxic mixture, and the Christian has no business getting involved with it, as Paul himself warned in 1 Corinthians 10.

It may be that 'the Nicolaitans' are, in fact, a small group who are teaching something very like this 'teaching of Balaam'. Some have suggested that, in the original languages, the names 'Balaam' and 'Nicolas' may have similar meanings. One way or another, the problem in Pergamum is that much of the church has lost its cutting edge, its ability to say 'no' to the surrounding culture. As the earliest Christians found in Acts, the church always has to be able to say 'We must obey God rather than human authorities', even if the 'authorities' in question are not the official magistrates (though the magistrates, too, may pose a threat if the Christians refuse to join in with state religion) but simply the insidious pressures of people saying 'but this is what everybody does'.

Jesus' response is clear. The Roman governor may wield the sword, but Jesus has the sharp two-edged sword coming out of his mouth (verses 12, 16, as in 1.16). His **word** will cut through the half-hearted spirituality that is happy to face both ways at once.

As ever, there is a promise, though in the case of Pergamum it is somewhat obscure. There are many early Christian texts which see the little churches like the Israelites in the wilderness. That, indeed, is the setting for the story of Balaam. That is the setting Paul uses for his very similar warnings in 1 Corinthians 10. On that wilderness journey, God fed his people with 'manna', bread that dropped down from the sky. I will do the same for you, promises Jesus here; the place where you live may seem to be starving you, but I will give you 'secret manna'.

Many Christians have clung on to this promise as they find themselves spiritually hungry in an alien environment. Many, too, have seen it as a pointer to the sacrament of Jesus' body and blood, again with parallels in 1 Corinthians 10.

In addition, there is the promise of a white stone with a new name written on it. Pergamum's great buildings were made of a black local stone. When people wanted to put up inscriptions, they obtained white marble on which to carve them. This was then fixed to the black buildings, where it stood out all the more clearly. In addition – and this may tie in with the 'hidden manna' – there was a custom of guests at a feast being given a stone with their name on as a ticket of admission.

What name, then, is written on the stone? Is it a new name for the person concerned, or is it 'the new name' of Jesus the **Messiah**, as opposed to the 'old names' of the local and imperial gods and goddesses? In favour of the second, it is possible that there may be an allusion here to the names of the tribes of Israel on the **high priest**'s clothing. These names would be summed up in that of the one true Israelite, Jesus the Messiah. But the fact that nobody knows this name except the one who receives it points, I think, to the first solution. Jesus is promising to each faithful **disciple**, to each one who 'conquers', an intimate relationship with himself in which Jesus will use the secret name which, as with lovers, remains private to those involved. The challenge to avoid the false intimacy of sexual promiscuity is matched by the offer of a genuine intimacy of spiritual union with Jesus himself.

REVELATION 2.18–29

The Letter to Thyatira

[18]"Write this to the angel of the church in Thyatira. "These are the words of the son of God, whose eyes are like flaming fire and whose feet are like exquisite brass. [19]I know what you have done: I know your love, your faith, your service and your

23

patience. I know that your works have been more impressive recently than they were before. [20]But I have something against you: you tolerate the woman Jezebel, who calls herself a prophet and teaches my servants (in fact, deceives my servants!) to practise fornication and to eat idol-food. [21]I gave her time to repent, but she had no wish to repent of her immorality. [22]Look! I am going to throw her on a bed, and those who have committed fornication with her will have great distress, unless they repent of the works into which she has led them. [23]I will utterly slaughter her children, and all the churches will know that I am the one who searches minds and hearts. I will give to each of you what your deeds deserve. [24]For the rest of you in Thyatira, those who have not held this teaching, who haven't discovered the so-called 'satanic depths': I'm not going to put any other pressure on you. [25]Just hold on tightly to what you have until I come. [26]To anyone who conquers, who keeps my works right through to the end, I will give authority over the nations, [27]to rule them with a rod of iron, as when clay pots get smashed! [28]That is the authority I myself received from my father. What's more, I will give them the morning star. [29]Let anyone who has an ear listen to what the spirit says to the churches.'"

Some cities are known by their industrial products. The city near where I grew up, Newcastle in the north-east of England, was famous for two hundred years as one of the chief suppliers of coal to the country, and to many places abroad. The phrase 'carrying coals to Newcastle' has become a proverbial way of referring to someone taking something to people who have quite enough of it already – a bit like 'selling sand to the Saudis', or 'selling ice to the Eskimos' (yes, I know: we might want to say 'Inuit' instead of 'Eskimo', which some (not all) find offensive). Sadly, Newcastle exports hardly any coal now, though there is still plenty underground in the region. We await a change of government policy which would allow the area once again to exploit one of its most obvious assets. Perhaps the proverb will continue until the reality once again

catches up, and Newcastle will again be known for the trade in
its celebrated local product.

The city of Thyatira was not as well known as the other six
to which these letters were addressed, but one of the things it
was famous for was its trade guilds, and not least its smelting
work in copper and bronze. That may well explain the choice
of the particular description of Jesus in verse 18, picking up
from 1.15: his feet are like exquisite brass. More important,
perhaps, the local deity in the area, who was the patron deity
of the bronze trade, was 'Apollo Tyrimnaeus', who appeared on
local coins together with the 'son of god', that is, the Roman
emperor. Granted these associations, there is particular power
in the letter's beginning, as it announces 'the words of the **son
of God,** whose eyes are like flaming fire and whose feet are like
exquisite brass'.

But the local industries, and the many trade and business
guilds which were formed around them, had become a major
problem for the church. As today with some kinds of business
and trade societies, various types of religious or quasi-religious
ceremonies were used as a way of celebrating the industry in
question and invoking divine blessing upon it. Again, as in our
own day, many people will have taken these ceremonies with
a pinch of salt. But in this letter Jesus makes it very clear
that this is not an option. Yes, the church in Thyatira has done
considerably better of late than it had before (verse 19). Love,
faith, service and patience – it reads like a Pauline list of the
virtues one should expect from a maturing Christian community. But there is still a major problem.

In the previous letter the problem in the church at Pergamum was identified by allusion to a famous biblical figure,
Balaam the prophet. This time another ancient villain plays
the same role: Jezebel, the wife of king Ahab, who seems to
have been the cause of some at least of her husband's wickedness. Their story is told in 1 Kings 16—22, ending with Ahab's
death; Jezebel's own story comes to its unpleasant end in

2 Kings 9. Jezebel, like the women of Moab whom Balaam and Balak used to seduce the Israelite men away from the pure worship of Yahweh, was a foreign woman who introduced the worship of Baal, a rival god, into Israel. That was at the heart of many other evils, summarized in 2 Kings 9.22 as 'whoredoms and sorceries'.

'Whoredoms' in that passage, like 'fornication' here, was a metaphor for the spiritual 'playing around' of communing with other gods. Certainly this is what is in mind in verse 22; it seems unlikely that church members themselves have been engaging in sexual activity with this first-century 'Jezebel'. But everything we know about ancient and indeed modern paganism inclines us to think that the sexual immorality noted in the Pergamum letter was a reality here as well. Certainly verse 20 seems to point in that direction. Once one admits (as Paul did not) that it is all right to attend events in pagan temples or near equivalents, then all the ancillary practices, which regularly included licentious sexual behaviour, would come with the territory. Almost literally: if you wanted to find a prostitute, the precincts of a pagan temple would be the natural place to look.

This makes it all the more shocking that the church was tolerating the woman here nicknamed 'Jezebel'. It isn't clear whether she was an official and accredited church teacher, but certainly she has had a powerful influence through what she claims is her prophetic gift. It seems that, within the young and muddled Christian community, some had become convinced that their spiritual freedom could appropriately be expressed both in sexual licence (one still hears, in some would-be Christian circles, the word 'prophetic' used to describe a call for sexual licence) and in attendance at pagan shrines, cult meals and the more ambiguous **fellowship** meals (still with religious overtones) of the trade guilds. Some may even have embraced a teaching according to which the Christian's freedom from sin means that he or she can, and perhaps should, explore the 'satanic depths' (verse 24), going boldly right into the enemy's camp just to show how invulnerable one was.

As far as Jesus is concerned, this whole approach is an absolute disaster. The church has no business compromising at any point with pagan worship and the practices that reflect and embody it. Here, as in the devastating scene in chapters 17, 18 and 19, where the 'great whore' is Babylon, the imperial city, judgment is pronounced on Jezebel and on all who have gone with her into wickedness. The throwing on a bed, great distress (verse 22) and utter slaughter (verse 23) that will follow are no doubt symbolic, but they are symbolic of the real and powerful action which the Lord will take, as the one whose flaming eyes search minds and hearts (verses 18 and 23), to purge his people of this multiple sin.

The authority which the Lord possesses, with which he can do all this, is summed up with a reference to Psalm 2, one of the great royal psalms in which the **Messiah** is given authority to rule the nations with a rod of iron, and smash them in pieces like a clay pot. Here (verses 26–27) this royal authority is to be shared with those who conquer. As frequently in Revelation, Jesus intends to make his people a 'royal priesthood'. What is required at the moment, for those who have not been drawn away by the teaching and practices of 'Jezebel', is that they 'hold on tightly'. That is a **word** for all those Christians today who find themselves in churches and fellowships where teaching and behaviour which they know is not the way of the Messiah is being eagerly embraced, and hailed as God-given.

One word more: Jesus promises to 'give them the morning star'. Since later in the book (22.16) it is Jesus himself who is the 'morning star', we probably have here another hint of the level of intimacy which he offers to his people. He will share his very identity with them, as we have just seen him do with his royal authority. But the 'morning star', most likely the planet Venus at its pre-dawn brightest, is a sign of the special vocation of Christians, not least those 'holding on' when others around them seem to be compromising, under pressure, with local pagan practices. Christian witness is meant to be a sign of the dawning of the day, the day in which love, faith, service and patience will have their fulfilment, in which idolatry and immorality will be seen as the snares and delusions they really are, and in which Jesus the Messiah will establish his glorious reign over the whole world.

REVELATION 3.1–6

The Letter to Sardis

[1]"Write this to the angel of the church in Sardis. "These are the words of the one who has the seven spirits of God, and the seven stars. I know what you have done. You have the reputation of being alive, but you are dead. [2]Wake up! Strengthen the things that remain – the things that are about to die – because I haven't found your works to be complete in the sight of my God. [3]So remember how you received the message, how you heard it and kept it – and repent! So if you don't keep awake, I will come like a thief, and you won't know what time I'm coming to you. [4]You do, however, have a few people in Sardis who haven't allowed their clothes to become dirty and polluted. They will be clothed in white and will walk with me, as they deserve. [5]Anyone who conquers will be clothed like this in white robes, and I won't blot their name out of the book of life. I will acknowledge their name in the presence of my father and in the presence of his angels. [6]Let anyone who has an ear listen to what the spirit is saying to the churches."'

You might be surprised to know that, in some parts of England, 'The Wars of the Roses' still live on. These wars were fought between the Houses of York (the white rose) and Lancaster (the red rose) in the fifteenth century. But, ever since, the great divide between Yorkshire, on the east side of northern England, and Lancashire, on the west, has continued in the minds of those born and bred in those counties. And, whenever Yorkshire meets Lancashire on the cricket field, the game is known as 'the Roses Match', and old loyalties are stirred once again.

From the fifteenth century to the twenty-first is a long time. It's nearly six hundred years since those wars took place. But if we in our modern world have long memories, they are as nothing beside the memory of great events cherished, for good or ill, by many in the ancient world. People might not have been able to tell you exactly when an event took place – it might have been, at the most, 'in the reign of King such-and-such' – but they knew more or less what had happened, allowing for some pardonable embellishment here and there.

The residents of Sardis knew very well what had happened to their city six hundred years before the Christian **gospel** reached them. The city had been thought, for a long time, completely impregnable. It was secure, sitting on top of its steep hill. Attackers might come and go, but the citizens were quite content to see them do so. They knew they could never be captured.

Until one night, during the reign of the famous King Croesus, the invading Persian army found a way in. Someone, greatly daring, got up part of the sheer cliff and managed a surprise attack. Because nobody was expecting it, the result was all the more devastating. Cyrus the Persian, who features in various biblical stories as well, conquered Sardis in 546 BC: a never-to-be-forgotten moment. Though Sardis remained an important city, the lesson had been learned.

Except that now Jesus is saying the Christian community in Sardis needs to learn it all over again! They have the reputation of being alive – of being a vibrant going concern, a **fellowship** where things are happening. But they have gone to sleep on their reputation, and need to wake up. All is not lost. There are some good things happening. But unless action is taken quickly they, too, will wither on the vine.

The more detailed charge against Sardis appears to be two-fold. First, their works have not been found to be 'complete'.

That may be a tactful way of saying that their performance of the gospel, their Christian way of life, 'leaves a lot to be desired'. But that's not the sort of thing Christian **faith** is. It's all or nothing: either Jesus really is the Lord, rightly asking for our absolute allegiance, or he is a sham and should be rejected outright. It simply won't do to bumble on, looking busy but achieving little or nothing. Reputation isn't enough.

The second charge emerges in verses 4 and 5, where Jesus acknowledges that some of the Christians in Sardis 'haven't allowed their clothes to become dirty and polluted'. This is hardly a comment on actual dirty linen, but it's not clear what in fact this image is being used for. It may just be a way of commenting on their spiritual laziness. Like people who can't be bothered to wash their clothes regularly, they are falling into slack habits. Or it may be a more specific reference to the toleration, within the community, of some sort of immoral behaviour.

If this continues, the church in Sardis will suffer the same fate as the city had suffered six centuries earlier. Jesus 'will come like a thief' (verse 3), and they won't know what time it will happen. This echoes similar sayings in Paul and Peter, and in the teaching of Jesus himself (1 Thessalonians 5.2; 2 Peter 3.10; Matthew 24.43). It was obviously a regular warning note sounded among the early Christians. The Jesus who holds the life of the churches – their angels, and the seven **spirits** of God which bring the churches to life (see 1.4; 4.5; 5.6) – will come. They won't know what's happening until it's too late.

Will this 'coming' be the final Day, the '**second coming**' properly understood? Probably not, though that too is in view as the ultimate backdrop. Throughout this book we glimpse other 'comings', which may consist in times of persecution (when Jesus is 'coming' to cleanse and purify his church) or of moments of comfort and restoration. Even Laodicea, as we shall see, is promised that if they open the door he will 'come in to them and eat with them' (3.20). Here it seems that the 'coming' may well be a time of persecution or simply of internal collapse, a church quietly drowning in its own inoffensiveness, unable to believe that its reputation for being alive is no longer deserved.

But the promise, to those who 'wake up', to those who 'conquer', and to those who have managed to keep their 'clothes' from being 'polluted', is that they will share the triumphal procession when Jesus comes as the conqueror. This theme will be taken up again and again later on in the book. They will wear white robes, as people did in triumphal processions, and as the newly baptized would do when they emerged from the water. They would, in other words, share the victory of Jesus over all (including ultimately death itself) that drags human life down into the dirt.

What's more, their names will stay where they are in 'the book of life'. This too is mentioned on various occasions later on in Revelation (13.8; 17.8; 20.12, 15; 21.27). The idea goes back within ancient Israelite thought to God's book, referred to in Exodus 32.32. That's not an encouraging reference, since there almost all the Israelites had deserved to be blotted out of that book, and it was only God's fresh act of mercy that rescued the situation. Closer to Revelation in time, many Greek cities had an official register of all citizens. Some places kept the grim custom that, when a citizen was to be condemned to death, his name would first be blotted out of the book, so that sentence could proceed without any stain on the city's reputation through one of its citizens facing the ultimate penalty. Here it appears that names at present in God's book can be blotted out: John is not advancing a theory about predestination, which in any case always has as its corollary that those who are to be saved turn out to be those who persevere. He is holding out a standard early Christian warning, going back to those of **John the Baptist**, Paul and Jesus himself. It's a warning against presuming that belonging to the community of the people of God, irrespective of behaviour within it, is all that is required.

To those who wake up, who stay unpolluted, and who conquer, Jesus finally reiterates another promise well known from the gospel tradition. He will 'acknowledge their names' before the father and his angels (see Mark 8.38; Luke 12.8). To be acknowledged by Jesus himself will be amazing. To have him acknowledge us before his father will be the moment of all moments. Let's wake up before it's too late.

REVELATION 3.7–13

The Letter to Philadelphia

[7]"Write this to the angel of the church in Philadelphia. "These are the words of the Holy One, the True One, the one who has the key of David, who opens and nobody shuts, who shuts and nobody opens. [8]I know your works. Look! I have given you an open door, right in front of you, and nobody can shut it, since you have a little power; you have kept my word, and you haven't denied my name. [9]Look: this is what I will do to the satan-synagogue, who call themselves Jews but who are frauds, nothing of the kind. Take note: this is what I will grant you – that I will make them come and worship before your feet, and they will know that I have loved you. [10]You have kept my word about patience, and so I will keep you from the time of trial that is going to come upon the whole world, to test out all the inhabitants of the earth. [11]I am coming quickly! Hold on to what you have, so that nobody takes away your crown. [12]Anyone who conquers, I will make them a pillar in the temple of my God. They will never go out of it again. I will write on that person the name of my God and the name of the city of my God, the new Jerusalem, which comes down out of heaven from my God, and my own new name. [13]Let anyone who has an ear listen to what the spirit is saying to the churches.""

I have been sitting here trying to imagine what it's like to find yourself in an earthquake. I was once in a hotel in Los Angeles, a few dozen floors up, and was alarmed to find detailed instructions in the room on what I should do if the building began to shake. It didn't. The closest I have been to even a small earthquake was a hundred miles away, and it only just rattled the china in the cupboard. So I still haven't experienced it.

And I don't want to, either. Tales from those who have felt a real tremor indicate that it is the stuff of ultimate nightmares: everything that you thought was fixed and secure is now moving. Houses, walls, streets, bridges, gardens, fields – everything suddenly going up and down. Nothing can be taken for granted.

Central Turkey, in the first century as much as any other time, was notorious for its earthquakes. Philadelphia had suffered one of the worst ones, fifty or more years before this book was written. Much of the city had been destroyed and had had to be rebuilt with a grant from the emperor. In a great city of that day, the fine public buildings would be particularly dangerous in such a crisis. Small, poor family homes might escape the worst of the damage; but imagine those splendid works of ancient architecture, civic structures and, not least, temples (of which ancient cities had plenty). Imagine the tall pillars shaking, cracking and then buckling as a huge marble pediment came crashing down. Not a good place to be.

Now imagine the effect, in a city like Philadelphia that knew plenty about earthquakes and collapsed temples, of promising the church there that those who conquered would be made pillars in the **temple** of God (verse 12). No stone, no marble will be involved: this, as in the writings of Paul and Peter, is a 'temple' made of living human beings, with Jesus himself as the foundation. This imagery was used from the earliest days of Christian **faith**. The first Christians, partly because of Jesus and partly because of the gift of the **spirit**, regarded themselves as the true Temple, the place where the living God had made his home. Sometimes the Jerusalem leaders had themselves been called 'pillars' (Galatians 2.9). That metaphor depends for its force on this idea of the church as the new Temple.

But now it is the ordinary Christians in Philadelphia, far away from Jerusalem, who are to be 'pillars' – in a city notorious for danger from earthquakes! A promise to cherish.

It goes closely with the comment, and the promise, at the start of the letter. Jesus is the one who, like the steward appointed over God's house in Isaiah 22.22, has 'the key of David': the royal key that will open, or lock, any and every door. Equipped with this regal power, Jesus has opened a door right in front of the Philadelphia Christians, and he is urging them to go through it. As with Paul's use of the same picture (1 Corinthians 16.9; 2 Corinthians 2.12; Colossians 4.3), the meaning is almost certainly that they have an opportunity not just to stand firm but to make advances, to take the **good news** of Jesus into places and hearts where it has not yet reached. The qualifications are all in place. They have some power; not very much, but with the backing of Jesus they have all they need. And they have been faithful, keeping his **word** and not denying his name (this implies that there had already been persecution of some sort). They must take courage and go through the door. They must grasp the opportunity they have while it's still there.

But there is something in the way. As in most cities of the region, there was almost certainly a significant Jewish community in Philadelphia; Sardis, not far away, was a major Jewish centre at the time. As in the letter to Smyrna, we have here an indication that the synagogue community was using its civic status to block the advance of the **message** about Israel's **Messiah**, Jesus, a message so very Jewish and yet so challenging to Jewish people. We should not imagine a 'church' on one street corner and a 'synagogue' on another, as in many cities today. We should imagine a Jewish community of several thousand, with its own buildings and community life, and a church of probably two or three dozen at most, holding on to the highly improbable, and extremely risky, claim that the God of Israel had raised Jesus from the dead. That imbalance goes some way to help us explain what is now being said.

34

Verse 9 is considerably harsher than the equivalent in the Smyrna letter (2.9). We remind ourselves again that it is not 'anti-Jewish'; what we have here is what we might call an inner-Jewish question. Which of these groups can properly claim to be the true Jews, bearing the torch of God's ancient people? This, as we saw, was a common enough question in other parts of first-century Judaism. Here Jesus is quite clear. Those who follow him, the Davidic Messiah, are the true Jews. Those who deny him are forfeiting their right to that noble name.

What is more (this is where the Philadelphia letter goes beyond the Smyrna one), there will be a dramatic reversal of roles. In Malachi (1.2) God declares to rebellious Israel, 'I have loved you', contrasting Israel, the descendants of Jacob, with Edom, the descendants of Jacob's brother Esau. Now we have a similar contrast: the unbelieving synagogue will realize that Jesus, their own Messiah, has loved *this little group that believes in him*. And, whereas ancient prophecy had spoken of times when foreign nations would come and bow before the people of Israel, acknowledging that the one true God was with them, now it's going to be the other way round. Like Joseph's brothers in Genesis 42, the Jewish people will bow down before the Jesus they had previously despised. Eventually it will be clear that the followers of Jesus are the ones who can go through the open door, the ones who are to be pillars in the new temple.

They are the ones, too, who carry the new name – now, the triple name of God, of the heavenly Jerusalem, and of Jesus himself, bearing his 'new name' of King and Lord. They are to be marked out publicly as God's people, as Jesus' people, as citizens of the city where **heaven** and earth will be joined for ever. No earthquakes there. Security, vindication, and the ultimate reward for patience. The time of trial is coming on the whole earth (verse 10), and like a powerful searchlight it will reveal who is holding on to Jesus and his promise of a 'crown' (verse 11) and who isn't. The Philadelphia Christians are holding on at the moment; they must go on doing so, and 'conquer' when the time comes. So must we.

REVELATION 3.14–22

The Letter to Laodicea

[14]"Write this to the angel of the church in Laodicea. "These are the words of the Amen, the faithful and true witness, the beginning of God's creation. [15]I know your works: you are neither cold nor hot. I wish you were either cold or hot! [16]So, because you are lukewarm, neither cold nor hot, I am going to vomit you out of my mouth. [17]You say, 'I'm rich! I've done well! I don't need anything!' – but you don't know that you are miserable, pitiful, poor, blind and naked. [18]This is my advice to you: buy from me gold refined in the fire – that'll make you rich! – and white clothes to cover yourselves and prevent your shameful nakedness being seen; and also healing ointment to put on your eyes, so that you will be able to see. [19]When people are my friends, I tell them when they're in the wrong, and I punish them for it; so stir up your spirits and repent! [20]Look! I'm standing here, knocking at the door. If anyone hears my voice and opens the door, I will come in to them and eat with them, and they with me. [21]This will be my gift to the one who conquers: I will sit them beside me on my throne, just as I conquered and sat with my father on his throne. [22]Let the one who has an ear listen to what the spirit is saying to the churches.'"

At the beginning of the year 2011, there were extraordinary floods in Australia. To begin with it was part of Queensland, the vast state in the north-east of the country. Then it was more of the state, and still more. Then the floodwaters extended southwards across the border into New South Wales. Hundreds of thousands of homes were ruined, and millions of people displaced. The effect on businesses will not be known, at the time I am writing this, for some while, if ever.

In late January, the Prime Minister of Australia announced that there would be a one-off tax to help the country to rebuild after the devastation. Nobody who had been affected would have to pay, nor would the very poor. It was the least Australians could do, to reach out and help those who had lost everything.

That sense of an emergency in which the state has to come to the rescue goes back a very, very long way, at least to the Roman world of the first century. As we saw in the previous letter, Philadelphia had been devastated in the earthquake of AD 17, and had gratefully accepted help from central funds in Rome. But when a later earthquake, in AD 61, did major damage to several cities in the Lycus valley, to the south of Philadelphia, one city was able to refuse imperial help. It was a proud thing to do. Most would have jumped at the offer. But Laodicea reckoned it didn't need outside help. It was quite rich enough, thank you very much.

That tells us one of the most important things we need to know about Laodicea, which stood at the junction of important trade routes running more or less north–south and east–west across the district of Phrygia. Like many towns similarly situated, Laodicea profited from the regular traffic. It was, in fact, the banking centre of the whole region, and we know today what that means. But there was more. The town boasted a fine medical school; people would come from far distances to train as doctors. In particular, the school specialized in ophthalmology, the healing of the eyes. Laodicea was a good place to get hold of a particularly popular Phrygian eye-powder.

Still there was more. The local farmers in Laodicea had developed a particular breed of black sheep whose wool was of especially fine quality. This seems to have generated a fashion, which the breeders were only too happy to support. Clothes made from the Laodicean wool were highly sought after.

The one thing the city did not have was good water. The river Lycus at that point is not strong, and sometimes it dries up altogether in the summer. There are, however, two other sources of water, one to the north and the other to the south-east. To the north, standing high on a dramatic cliff, is the city of Hierapolis. It boasts to this day a set of hot springs to which tourists come from all over the world; the hot, chemically charged water comes bubbling out of the ground (channelled, today, into the bathing pools of various hotels), and spills over the cliff, leaving a white mineral deposit visible from miles around. In the first century they built aquaducts to bring this water across to Laodicea in the centre of the valley, four or five miles away. They can still be seen today – with their insides covered in hardened mineral deposit. But by the time the water arrived in Laodicea it was no longer hot. It was merely lukewarm. What was worse, the concentrated chemicals made it unsuitable to drink, unless for medicinal reasons you wanted to make yourself physically sick.

To the south-east of Laodicea was the town of Colosse. It, too, had suffered badly in the earthquake of AD 61, but had not been rebuilt. Colosse, however, had a splendid supply of water, flowing down from high, snow-capped Mount Cadmus: fast-flowing, chilly streams of almost Alpine quality. But by the time the water reached Laodicea, 11 miles away, the normal Turkish heat meant that it, too, had become lukewarm.

It is this remarkable feature of Laodicea – hot water that has cooled down, and cold water that has heated up – which forms the most famous part of this most famous of the seven letters. Indeed, the word 'Laodicean' has become proverbial for 'luke-warmness', with the meaning of 'apathetic', 'neither one thing nor the other'. So Jesus addresses the church with a mixture of sorrow and, it seems, real anger: 'You are neither cold nor hot. I wish you were either cold or hot! So, because you are lukewarm, I am going to vomit you out of my mouth.' 'Vomit' is not too strong a word here. Jesus is disgusted at the taste of Laodicean Christianity. It makes him sick.

The 'local colour' of this letter continues in full strength. 'You say, "I'm rich! I've done well! I don't need anything!"'

Apparently the smug, well-off attitude of the town as a whole had rubbed off on the Christians. But Jesus leaves them in no doubt. They are, in fact, miserable and pitiful (two general terms for their actual condition, even though it didn't feel like that): they are, more specifically, poor, blind and naked. They need the sort of gold that only Jesus can give. They need the kind of fine clothes – white ones, rather than the black ones so popular locally! – that only he can provide (white robes, we remind ourselves, were worn by the newly baptized, signalling their commitment to a new, holy **life**). They need a new kind of eye-salve; the Phrygian speciality won't do to heal the spiritual blindness of the place and the people. This is devastating stuff, all the more so for its multiple echoes of local culture.

Saint Teresa of Avila once complained to the Lord about what she was suffering. 'This', he is said to have replied, 'is how I treat my friends.' Teresa, who by then prayed in the good, direct and biblical style, retorted, 'Then you shouldn't be surprised that you have so few of them.' Verse 19 has just the suggestion of that kind of wry humour: after the withering denunciations of verses 15–18, Jesus now says, in effect, 'Now you know how I treat my friends!' It is because the Laodicean Christians are still, despite everything, on Jesus' list of friends – and Jesus is a faithful friend, even if we are not – that he will tell them sharply and truly when they are in the wrong. Because he is not only a friend but their Lord, he will also punish them, not to devastate them but to bring them to their senses. 'Stir up your spirits and repent!' One might say to many parts of today's church: if the cap fits, wear it.

As well as local colour, the letter to Laodicea carries the most striking descriptions of Jesus himself, and the most powerful promise. Strange, perhaps, that the one church that was in real trouble drew from the Lord the most intimate and loving promise. Perhaps there's a lesson there too. Jesus describes himself as 'the Amen', the one who stays true to his **word**, 'the faithful and true witness', and, more remarkably, 'the beginning of God's creation'. This echoes Colossians 1.15–20 (in a letter which was designed to be forwarded to Laodicea, as Colossians 4.16 indicates): Jesus is the one through whom God's world came to be, and also the one in whose **resurrection** the new creation has been launched. That cosmic plan puts the Laodicean lukewarmness into even more embarrassing perspective. Here is Jesus, the lord of the cosmos, and here are you, smug and self-satisfied but in fact poor, naked and blind!

And then there come the two closing promises. I said that verse 15 was the most famous verse in the letter, but verse 20 runs it close: 'Look! I'm standing here, knocking at the door.' I must have heard dozens of talks and sermons on that verse, all encouraging the hearers to open the door of their hearts, of their lives, and to let Jesus come in. Wonderful. Vital. Absolutely necessary. But, sadly, not quite what this passage is about. The echoes of stories in the **gospels** suggest that the one knocking on the door is the master of the house, returning at an unexpected hour (as in the warning to Sardis in 3.3), while the one who should open the door is the servant who has stayed awake. It is, then, Jesus' house in the first place; our job is simply to welcome him home. And the echoes of the ancient scriptures suggest a different but related image. This is the bridegroom, knocking on the door of the house where his beloved lies asleep (Song of Solomon 5.2). A glance at Revelation 21.2 suggests that this may have been in mind as well.

And again there is more. For some reason, all those talks and sermons I used to hear never got around to the second half of the verse: 'I will come in to them and eat with them, and they with me.' No early Christian could have heard those words without thinking of the regular meal, the bread-breaking, at which Jesus would come powerfully and personally and give himself to his people. Such meals anticipate the final messianic banquet (see 19.9). They are advance 'comings' of the one who will one day come fully and for ever.

Those who share this meal, and who are thereby strengthened to 'conquer' as Jesus 'conquered' through his death, will have the most extraordinary privilege. It is already quite mind-blowing to think of Jesus sharing the throne of God – though the early Christians saw this as the fulfilment of Psalm 110 and Daniel 7. But now it appears that 'those who conquer' are going to share Jesus' throne as well. They will (that is) share his strange, sovereign rule over the world, the rule to which he came not by force of arms but by the power of suffering love. This is what it means to be 'a royal priesthood'.

The seven letters are ended. Let anyone with an ear listen, today as much as in John's day, to what the **spirit** is saying to the churches.

REVELATION 4.1–6a

In the Throne Room

¹After this I looked – and there was a door in heaven, standing open! The voice like a trumpet, which I had heard speaking with me at the beginning, spoke again. 'Come up here,' it said, 'and I will show you what must take place after these things.'

²At once I was in the spirit. There in heaven stood a throne, and someone was sitting on it. ³The seated figure had the appearance of a jasper stone or a carnelian, and there was a rainbow around the throne, looking like an emerald. ⁴Around the throne were twenty-four thrones, and sitting on the thrones were twenty-four elders, clothed in white robes, and with golden crowns on their heads. ⁵Flashes of lightning, rumblings and thunderclaps were coming from the throne, and in front of the throne seven lampstands, which are the seven spirits of God, were burning with fire. ⁶ᵃ In front of the throne there was something like a sea of glass, like crystal.

We were walking into the cathedral as part of a great procession. My companion, a senior clergyman, was looking at the service paper we had been given.

'Ah!' he said. 'I see we have Revelation chapter 4 as the second reading.'

He smiled. 'One of the two most wonderful chapters in the Bible!'

Knowing I was setting myself up, I asked the obvious question.

'What's the other one, then?'

His smile grew even broader.

'Revelation chapter 5, of course!' he said, triumphantly.

I have often thought of that exchange as I have studied, and preached on, these two chapters. The letters to the seven churches in chapters 2 and 3 are powerful enough, to be sure. The opening vision of Jesus in chapter 1 is enough to make the serious reader react like John himself, and fall down in awe and worship. But now we realize that even these three opening chapters have only been preparation. Chapter 4 is where the story really starts. This is where John is given the 'revelation' that gives the book its title. Everything from this point on is part of the vision which is granted to him as he stands there in the heavenly throne room.

This short opening passage tells us, with every line, a wealth of detail about where John has been taken, and what it all means. It's worth going slowly through it, almost phrase by phrase.

What do you think of when you read about 'a door in **heaven**'? For many years I imagined that John looked up to the sky and saw, far away, tiny but bright like a distant star, an open door, through which he was then invited to enter into the heavenly world. I now think of it quite differently.

'Heaven' and 'earth', as I have often said, are not, in biblical theology, separated by a great gulf, as they are in much popular imagination. 'Heaven', God's sphere of reality, is right here, close beside us, intersecting with our ordinary reality. It is not so much like a door opening high up in the sky, far away. It is more like a door opening right in front of us where before we could only see this room, this field, this street. Suddenly, there is an opening leading into a different world – and an invitation to 'come up' and see what's going on.

This is not, as some people have supposed, anything to do with God's people being snatched away to heaven to avoid awful events that are about to take place on earth. It is about a prophet being taken into God's throne room so that he can see 'behind the scenes' and understand both what is going to take place and how it all fits together and makes sense. These two wonderful chapters, Revelation 4 and 5, do not stand alone. At one level, they introduce the whole sequence of prophecies that will take us through the rest of the book. At another level, they introduce more particularly the first of the sequences of prophecies, the 'seven seals' which must be broken open if the 'scroll' of God's purposes (5.1) is to be unrolled.

It may help us to keep our balance in the rich mixture of imagery in the following chapters if we see the book like this, structured around its sequences of 'sevens'. We have already had the seven letters to the churches. Now we are to be introduced to the seven seals, which are opened between 6.1 and 8.1. The seventh introduces a further sequence, the seven trumpets, which are blown one by one from 8.6 to 11.15. Then, at the centre of the book, we find visions which unveil the ultimate source of evil and its chief agents: the Dragon, the Beast from the Sea and the Beast from the Land – and also a vision of those who have somehow defeated these monsters (chapters 12—15). This then leads into the final sequence of seven: the seven bowls of God's wrath, the final plagues which, like the plagues of Egypt (15.1), will be the means of judging the great tyrannical power and rescuing God's people from its claws. These bowls of wrath are poured out in chapter 16, but their effect is described more fully in chapters 17 and 18, leading to the celebration of victory over the two Beasts in chapter 19. That only leaves the old Dragon himself, and the last twists of his fate are described in chapter 20. This then clears the stage for the final unveiling of God's eventual plan:

the New Jerusalem in which heaven and earth are joined fully and for ever.

What we are witnessing in chapters 4 and 5, then, is not the final stage in God's purposes. This is not a vision of the ultimate 'heaven', seen as the final resting place of God's people. It is, rather, the admission of John into 'heaven' *as it is at the moment*. The scene in the heavenly throne room is the present reality; the vision John is given while he is there is a multiple vision of 'what must take place after these things' – not 'the end of the world' as such, but those terrible events which were going to engulf the world and cause all the suffering for God's people about which the seven churches have just been so thoroughly warned.

John is summoned into the throne room because, like some of the ancient Israelite prophets, he is privileged to stand in God's council chamber and hear what is going on in order then to report it to his people back on earth. Like Micaiah ben Imlah in 1 Kings 22, he sees God himself sitting on his throne, with his hosts around him, and is privy to their discussions and plans. But this scene reminds us, too, of Ezekiel 1, where the prophet is given a vision of God's throne-chariot, carried to and fro on whirling, fiery wheels. The rainbow (verse 3) reminds us of that, but also takes us back to the story of Noah in Genesis 9, where the great bow in the sky was God's visible promise of mercy, never again to destroy the earth with a flood. A 'rainbow looking like an emerald' is a challenge to the imagination – not the only such challenge in these chapters, as we shall see! – but the effect is a rich and dense combination of mercy, awe and beauty.

As in some other ancient visions, so here John sees God's council: twenty-four elders, sitting on separate thrones. They represent, almost certainly, the combination of the twelve tribes of Israel and the **twelve apostles**. They are, as it were, the embodied perfection of the people of God, sharing now in the rule of God over the world. Their white robes indicate purity and victory; their crowns reveal them as the representatives of the 'royal priesthood' (1.6; 5.10; 20.6). It is not (to say the least) a placid scene. Lightning, thunder and fire are sparkling and booming – something that happens at significant moments throughout the book (8.5; 11.19; 16.18). When God's purposes are being disclosed, we are to expect things to be shaken up alarmingly.

The final detail of this opening description of the throne room is 'something like a sea of glass'. This is deeply mysterious. Solomon's **Temple** had a 'sea', a huge bronze bowl (1 Kings 7.23–26), and this may have been part of the point. But in 15.2 the 'sea of glass' has become more like the Red Sea, through which the children of Israel have passed to safety. The other 'sea' in Revelation is the one from which, as in Daniel 7, the great Beast emerges (13.1), while the Dragon stands beside the shore apparently presiding over the Beast's appearing (12.18). Then, of course, in the New Jerusalem itself there is 'no longer sea' (21.1). All this seems to indicate that the 'sea' within the throne room is a kind of symbolic representation of the fact that, within God's world as it currently is, evil is present, and dangerous. But it is contained within God's sovereign purposes, and it will eventually be overthrown.

I have spoken of this scene so far in terms of God's throne in heaven, and John's appearing before it like an Old Testament prophet. But the idea of a throne room, with someone sitting on the throne surrounded by senior counsellors, would instantly remind John's readers of a very different court: that of Caesar. We have already heard hints of the power struggle (the **kingdom of God** against the kingdoms of the world) in the opening three chapters. Now, by strong implication, we are being invited to see that the powers of the world are simply parodies, cheap imitation copies, of the one Power who really and truly rules in heaven and on earth. As John's great vision unfolds, we will see how it is that these human kingdoms have acquired their wicked, cruel power, and how it is that God's radically different sort of power will win the victory over them.

This is the victory in which the seven letters were urging the churches to claim their share. We now discover how that victory comes about.

It begins with the unveiling of reality. Behind the complex and messy confusions of church life in ancient Turkey; behind the challenges of the fake synagogues and the threatening rulers; behind the ambiguous struggles and difficulties of ordinary Christians – there stands the heavenly throne room in which the world's creator and lord remains sovereign. Only by stopping in our tracks and contemplating this vision can we begin to glimpse the reality which not only makes sense of our own realities but enables us, too, to win the victory.

REVELATION 4.6b–11

Praise to the Creator

[6b]In the middle of the throne, and all around the throne, were four living creatures, full of eyes in front and behind. [7]The first creature was like a lion, the second creature was like an ox, the third creature had a human face, and the fourth creature was like a flying eagle. [8]Each of the four creatures had six wings, and they were full of eyes all round and inside. Day and night they take no rest, as they say,

'Holy, holy, holy,
Lord God Almighty,
Who Was and Who Is and Who Is to Come.'

[9]When the creatures give glory and honour and thanksgiving to the one who is sitting on the throne, the one who lives for ever and ever, [10]the twenty-four elders fall down in front of the one who is sitting on the throne, and worship the one who lives for ever and ever. They throw down their crowns in front of the throne, saying, [11]'O Lord our God, you deserve to receive glory and honour and power, because you created all things; because of your will they existed and were created.'

Scientists and anthropologists have often asked themselves, 'What is it that humans can do that computers can't do?' Computers, after all, can play chess better than most of us. They can work out answers to all kinds of questions that would take us a lot longer. Some people have boldly declared that, though at the moment computers can't do quite everything that we can, they will one day overtake us.

The writer David Lodge wrote a powerful novel on this theme, entitled *Thinks* ... The heroine eventually discovers the answer: humans can weep; and humans can forgive. Those are two very powerful and central human activities. They take place in a quite different dimension from anything a computer can do. But without them, we would be less than human.

A similar question is often posed: 'What can humans do that animals can't do?' Again, some scientists have tried to insist that we humans are simply 'naked apes', a more sophisticated version perhaps, but still within the same continuum. This is a trickier question than the one about computers, but to get straight to the point: in our present passage, the main difference is that humans can say the word 'because'. In particular, they can say it about God himself.

Consider the two songs of praise in this passage, the first in verse 8 and the second in verse 11. The first one is the song which the four living creatures sing round the clock, day and night. They praise God as the holy one; they praise him as the everlasting one. The four creatures deserve our attention for other reasons, too. They seem in some ways to resemble the seraphim who surround God in Isaiah's vision in the **Temple** (Isaiah chapter 6), and they are also quite like the four creatures of Ezekiel's vision (Ezekiel 1). They represent the animal creation, including humans but at this stage with the human-faced creature being simply one among the others, alongside the king of the wild beasts (the lion), the massive leader of tamed animals (the ox), and the undisputed king of the birds (the eagle). (In some early Christian traditions, these animals represent the four **gospel** writers, so that Matthew (the human face), Mark (the lion), Luke (the ox) and John (the eagle) are thought of as the living creatures who surround, and worship, the Jesus of whom they speak.) These remarkable creatures seem to be not merely surrounding God's throne but ready to do his bidding. Twice John tells us that they are 'full of eyes': unsleeping, keeping watch for God over his whole creation.

The song of these living creatures is simply an act of adoring praise. We are meant, reading this passage, to see with the Psalmist that all creation is dependent on God and worships him in its own way. That alone is worth pondering as a striking contrast to how most of us view the animal kingdom. But the contrast with the twenty-four elders is then made all the more striking. Creation as a whole simply worships God; the humans who represent God's people *understand why they do so*. 'You *deserve*,' they say, 'to receive glory and honour and power, *because* you created all things.' There it is: the 'because' that distinguishes humans from other animals, however noble those animals may be in their own way. Humans are given the capacity to reflect, to understand what's going on. And, in particular, to express that understanding in worship.

Worship, after all, is the most central human activity. Certainly it's the most central Christian activity. When I was a student, many of us busied ourselves with all kinds of Christian activities – teaching and learning, studying scripture, evangelism, prayer meetings and so on. We went to church quite a lot, but never (I think) reflected much on what we were doing there. There was, after all, a sermon to learn from, and the hymns were good teaching aids as well. It was a time of learning and **fellowship**. When a friend suggested at one point that worship was actually the centre of everything, the rest of us looked at him oddly. It seemed a bit of a cop-out.

Now, of course, I know he was right. Worship is what we were made for; worship with a *because* in it is what marks us out as genuine human beings. This scene remains the foundation for everything that follows in the rest of this powerful and disturbing book. All that is to come flows from the fact that the whole creation is called to worship the one true God as its creator. The profound problems within that creation mean that the creator must act decisively to put things right, not because creation is bad and he's angry with it but because it's good and he's angry with the forces that have corrupted and defaced it, and which threaten to destroy it (11.18).

These short songs of praise are the beginning of one of the most remarkable features of the book. Revelation contains several passages which, like these ones only often considerably longer, offer praise and prayer to the creator God. They grow out of the worshipping life of ancient Israel, often echoing the psalms, the prophets, and other worship songs such as the song of Moses and Miriam in Exodus 15. Many have guessed, probably rightly, that these songs and prayers are similar to those which the earliest Christians used, though the logic of John's vision is not that what he sees in the heavenly dimension is merely reflecting what is going on in the life of the church, but rather that what he sees in **heaven** is what *ought to be* going on here on earth. Heaven is in charge; heaven gives the lead. It isn't simply 'the spiritual dimension' of what we happen to choose to do.

There is much more to learn about heaven, and about worship, in the passages which follow at once. But perhaps we should pause here and reflect carefully. Do we, in our private prayers and worship, and in our public services and liturgies, give sufficient weight to praising God as the creator of all things? Do we allow ancient poems like the song of the three men in the fiery furnace (sometimes called the 'Benedicite') to inform and colour our praises, so that we consciously celebrate with all the different elements of creation? Do we then view creation itself as a theatre of praise, and live appropriately within such an awesome place?

In particular, are we conscious of our vocation to worship with a 'because'? Do we (in other words) allow our thinking about God to inform our praise? Do we think through the fact that he *deserves* 'glory, honour and power' because of what he has done?

All this may seem rather obvious. But actually it's anything but. The world has been full of movements, systems, philosophies and religions that have ignored creation as shabby, or irrelevant to 'spiritual' life, or that have vilified it as a nasty, dark and dangerous place, full of evil and death. Equally, the world has been full of movements which, instead of worshipping the God who made the world, have worshipped the world itself, or forces within it (money, sex, war, power – the usual lot). Revelation sets out the delicate but decisive balance. All creation worships God; we humans are called to worship him with mind as well as heart, recognizing that he is worthy of all praise as the creator of all things.

REVELATION 5.1–7

The Lion, the Lamb

¹I saw that there was a scroll in the right hand of the one sitting on the throne. The scroll was written on the inside and the outside, and it was sealed with seven seals. ²I saw a strong angel announcing in a loud voice, 'Does anybody deserve to open the scroll, to undo its seals?' ³And nobody in heaven or on the earth or under the earth could open the scroll or look at it. ⁴I burst into tears because it seemed that there was nobody who was worthy to open the scroll or look inside it. ⁵One of the elders, however, spoke to me. 'Don't cry,' he said. 'Look! The lion from the tribe of Judah, the Root of David, has won the victory! He can open the scroll and its seven seals.'

⁶Then I saw in the midst of the throne and of the four living creatures, and in the midst of the elders, a lamb. It was standing there as though it had been slaughtered; it had seven horns and seven eyes, which are the seven spirits of God sent out

into all the earth. ⁷The lamb came up and took the scroll from
the right hand of the one who was sitting on the throne.

We stood and stared at the letter as it lay on the doormat.
It was a smart envelope, good quality paper, with clear, bold
typewritten name and address. And at the top, in even larger
letters, we saw the words: TO BE OPENED BY ADDRESSEE
ONLY. And the addressee was not at home. We hardly dared
touch it.

But supposing the envelope had said, TO BE OPENED BY
THE PERSON WHO DESERVES TO DO SO? That would
have been even more intriguing, and would have posed a
different kind of challenge. How do you know if you deserve
to open it? As one writer put it, we are all overdrawn at the
moral bank. The thought of being sufficiently 'deserving' for
any task at once makes us search our consciences and discover,
no doubt, all kinds of things which might well disqualify us for
whatever task is at hand.

That is the situation at the start of this scene. We are still
looking, through John's eyes, at the heavenly throne room, and
it is not simply one long round of endless, repetitive praise.
This is the throne room of God the creator, and his world
is not merely a tableau, a living picture to be enjoyed. It is a
project. It is going somewhere. There is work to be done.

In particular, there is work to be done to rescue the creation
from the deadly dangers that have taken root within it. There
is work to be done to overthrow the forces that are out to
destroy the very handiwork of God. That will be a terrible task,
and one might well shrink from it in itself. But of course we
have all made it worse by being, ourselves, part of the problem
rather than part of the solution.

This is at the heart of the challenge issued by the 'strong
angel' of verse 2. God, the creator, has a scroll in his right hand,
like an architect with a rolled-up design for a building, or
a general with a rolled-up plan of a campaign. The scroll is

sealed with seven seals. We rightly guess, however, that it contains God's secret plan to undo and overthrow the world-destroying projects that have already gained so much ground, and to plant and nurture instead the world-rescuing project which will get creation itself back on track in the right direction. Is there anybody out there who deserves to open this scroll? Is there anybody who has not, themselves, contributed in some way to the problems of creation, to the age-old spoiling and trashing of God's beautiful world?

John's answer shows that he, like the other New Testament writers, had a realistic view of the deep-rooted problem of all the human race – and, it seems, all other creatures as well (verse 3). Nobody deserves to open the scroll.

But that constitutes a major problem. God the creator committed himself, back in Genesis 1 and 2, to work within his creation *through obedient humankind*. That is how the world was designed to work. For God then to say, 'Well, humans have failed, so I'll have to do it some other way,' would be to unmake the very structure of his good creation, to turn it into a different sort of world entirely. Someone must be found.

From within the traditions of Israel, one answer would have been: Israel itself is called to be God's true humanity, to put God's rescue plan into operation. True. But, though John doesn't say so explicitly, here we meet the second level of the problem. Israel too has failed, has let God down. And here again God appears to be faced with a dilemma. If he says, 'Well, Israel hasn't done what I hoped, so I'll have to cut out that bit of my plan', it would look as though he has blundered, has been flailing around with different ideas, none of which have worked. God has made the world in such a way that his plans for the world must be executed by a human being. Since human sin now means that those plans require a rescue operation, God has called one human family to be the means through which this rescue will be put into effect. God has, in other words, determined to *run* the world through *humans*, and to *rescue* the world through *Israel*. Both have let him down. What will he now do? 'Does anybody deserve to open the scroll?'

We might well join John in floods of tears at this point. Can nothing be done? But already the plan, to wipe away all tears from all eyes (7.17; 21.4) has begun. 'Don't cry,' says one of the elders. 'Look!' he says. 'Here is the one who can do it.' And before we even look we know who this is. It is the truly human one. It is the true Israelite. It is the **Messiah**.

But in John's vision nothing is ever said straightforwardly, because everything must be seen in its multidimensional glory. John is invited to look at 'the lion from the tribe of Judah, the Root of David'. The echoes that rumble like thunder around the cave walls of our scriptural memories conjure up prophecies and visions. The Messiah will come from David's tribe, the tribe of Judah; Judah was described in Genesis 49.9 as a lion's cub; this was picked up in later visionary writing in which the Messiah appears as a lion to attack the 'eagle' of the Roman empire (2 Esdras 11 and 12, in the Apocrypha). No first-century Jew would miss the reference, or fail to understand 'the Root of David', a phrase which, as in 22.16, echoes the great messianic prophecy of Isaiah 11.1–10. And, as we would expect of the true Messiah, we are told not just that he 'deserves' to open the scroll, but that he 'has won the victory'. The Messiah, it was thought, would fight and win the decisive battle against the last great enemy of God's people, and so liberate them once and for all. Well, says the elder to John, he has done it! Here he is!

And now we come to one of the most decisive moments in all scripture. What John has *heard* is the announcement of the lion. What he then *sees* is the lamb. He is to hold what he has heard in his head while gazing at what he now sees; and he is to hold what he is seeing in his head as he reflects on what he has heard. The two seem radically different. The lion is the symbol both of ultimate power and of supreme royalty, while the lamb symbolizes both gentle vulnerability and, through its

sacrifice, the ultimate weakness of death. But the two are now to be fused together, completely and for ever. From this moment on, John, and we as his careful readers, are to understand that the victory won by the lion is accomplished through the sacrifice of the lamb, and in no other way. But we are also to understand that what has been accomplished by the lamb's sacrifice is not merely the wiping away of sin for a few people here and there. The victory won by the lamb is God's lion-like victory, through his faithful Israel-in-person, through his obedient humanity-in-person, over all the forces of corruption and death, over everything that would destroy and obliterate God's good, powerful and lovely creation.

There have been, down the years, plenty of lion-Christians. Yes, they think, Jesus died for us; but now God's will is to be done in the lion-like fashion, through brute force and violence, to make the world come into line, to enforce God's will. No, replies John; think of the lion, yes, but gaze at the lamb.

And there have been plenty of lamb-Christians. Yes, they think, Jesus may have been 'the lion of Judah', but that's a political idea which we should reject because **salvation** consists in having our sins wiped away so that we can get out of this compromised world and go off to **heaven** instead. No, replies John; gaze at the lamb, but remember that it is the lion's victory that he has won.

And remember, as we listen and look, that the lamb has seven horns and seven eyes. He is, that is to say, all-powerful and all-seeing. And he has the right to take the scroll and open it. Everything else follows from this moment.

REVELATION 5.8–14

Worthy Is the Lamb!

[8]When he took the scroll, the four living creatures and the twenty-four elders fell down in front of the lamb. They each had a harp, and they each had golden bowls full of incense,

which are the prayers of God's holy people. [9]They sing a new song, which goes like this:

'You are worthy to take the scroll;
you are worthy to open its seals;
for you were slaughtered and with your own blood
you purchased a people for God,
from every tribe and tongue,
from every people and nation
[10]and made them a kingdom and priests to our God
and they will reign on the earth.'

[11]As I watched, I heard the voice of many angels around the throne, the living creatures and the elders. Their number was ten thousand times ten thousand, thousands upon thousands, [12]and they were saying in full voice,

'The slaughtered lamb has now deserved
to take the riches and the power,
to take the wisdom, strength and honour,
to take the glory, and the blessing.'

[13]Then I heard every creature in heaven, on the earth, under the earth, and in the sea, and everything that is in them, saying,

'To the One on the throne and the lamb
be blessing and honour and glory
and power for ever and ever!'

[14]'Amen!' cried the four living creatures. As for the elders, they fell down and worshipped.

Think of it as another visit to the theatre. You are sitting in the dark when the drum begins. A slow, steady rhythm. It's telling you something. It's going somewhere. It builds up, louder and louder. Then the voices join in. Wild, excited singing, rich and vivid. That too builds up, louder and louder. Then, as the stage lights come on, the musicians join in as well: the rich brass, the shimmering strings, the sharp, clear oboe and the flute fluttering like a bird to and fro over the top of it all. The music is designed to set the scene, to open the play, to make you realize that this is drama like you've never seen it before.

And the actors? Now for the shock. John, in describing this scene, has hinted that *we are the actors*. We are listening to the music so that we can now come on stage, ready or not, and play our part.

It's there in the opening of the music that he describes. When the elders fall down in front of the lamb, each of them was holding two things: a harp, and a golden bowl of incense. John tells us what the incense is: it's the prayers of God's people, that is, of you and me. The heavenly scene is umbilically related to the earthly. The ordinary, faithful, humble prayers of Christians here on earth appear in **heaven** as glorious, sweet-smelling incense. I suspect the same is true of the music, with the heavenly harps corresponding to the song, however feeble and out of tune, which we sing to God's praise here and now. Then, in the first of the three songs in this passage, we find that the lamb is being praised, not just for rescuing us but for turning us from hopeless rebels into useful servants, from sin-slaves into 'a **kingdom** and priests'. From rubbish into royalty. This is our play. The lamb has set us free to stop being spectators and to start being actors.

We hear this crescendo of songs, then, not merely with excitement and eager fascination but with a sense of vocation. First, the praise of the lamb for what he's done (verses 9 and 10): he is indeed worthy to take and open the scroll and its seals. He is worthy (that is) to be the agent to carry forward God's plan to destroy the destroyers, to thwart the forces of evil, to confront the seemingly all-powerful and to establish his new order instead. And the way the lamb has done this is through his own death, his own blood.

Any first-century Jew would know that this meant 'through his death seen as a **sacrifice**'. Similarly, they would know that a sacrifice through which God 'purchased a people . . . to be a kingdom and priests' is the ultimate Passover sacrifice, the final fulfilment of what God had done close up in history when he set his people free from their slavery in Egypt, 'purchasing' them like slaves from a slave-market, in order to establish them as a 'royal priesthood', as the people through whom he would accomplish his worldwide purposes. That much is clear in the book of Exodus (19.4–6).

But John, as so often, isn't just evoking one biblical passage. This first song also echoes the great passage in Daniel 7 where, after the raging of the monsters and the vindication of 'one like a **son of man**', God establishes his rule over the whole earth in and through the 'people of the holy ones of the Most High' (7.22, 27). The rescue effected in Daniel is, as it were, the great new **Exodus**, with the monsters who have oppressed God's people taking the place of Pharaoh in Egypt. John is picking up the same storyline, only now putting together the slaughtered Passover lamb and the vindicated son of man. This breathtaking move is made possible, indeed obvious, by the rushing together of both vocations in Jesus himself.

The first song, then, praises the lamb for rescuing a people by his death so that they could then take forward God's royal and redemptive purposes ('kingdom and priests') for the wider world. The second song, in which thousands upon thousands of angels join, turns from what the lamb has *achieved* to what he has *deserved*, namely, all the honour and glory of which creation is capable. The wealth and strength of the nations belongs to him; everything that ennobles and enriches human life, everything that enables people to live wisely, to enjoy and celebrate the goodness of God's world – all this is to be laid at his feet. Sadly, there are many Christians who think of Jesus purely in terms of their own comfort and hope ('he has rescued us; he is with us as a friend') and who fail completely to see the sheer scope of his majesty, the sweep of his glory. Many rest content to have Jesus around the place for particular 'spiritual' purposes, but continue to assign riches, power, glory and the rest to earthly forces and rulers. Perhaps one of the reasons why Revelation is marginalized in some churches is precisely because it so strongly challenges this attitude.

And so to the third song, in which every creature in every part of God's creation joins in, much as in Paul's vision in Philippians 2.9–11. This time the praise of the lamb has been joined together with the praise of God the creator, as in chapter 4. In thunderous worship the whole creation praises 'the One on the throne and the lamb'.

And, if we are not either overwhelmed with the vision or exhausted with trying to understand it, we may glimpse here the most profound truth of all, which like everything else in chapters 4 and 5 continues to inform the whole of the rest of the book. The lamb *shares the praise which belongs to the one and only God*. This is John's own way of glimpsing and communicating the mind-challenging but central truth at the heart of Christian **faith**: Jesus, the lion-lamb, Israel's Messiah, the true man – this Jesus shares the worship which belongs, and uniquely and only belongs, to the one creator God.

But notice what this means. The affirmation of the full, un-equivocal divinity of the lion-lamb comes, and only comes, in the context of the victory of God, through the lion-lamb, over all the powers of evil. It isn't enough just to agree with the idea, in the abstract, that Jesus is, in some sense or other, God. (People often say to me, 'Is Jesus God?', as though we knew who 'God' was ahead of time, and could simply fit Jesus in to that picture.) God, as we have already seen in Revelation, is the creator, who is intimately involved with his world, and worshipped by that world. God has plans and purposes to deliver his world from all that has spoiled it; in other words, to re-establish his sovereign rule, his 'kingdom', on earth as in heaven. It is at the heart of those plans, and only there, that we find the lion-lamb sharing the throne of the one God. The church has all too often split off a bare affirmation of Jesus' 'divinity' from an acceptance of God's kingdom-agenda. To do so is to miss the point, and to use a version of one part of the truth as a screen to stop oneself from having to face the full impact of the rest of the truth. We discover, and celebrate, the divinity of the lion-lamb Messiah only when we find ourselves caught up to share his work as the royal priesthood, summing up creation's praises before him but also bringing his rescuing rule to bear on the world.

REVELATION 6.1–8

Four Horsemen

[1]The next thing I saw was this. When the lamb had opened one of the seven seals, I heard one of the four living creatures say in a voice like thunder, 'Come!' [2]And, as I watched, there was a white horse. Its rider was holding a bow. He was given a crown, and he went off winning victories, and to win more of them.

[3]When the lamb opened the second seal, I heard the second living creature say, 'Come!' [4]And another horse went out, fiery red this time. Its rider was given permission to take peace away from the earth, so that people would kill one another. He was given a great sword.

[5]When the lamb opened the third seal, I heard the third living creature say, 'Come!' As I watched, there was a black horse. Its rider held a pair of scales in his hand. [6]I heard something like a voice coming from the midst of the four living creatures. 'A quart of wheat for a denarius!' said the voice. 'And three quarts of barley for a denarius! But don't ruin the oil and the wine!'

[7]When the lamb opened the fourth seal, I heard the voice of the fourth living creature say, 'Come!' [8]As I looked, there was a pale horse, and its rider's name was Death. Hades followed along behind him. They were given authority over a quarter of the earth, to kill with the sword, and with famine, and with death, and by means of earth's wild animals.

All doctors, and all pastors, know that when someone comes to them with a problem, the problem they talk about may not be the only problem they have. The pain that gets someone into the doctor's surgery may well be only a symptom of much deeper ills, medical or psychological. The fear, depression or guilt that makes someone knock on the pastor's door is quite likely to be a second- or third-order anxiety which won't be solved until the first-order ones have been exposed and addressed.

This often lands the patient, or the person seeking counselling, in a position very like the reader of Revelation 6. We finally pluck up courage to go to the doctor. We finally admit we've got a problem, and make an appointment with the pastor. Now everything will be sorted out! Now I'm going to feel well again, happy again! This visit will put me back on track! And, again and again, the wise doctor or pastor knows that they must disappoint, for the moment, in order to get to the root of the problem and effect the lasting cure. First we must enquire about other symptoms. First we must find out a bit more about the background: when have you felt like this before? What have you been most afraid of? Soon the person answering the questions will feel uncomfortable. I didn't know we were going to get into all *that*. Surely we don't need to bring those things up again? It was a long time ago, and besides . . .

Sorry, but we do need to. Unless we lay out the problems to their full extent, no real healing can take place. Unless the ills of the world are brought out, shown up in their true colours, put on display and allowed to do their worst, they cannot be overthrown. Unless the four horsemen ride out and do what they have to do, the scroll cannot be read. The victory of the lion-lamb will not be complete.

This is the answer (like all answers to do with Revelation, it remains partial and puzzling: this is a book designed to go on making you ponder and pray, not one designed to answer everything to your satisfaction) to the problem that many readers have when they get to Revelation 6. We have just celebrated the magnificent scene in the throne room with the whole of creation singing a glorious, thunderous hymn of praise to the creator God and to the slaughtered lamb. We have celebrated the fact that he has won the victory: now God's plan to rescue the whole world can go ahead! So, surely, all we have to do is to turn the page and there we will find . . .

And there we will find that the dark powers of evil are given their head. Things have to be exposed before they can be dealt with. Things have to come to the light before the surgeon can perform the operation. Ancient memories of guilt and sorrow must be raked up, however painfully, before they can be prayed through and healed. Revelation is, as it were, a cosmic version of the tough pastoral struggle over the deeply wounded soul. The soul of the world is aware of immediate problems and pains; but unless we look deeper, to the ancient patterns of conquest, violence, oppression and death itself we shall not begin to understand what needs to be done if the world is to be healed, really healed rather than merely patched together for a few more years.

Thus, when the lamb opens the first four seals on the scroll, instead of four glorious remedies for the world's ills we find the four living creatures summoning four horses and riders, each (so it seems) to make matters worse. (The four strange horsemen owe something to Zechariah's visions in his chapters 1 and 6, but are here given quite a new role.) The first, the white horse with the rider and his bow, is sometimes supposed to be the **Messiah** himself, on the basis of the partial parallel in 19.11. This is not impossible, but I think it's more likely that he symbolizes the conquering kings of the earth who have charged to and fro, overcoming mighty nations and claiming sovereignty (the 'crown') over them. What happens when the 'seals' are opened is that the forces of human conquest and oppression are allowed to do their worst, before the divine purpose, which is to deal with the world's ills, can be read from the scroll.

61

This fits well, too, with the second, third and fourth horsemen. The second, the fiery red horse whose rider takes from the earth even the superficial appearance of peace, is well known in every century. The black horse, third in line, signifies the economic problems which so often lie at the root of violence within and between nations. Ordinary commodities, the staple diet of poor people, shoot up in price; luxury items, oil and wine, stay the same, allowing the rich once more to get richer at the expense of the poor. The pale horse, carrying Death on its back and with Hades, the abode of the dead, as a personified creature following behind, is the ultimate threat of every tyrant and every anarchist. Human history records that again and again war, famine and a thousand other things have carried people off before their time.

These four are the basic ills which humans inflict upon one another. They charge off around the world, and must be allowed to do this in order that the saving **message** of the scroll can have its full effect. I have suggested, and we must follow this through in due course, that they are allowed to do their worst because the problems they represent need to be tackled head on, not side-stepped. For too long, over the last century at least, mainline Western churches have healed the wounds of the human race lightly, declaring 'peace, peace' when there is no peace except at the superficial level. We have been unwilling to look below the surface and see the dark forces at work. But if God's new creation is to be brought to birth, the deepest ills of the old one must be exposed, allowed to come out, and be dealt with.

This is a good moment at which to think about how the symbolism of chapters like this works. Obviously the four horsemen, and their riders, are symbols. John does not expect that his readers will shortly look out of the window and see these sinister characters riding by on the streets of Ephesus or Smyrna. But the sequence, too, is symbolic. John does not suppose that conquest is followed by violence, violence by economic disaster, and economic disaster by widespread death. They are connected, but not so tidily.

This is one of the differences between writing something with words and writing it with music. In music, you can have several lines which all happen at the same time; but with words you have to say everything in sequence. This sevenfold sequence (four down, three to go, so far) is not chronological. It is an exposition of a sevenfold reality.

In the same way, we should not suppose that this sevenfold sequence of 'seals' being opened is supposed to take place *before* the subsequent sequences of the trumpets (chapters 8—11) and the bowls of wrath (chapter 16). Rather, each of the sequences – and the material in between, too – is a fresh angle of vision on the same highly complex reality. If we look at the problems and pains of the world from *this* angle, God's answer is to draw out the arrogant wickedness of humans to its full extent and show that he is bringing his people safely through (chapter 7). If we look at those same problems and pains from the *next* angle of vision, God's answer is to allow the forces of destruction to do their worst, so that he can then establish his **kingdom** fully and finally over the world (chapters 8—11). And if we take a deep breath and begin the story again from yet a third angle of vision (chapters 12 and 13), we see the full depth and horror of the problem, to which God's answer will be to inflict on the rebellious world the equivalent of the plagues of Egypt, before finally rescuing his people and judging the dark powers that have for so long enslaved them (chapters 12—19).

Then and only then can the darkest power of all be dealt with (chapter 20). And then and only then can the new **heaven** and the new earth be established, without any fear that there may be lingering sicknesses still unhealed, buried sadnesses still to produce grief. Revelation 6—20 is not what we wanted to hear, just as the news from the doctor or the pastor may not be what we wanted to hear. But it is what we must hear if the world is to be healed.

REVELATION 6.9–17

The Day Is Coming!

[9]When the lamb opened the fifth seal, I saw under the altar the souls of those who had been killed because of the word of God and because of the witness which they had borne. [10]They shouted at the tops of their voices. 'Holy and true Master!' they called. 'How much longer are you going to put off giving judgment, and avenging our blood on the earth-dwellers?' [11]Each of them was given a white robe, and they were told to rest for a little while yet, until the full number of those to be killed, as they had been, was reached – including both their fellow-servants and their kinsfolk.

[12]As I looked, he opened the sixth seal. There was a great earthquake, the sun turned black like sackcloth, the whole moon became like blood, [13]and the stars were falling from heaven onto the earth as when a fig tree, shaken by a strong wind, drops its late fruit. [14]The heaven disappeared like a scroll being rolled up, and every mountain and island was moved out of its place. [15]The kings of the earth, the leading courtiers, the generals, the rich, the power-brokers, and everyone, slave and free, all hid themselves among the caves and rocks of the mountains. [16]'Fall upon us!' they were saying to the mountains and the rocks. 'Hide us from the face of the One who sits on the throne, and from the anger of the lamb! [17]The great day of their anger has come, and who can stand upright?'

There are three ways of ending a game of chess. The first is that one player or the other simply wins the game. There is no question: this is checkmate, and that's the end of it. The second is that both players realize the game is unwinnable, and they agree to a draw. The third is that one of the players loses his or her temper, kicks the board over and stalks off. Highly unsatisfactory – except, no doubt, for the short-lived pleasure of letting off steam.

There are plenty of people who think that God, faced with the long chess game of rescuing the world, should simply kick the board over and leave it at that. The game has become so stupid and complicated, with so many crazy people doing so many idiotic things, with so much suffering and pain and anger and violence – isn't it time, they think, for him to step in and do something? Shouldn't he, as it were, send in the tanks and sweep all opposition aside? Wouldn't that be better than letting things run on?

This objection is regularly heard from people who have given up believing in God, or perhaps never believed in the first place. How can they believe, they ask, in a 'God' who seems to do nothing when faced with the terrors and torments of this world? How can we claim he's sovereign over the world when the world is in such a mess? Surely he should simply reach out a divine foot and kick all the recalcitrant chess pieces into the fire?

The problem is also regularly voiced by those who, though they believe in God, find the present suffering virtually intolerable. Here there is a long tradition, going back through the Psalms and the prophets to the children of Israel in Egypt, crying to their God to do something at last (Exodus 2.23). This cry ('How long, O Lord, how long?') echoes down the centuries, and is heard again as the fifth seal is opened and we are confronted, not now by another horseman or any other violent image, but by the **souls** of those who had been killed because they had borne faithful witness to God's **word**.

This is a fascinating passage for many reasons, not least because it is the only place in the New Testament where anything definite is said about the present state and location of the Christian dead. They are 'under the altar' – John hasn't mentioned an 'altar' before this, but we shall gradually discover that the throne room where he is receiving his vision is also the heavenly **temple**. These 'souls' are conscious of the fact that the world is still unjudged and unhealed. Wickedness, including the wickedness that brought them to their martyrs' deaths, still goes unchecked. They long for justice, as all who have been deeply wronged long for it; this is not petty or spiteful vengeance, but the heartaching desire to see the world brought back into balance at last, and their own harsh verdict and sentence being shown up as unjust.

And they are told that they must wait. There are plenty of calls for patience in Revelation, and here is another. They are given a white robe – how a 'soul' puts on a 'robe' might baffle the imagination, but of course John is as usual writing in symbols, and the white robe indicates both purity and victory – and told that something else still has to happen before God's justice will have worked itself out. Only when that happens, as we discover later in the book, will the new world appear, the world in which they will be raised from the dead, with justice done at last and seen to be done.

The 'something else' which still has to happen is the point at which we discover the way in which God actually runs the world, as opposed to the way most people assume he ought to run it. To use the (admittedly dangerous) image of the chess match, this is where we discover that God is not the sort to kick the table over. Nor will he settle for a draw. His opponent has many things going for him, but God is playing the long game and will go all out for the win.

What has to happen, it seems, is for evil to do its worst, to reach its height, and so to be at last ripe for the judgment that wise and faithful people know, in advance, it deserves. Way back in scripture, God tells Abraham that his family will have to wait for four generations before coming to possess their promised land, because 'the iniquity of the Amorite is not yet complete' (Genesis 15.16): in other words, God will not judge them until they are fully and thoroughly deserving of it. Here, it seems, two things go together. First, the evil represented by the four horsemen must reach its height with the martyrdom of yet more believers. Second, though, that martyrdom will itself be part of the means of God's just judgment. As we shall see, this is how the lamb's victory is worked out in practice.

In case we might think that the taking off of the seals is simply more bad news for God's people, the sixth seal (verses 12–17) shows a different side to the picture. Once again we must be careful about the symbolism. It is true that many in the ancient world saw eclipses, earthquakes, shooting stars and the like as signs and portents. John may be happy for people to hear those echoes. But in the Old Testament, language about the sun turning black and the moon becoming like blood, the stars falling from **heaven**, and so on, was regularly employed as a way of speaking about what we would call 'earth-shattering events' – not at all meaning actual earthquakes, but rather tumultuous events such as the fall of the Berlin Wall or the smashing of the Twin Towers on September 11, 2001: events for which it is hard to find appropriate language except through vivid symbol and metaphor.

This is certainly how it is here. If heaven and earth were really disappearing, if this was actually the end of the universe of space, time and matter, why would the rich and famous be hiding in caves? Rather, we should see the fresh revelation given by the undoing of the sixth seal as a time of huge political and social turbulence, resulting in a scene which many ancient prophets had described (e.g. Hosea 10.8). Those we call 'the great and the good', and many more besides, are thrown into a sudden panic. They realize they are entirely at the mercy of the God who rules the world. Their own schemes have come to nothing; what is now to become of them?

The thing of which they are most afraid is the combination of the creator's gaze and the lamb's anger. Here there is, once more, a deep mystery. The phrase 'the anger of the lamb' sounds like a contradiction in terms. Just as John has to learn to see the lion in terms of the lamb (and just as the two **disciples** on the road to Emmaus in Luke 24 had to learn to see their hopes for the **Messiah** redefined around the scriptural story of suffering and vindication which Jesus told them), so the very notion of 'anger' is radically redefined by the fact that it is the lamb's anger. It is the anger of the one who has embodied, in his own death, God's own self-giving, self-sacrificial love.

They, however, do not see this – just as, today, those who reject God vilify him, charging him with all sorts of wickedness. Someone once asked the novelist Kingsley Amis if he believed in God. 'No,' he replied, 'and I hate him.' That is the tone of voice of the people we see here. They are right that God – the creator God, the God we know in and through Jesus – is calling the world to account. They are wrong to imagine him as a capricious or vengeful tyrant. God is indeed angry at everything that has so horribly spoiled his wonderful world. His gaze from the throne is a deep, inexpressible mixture of sorrow and anger. But the lamb's anger is the utter rejection, by Love incarnate, of all that is unloving. The only people who should be afraid of it are those who are determined to resist the call of love.

REVELATION 7.1–8

Sealing God's People

¹After this I saw four angels, standing at the four corners of the earth, holding back the four winds of the earth to stop any wind from blowing on earth, or on the sea, or on any tree. ²And I saw another angel coming up from the east, holding the seal of the living God. He shouted out in a loud voice to the four angels who had responsibility for harming the earth and the sea. ³'Don't harm the earth just yet,' he shouted, 'or the sea, or the trees. Don't do it until we have sealed the servants of our God on their foreheads.'

⁴I heard the number of the people who were sealed: it was a hundred and forty-four thousand who were sealed from all the tribes of the children of Israel. ⁵Twelve thousand were sealed from the tribe of Judah, twelve thousand from the tribe of Reuben, twelve thousand from the tribe of Gad, ⁶twelve thousand from the tribe of Asher, twelve thousand from the tribe of Naphtali, twelve thousand from the tribe of Manasseh,

7twelve thousand from the tribe of Simeon, twelve thousand
from the tribe of Levi, twelve thousand from the tribe of
Issachar, 8twelve thousand from the tribe of Zebulun, twelve
thousand from the tribe of Joseph and twelve thousand from
the tribe of Benjamin. That is the number that were sealed.

Just when you think you are nearly at the top of the mountain,
you crest a ridge and there . . . is another ridge half a mile
ahead, steeper than the one you've just climbed. That is how
it feels to get to this point in the sequence of the 'seals' which
have kept the purposes of God, written on the scroll, from
being put into effect. So far the lamb has opened six of the
seals, and we are all agog for the seventh, which will surely
bring a decisive climax, as the scroll can at last be read. But
instead John keeps us in suspense, a trick he will play more
than once more. Like the souls under the altar, we must wait
and watch while something else happens first.

What happens is a quite different sense of 'seal'. The 'seals'
on the scroll were the kind of sticky wax whose purpose, in
the ancient world and sometimes in the modern as well, was
to keep important documents secure against prying eyes. You
could always tell if the seal had been broken, since it would
have been stamped with the mark of the one who had sealed
it up. But a 'seal' of that kind could also have the purpose
of putting an identification mark on something, in the way
that some people like to put their own bookplate inside the
front cover of all the books in their personal library. From
there it is a short step to the kind of 'seal' which marks out
an item, be it a book, an animal or (as in this case) a human
being, for special treatment.

The special treatment here is, to put it in a single word,
rescue. Just as the children of Israel were spared the attack
of the angel of death because they had put the blood of the
Passover lamb on their doorposts (Exodus 12), so these people
are to be spared the suffering which will come upon the whole

world as evil is allowed to do its worst. In the same way, the few righteous people in Ezekiel 9 are to be 'sealed' so as not to be killed in the violent judgment which is coming upon the idolaters.

The created order needs to be purified, it seems, in this case by a violent wind which will scorch the earth, stir up the sea and uproot trees. Like the other symbols of divine judgment, these images from the natural world are to be taken symbolically in terms of the great shaking that will pass through the whole world of human affairs as God's judgments start to take hold. While that is about to happen, God's people need to be reassured that they will come safely through, marked on their foreheads with the special seal that declares that they belong to God and are not to be harmed.

Not that they will escape suffering. Most readers of Revelation (not all) agree that the list of people who are 'sealed' in this way in verses 4–8 refers to the same people who are then described as a great, uncountable crowd in verses 9–17. As with the lion and the lamb in chapter 5, we notice that John *hears* the number – 144,000, broken down into twelve twelves – but then, when he looks (verse 9), he *sees* the great, uncountable crowd. This strongly suggests that they are the same people, symbolically represented as the complete people of God (twelve thousand times twelve), but actually consisting of a much larger number which nobody could count. And the people in this great crowd, as we shall see, have not escaped suffering. They have come through it to safety the other side, as Jesus himself passed through death to the immortal physical **life of resurrection.**

We should not suppose, then, that this 144,000 consists simply of ethnic Jews. For John, the people of God now consists of all those, including of course the Jews who remain at the heart of the family, who believe in Jesus, who acknowledge him as Lord. Just as the New Jerusalem has the names of the twelve tribes of Israel inscribed on its gates (while the foundations have the names of the twelve **apostles**) (21.12–14), so here the twelve tribes do not indicate ethnic Jews over against a large crowd of **Gentile** Christians in verses 9–17, any more than the description of that great crowd in verses 14–17 in particular should be thought to apply to Gentile Christians only, not to Jewish followers of the **Messiah**. Rather, as always, John is using the rich symbolism of Israel's identity to mark out those who, through the Messiah, belong to God's renewed and rescued people, no matter what their ancestry.

The list of the twelve tribes is peculiar when we compare it with the great biblical lists (e.g. Genesis 49 or Deuteronomy 33). We can easily explain the first strange feature, namely that Judah has been promoted to first place rather than the first-born Reuben. This presumably indicates that this is the people of God as renewed by the Messiah, the 'lion of Judah' (5.5). Another feature – the omission of the tribe of Dan – may perhaps be explained on the grounds that in some Jewish traditions it was thought that the Antimessiah would come from that tribe. A third feature is harder to explain: why is Manasseh, one of Joseph's children, included in the list? Perhaps because Manasseh did become, in effect, a separate tribe, and John simply wanted to make up the twelve after dropping Dan.

The idea of 'harming' the earth, the sea and the trees in verse 3 is harsh. This, we remind ourselves, is God's good creation, the natural order of which God said 'very good' in Genesis 1 and from which, as we have seen, ceaseless praise arises before God's throne. We seem here to be in the presence of yet another mystery. The only sense we can make of it, I think, is to hold in our minds the possibility that somehow the very stuff of the natural world has itself been infected with the disease of human rebellion and wickedness. The earth itself, and the sea and the trees, need to be purified, to be shaken hard by the great winds that will blow upon them. (It is one of the many tantalizing features of Revelation that we are never told when these winds blow, or what happens when they do.)

The point of the present passage, coming as it does in the pause between the opening of the sixth and the seventh seals, is to affirm that even though evil must be allowed to come to its full height, in order eventually to be fully and finally overthrown, God will not allow this process to put in jeopardy the ultimate rescue of his true people. This true people, redefined as they are around the lion of Judah, are to be marked out. The events around them will no doubt be terrifying, but they may rest assured that God has them in his care.

REVELATION 7.9–17

The Great Rescue

[9]After this I looked, and lo and behold a huge gathering which nobody could possibly count, from every nation and tribe and people and language. They were standing in front of the throne, and in front of the lamb. They were dressed in white robes, holding palm branches in their hands. [10]They were shouting out at the tops of their voices, 'Salvation belongs to our God, to the one who sits on the throne, and to the lamb!' [11]All the angels who were standing around the throne and the elders and the four creatures fell down on their faces before the throne and worshipped God. [12]'Yes, Amen!' they were saying. 'Blessing and glory and wisdom and thanks and honour and power and strength be to our God for ever and ever! Amen!'

[13]One of the elders spoke to me. 'Who are these people dressed all in white?' he asked. 'Where have they come from?'

[14]'Sir,' I replied, 'you know!'

'These are the ones', he said, 'who have come out of the great suffering. They have washed their clothes and made them white in the blood of the lamb. [15]That is why they are there in front of God's throne, serving him day and night in his temple. The one who sits on the throne will shelter them with his presence. [16]They will never be hungry again, or thirsty again. The sun will not scorch them, nor will any fierce heat. [17]The lamb, who is in the midst of the throne, will be their shepherd. He will lead them to springs of running water, and God will wipe away every tear from their eyes.'

I stopped sleepwalking some time in my mid-twenties, but I can still remember the mixture of fear and excitement I used to feel when, eventually, I would wake up. In my dream, I had been in a room, in a house, in a corridor, somewhere which was part memory, part imagination. There were people there I had to meet; there were things I had to do. But then, as I gradually emerged from sleep, I had to adjust my mind and imagination to realize that, instead of the place where I had been in my dream, I was in fact in *this* room, in *this* passage, and had to navigate my way back to my bed. Often the dream would still be powerfully present, and sometimes more appealing than the humdrum reality I actually faced. But I had to tell myself that this was the reality.

Sometimes, of course, it's the other way round. Sometimes you're in the middle of a nightmare which seems so real, so powerful and so horrible that when you wake up you can hardly dare to believe that it was only a dream, that the accident didn't happen, that so-and-so is still alive after all, that the monster attacking you was just in your imagination. Again, the clash of dream and reality is powerful. To begin with, it may be difficult to tell which is which.

John is facing a similar problem with the little communities to whom he is sending this book. They are about to face a nightmare. Persecution is on the way, and they must be ready for it. What he is offering them here is part of his continuing vision; and it's a vision not of nice dreams in his head, but of the heavenly reality which is the absolute, utter truth against which the nightmare must be measured. This, he says, is the ultimate reality of the situation, and you must hold on to it for dear life as you plunge back into the nightmare. The reality is that the creator God and the lamb have already won the victory, the victory which means that those who follow the lamb

73

are rescued from harm. The reality is that the people who claim the lamb's protection may well have to come through a time of great suffering, but they will then find themselves in the true reality, in God's throne room, worshipping and serving him day and night with great, abundant and exuberant joy.

This vision, then, is the thing which John 'sees' (verse 9), after having 'heard' the list of the 144,000 in verses 4–8. Formally speaking, this is the complete people of God, twelve times twelve times a thousand. In reality, this is a huge throng which nobody could ever count (think of the journalists' estimates of a great crowd filling a city square; then multiply that crowd by a few hundred, or a few thousand, so that the counters simply give up with a smile). Clothed in white, for victory and purity, this crowd is carrying palm branches as a further sign of victory celebration, and they can't restrain their enthusiasm: they are shouting out their delight and praise and thanks to God and the lamb, because they have won the victory which has brought them their rescue.

The word '**salvation**' in verse 10 literally means 'rescue'. But often in the Old Testament the word seems to mean 'the victory through which rescue is won'. So it seems to be here. The shout of praise continues into verse 12, where the great crowd of the redeemed recognize with joy that everything good, noble, powerful and wise comes from God himself. In technical language, this is what true monotheism looks like: not a bare, dry acknowledgement that there is only one God, but the uninhibited shout of praise to the God from whom all blessings flow.

There then follows one of those little conversations with which the dream-writing and vision-literature of the time is peppered. John, we remind ourselves, is in the heavenly throne room, which (as it now more fully appears from verse 15) is also the heavenly temple, the counterpart to the **Temple** in Jerusalem. He is not simply looking on from a great distance in a fly-on-the-wall fashion; he is right there, with the four living creatures and the twenty-four elders. And one of those elders now speaks to him, asking him the question which John's reader wants to ask. Who are these people?

The elder himself supplies the answer – the answer that John's communities badly need to hear. *These are those who have come out of the great suffering.* They have lived through the nightmare and can now wake up to a glorious, fresh new morning. The reason their clothes are white is not because they necessarily lived lives of total holiness and purity, but because the blood of the lamb, the sacrificial Passover-like death of Jesus himself, has rescued them from slavery to sin, making them able at once to stand in the very presence of the living God. No need to wait, then; no fear of a lengthy post-mortem clean-up period. The death of Jesus, and the suffering they have already endured, have done all that is required.

God will not only allow them, welcome them, into his presence. He will '*shelter* them with his presence'. God's 'presence' is a way of speaking of his glorious presence in his temple, and the word for 'shelter them' means literally that God will 'pitch his tent over them', as he pitched his tent in the midst of the Israelites during their wilderness wanderings. All the blessings of the Jerusalem Temple, in other words, will be theirs.

And more besides: because at this point John glimpses the further future, the vision of the New Jerusalem itself. We are not there yet, because there is still a 'temple' here, and there won't be one in the final city (21.22). But, as so often in Revelation (and in Christian thinking generally), present and future overlap and interlock in various confusing ways, and already some of the blessings of the final city are to be experienced by these people – by these people who, John is eager to say, are *you*, you who are about to suffer in Ephesus, or Smyrna, or Pergamum, or wherever. God will protect them from the elements, and from hunger and thirst (the same promise given by Jesus to the crowds in John 6.35). And, in a wonderful role reversal, the lamb will turn into a shepherd, assuming the royal role of John 10 (the 'good shepherd') and indeed the divine role of Psalm 23 (God as the shepherd who leads his people to springs of living water).

And, in a final anticipation of the New Jerusalem (21.4), God himself 'will wipe away every tear from their eyes'. There is an intimacy about that promise which speaks volumes for the whole vision of God throughout the book. Yes, God is rightly angry with all those who deface his beautiful creation and make the lives of their fellow humans miserable and wretched. But the reason he is angry is because, at his very heart, he is so full of mercy that his most characteristic action is to come down from the throne and, in person, wipe away every tear from every eye. Learning to think of this God when we hear the word 'God', rather than instantly thinking of a faceless heavenly bureaucrat or a violent celestial bully, is one of the most important ways in which we are to wake up from the nightmare and embrace the reality of God's true day.

REVELATION 8.1–5

The Golden Censer

[1]When the lamb opened the seventh seal, there was silence in heaven, lasting about half an hour. [2]I saw the seven angels who were standing in front of God; they were given seven trumpets. [3]Another angel came and stood before the altar. He was holding a golden censer, and he was given a large quantity of incense so that he could offer it, along with the prayers of all God's holy people, on the golden altar in front of the throne. [4]The smoke of incense, with the prayers of the saints, rose up from the hand of the angel in front of God. [5]Then the angel took the censer, filled it with fire from the altar, and threw it on the earth. There were crashes of thunder, loud rumblings, lightning, and an earthquake.

Bernard Levin was one of the greatest London journalists of the last generation. In his later years he wrote mostly for *The*

Times, at one point producing three columns a week so varied, so lively, and sometimes so controversial, that for numerous readers those three days each week had a special flavour. I have lots of his columns cut out and filed away, and many volumes of his collected pieces.

One of his great loves was music; and one of his musical heroes was Schubert. Levin relished the great moments of classical music, the operas of Mozart and Wagner in particular. He was no stranger to thunderous applause, standing ovations, the celebration of a delighted audience after a majestic performance. But on one occasion, at the end of a recital of Schubert songs by one of the finest singers of the day, he described how the audience simply sat in silence, and then, still in silence, got up slowly and left the concert hall. The spell of the music had been so powerful that nobody dared to break it with anything so mundane as clapping.

Such moments are precious and rare, and remind us, in our noise-soaked world, that silence can be not simply the absence of noise, a temporary and unwelcome piece of boredom, but a profound, still, deep experience in which one can sense aspects of reality which are normally drowned out by chatter and babble. That is the spirit in which we should hear what John has to say, that when the lamb opened the seventh seal 'there was silence in **heaven**, lasting about half an hour'. A sense of awe, expectation and anticipation. The otherwise ceaseless praise of the four living creatures dies away. The song of the elders, the angels and the huge, countless crowd falls quiet. Everyone seems to be holding their breath. This, we sense, is the moment they've all been waiting for. We watch, hardly daring to breathe ourselves.

We have, after all, waited long enough, or so we might think. Throughout chapter 6 we watched, perhaps in dismay, as the lamb removed the seals from the scroll which had been handed to him by the figure seated on the throne. The four horsemen; then the souls under the altar; then the terror seizing earth's inhabitants. Then there was a pause, with God's faithful people being 'sealed' so that the great damage that was bound to be done upon earth when God's judgment came sweeping through would not harm them. And in that pause we were privileged to glimpse, for the encouragement of those undergoing persecution, a vision of the heavenly reality in which, instead of a little bedraggled group, beaten up by a vicious mob or 'judicially' tortured and killed by an oppressive regime, God's people appeared as a huge crowd, celebrating God's victory and their own deliverance, with God himself looking after them and protecting them.

But now we come to the seventh seal. If we were expecting something even more spectacular than the great display of praise and worship around the throne, we might be disappointed by this sudden silence. But the unexpected hush in heaven ought to tell us that something huge, something powerful, something utterly decisive, is now going to happen.

So, indeed, it is; but again the way must be prepared. To begin with, we are introduced to the next cycle of seven. After the seals (and as part of the fulfilment of the seventh seal) we have the seven trumpets. Trumpets were used for various purposes in ancient Judaism, sometimes in worship (especially at certain festivals) and, not unnaturally, in battle. One of the most celebrated of the latter occasions was when the Israelites circled Jericho and then, at the blast of their trumpets, the walls fell down flat (Joshua 6). More generally, trumpets were blown for warning, to sound the alarm (e.g. Joel 2.1; Amos 2.2; 3.6). That seems to be the point here. The trumpets herald great plagues, the worldwide version of the plagues of Egypt at the time when God was making ready to rescue his people from slavery.

But before the trumpets can sound, and to round off the sequence of the seven seals, something else must happen, something in which, as so often in Revelation and writings like it, heaven and earth come together in a new way. An angel appears, carrying a golden censer.

We have already heard (5.8) that the prayers of God's people on earth are presented before God like incense, so that the sense of smell in the heavenly throne room is just as delighted and satisfied as those of sight and sound. Now the angel approaches once more, and this time he is given a large quantity of incense. The incense and the prayers, it seems, are not exactly the same thing. The prayers are, perhaps, like the charcoal on which the incense will burn. One way or another, the prayers of God's people, not least the prayers of the martyrs who lie under the altar itself (6.9–11), are coming before God's throne.

Perhaps there is another dimension to the 'silence' of the first verse. In some Jewish thinking, the praises of heaven must pause for a while so that the prayers of earth may be given a proper hearing. The main point, however, is that the seven trumpets and what they bring will be part at least of God's answer to the prayers of his people. The sequence of divine judgments, necessary for evil to be conquered and God's glorious new world to emerge, is not a mechanical plan which will grind forward irrespective of human agency. God, as we have seen, is committed to working in the world through human beings. Prayer, even the anguished prayer of those who do not understand what is going on, is a vital element in this mysterious co-operation (see Romans 8.26–27).

If prayer from on earth is presented by means of the golden censer, the immediate answer is given in the same way. The angel, having offered the incense, now fills the censer with fire from the altar and throws it on the earth. Until evil has been judged, condemned and radically uprooted from the earth, the only word that earth as a whole can hear from heaven is that of judgment. The 'thunder, rumblings, lightning and earthquake' come at the close of each section of the book, picking up from their initial appearance in front of God's throne (4.5). Here they appear at the close of the seven seals; at 11.19, after the seven trumpets have sounded; and at 16.18, once the seven bowls of wrath have been poured out. We are to understand that the commerce between heaven and earth, though vital for God's purpose and central to his eventual plan (21.1–8), will always be a matter of awe and wide-eyed wonder, and in the present time a matter for proper fear and trembling. Only the foolish and arrogant think they can scale the heights of heaven on their own behalf (Genesis 11). God remains sovereign, and as long as earth remains the haunt of evil, his answer to it must be fire. Jesus himself declared that he had come 'to throw fire upon the earth' (Luke 12.49). Here the angel with the golden censer continues the lamb's strange work.

REVELATION 8.6–13

The Plagues Begin

[6]Then the seven angels who had the seven trumpets got ready to blow them. [7]The first angel blew his trumpet, and hail and fire, mixed with blood, were thrown down on the earth. A third of the earth was burnt up, a third of the trees were burnt up, and so was every blade of green grass. [8]Then the second angel blew his trumpet, and something like a huge mountain, flaming with fire, was thrown into the sea. A third of the sea turned into blood, [9]a third of all living sea-creatures died, and a third of the ships were destroyed. [10]Then the third angel blew his trumpet, and a huge star, burning like a torch, fell from the sky, falling on a third of the rivers and on the springs of water. [11]The name of the star is Poisonwood: a third of the waters turned to poison, and many people died because of the waters that had become bitter. [12]Then the fourth angel blew his trumpet, and a third of the sun was struck, and a third of the moon, and a third of the stars, so that a third of their light would be darkened, with a third of the day losing its light and a third of the night as well. [13]Then I looked, and I heard a lone eagle flying in mid-heaven, and calling out loudly. 'Woe, woe, woe to the earth-dwellers,' it called, 'because of the sound of the other trumpets that the last three angels are going to blow!'

'Many people want to serve God,' said the sign outside the church, 'but only in an advisory capacity.' And this is one of the moments in Revelation when some at least would give rather firm advice to the one who sits on the throne: 'Don't do it! What is the meaning of all this wanton destruction?'

The point is well taken, especially when we consider the way in which the four living creatures, and the elders, have praised God for his goodness and power in making the world (chapter 4). This is his creation: he made it, he made it good, and he loves it. How then can he sanction these apparently meaningless destructions of a third of the earth, the trees, the sea and its creatures, the rivers, and even the sun, moon and stars?

Three preliminary answers may point us in the right direction. First, as a wise old writer put it, 'You haven't yet considered the seriousness of sin.' Even after a century of war, terror and high-tech genocide, we are still inclined, in the Western world at least, to pretend to ourselves that the world has really become quite a pleasant place, with 'evil' merely a blip on the horizon with which we can deal easily enough. However great the contrary evidence, this modern myth of the eradication of evil through 'enlightenment', leaving only a few minor mopping-up operations (preferably in far-away places) before Utopia finally arrives, has taken such a hold on popular imagination that any idea of God having to do anything powerful and destructive to address the problem is regarded as far too drastic, far too dramatic. But none of the early Christians, and certainly not Jesus himself, would have colluded with this glossing over of the seriousness of evil.

The second answer is, as always in Revelation, that we should not mistake symbol for reality. The stylized way in which the effects of the seven trumpets are described ought to remind us of what John's first readers certainly knew, that he wasn't actually talking about one-third of the earth, the seas and so on. He was talking about God's drastic action to purify the world, to cut it back as one would with a tree that had become

81

dangerously diseased, removing the deadly cancer so that the rest may be saved. He was talking about the necessary work of radically upsetting the human systems by which millions had been enslaved and degraded, but which were kept in place by structures of apparent beauty, nobility and high culture. A little modification will not be enough. Only major surgery will do.

The third answer is that with these plagues, and continuing on into those which occur when the 'bowls of wrath' are poured out in chapter 16, we are seeing a major rerun of the plagues with which God afflicted the Egyptians at the end of the Israelites' four hundred years of slavery. In Exodus 7—12 there are ten plagues, which strike both the people and the land, functioning as a warning to the Egyptians of the power of the God of Israel, and finally as the dramatic means by which, at Passover, Israel escapes (and then only because of the shed blood of the lamb). The plagues which John now envisages would resonate, in the minds of his hearers, with the ancient Egyptian plagues, and assure them of the same result. We have already seen that Passover plays a significant part in the story John is telling. Indeed, the lamb himself is who he is because he is the true Passover lamb. We should not be surprised, then, that just as Egypt was smitten with plagues as both a warning and a means of liberation, so the whole world is to be smitten with similar plagues in order to warn its inhabitants and to deliver God's people.

The ten plagues of Egypt were as follows. First, the waters were turned to blood. Then there were frogs, then gnats, then flies, each of them inflicting damage and destruction. (Each time, too, Pharaoh hardened his heart and would not let the people go.) Then a deadly pestilence struck the Egyptian livestock; then the people were afflicted with festering boils; then thunder and hailstorms devastated the crops; then came a plague of locusts; and then, building up to the final terror, a plague of darkness came over the whole land for three days.

82

At last came the judgment of Passover night, when the angel of death passed through the land, and the firstborn of every family (and every herd) was killed, while the Israelite firstborn were spared, because of the lamb's blood on the doorposts of the house. That was the final straw, and Pharaoh drove the Israelites out of the land – only then to change his mind and pursue them, leading to the second great act of rescue, when the Israelites walked dry-shod through the Red Sea but the pursuing Egyptian army were drowned (Exodus 14).

John has all this in mind, and expects his readers to do so too, as he describes the plagues, both here and in the chapters that follow. He is not repeating them one by one, but we cannot miss the echoes. When, eventually, we find the rescued people 'singing the song of Moses, and the song of the lamb' in 15.3, we ought not to be surprised. This is perhaps the major key to some of the most difficult passages in the book.

The particular plagues which come at the blast of the first four trumpets (following one another in quick succession, like the four horsemen) begin with two which echo the Egyptian plagues, but which obviously apply much more widely. This is the serious divine warning, not just for one country but for all humankind. Hail and fire devastate a third of the earth and its vegetation. A third of the sea, not just the river Nile, turns to blood. The poisoned waters of the third plague likewise remind us of Egypt. The fourth plague echoes the ninth Egyptian one, bringing darkness for one-third of the time when before there had been light. Imagery from other sources crowds in as well: the idea of a huge mountain being thrown into the sea is an image used by Jesus himself on occasion, for example, Mark 11.23, and was familiar from other Jewish writings of the time. So, too, the picture of a giant star falling from the sky has resonances with the old story of a fallen angel being cast out of **heaven** (Isaiah 14.12). In Isaiah, this ancient picture has been freshly applied to the king of Babylon. John, well aware of this, sees the fall of the great star in this passage

83

as an advance signpost towards the great denouement at the end of his own book.

But for the moment the point is that the fire cast upon the earth, following the prayers of God's suffering people (8.3–5), begins the long process of catastrophic events which are meant to function as warnings to the 'earth-dwellers' (verse 13). There is nothing wrong with being an earth-dweller. But the point John is making, again and again, is that there are many who have lived on earth as though there were no heaven, or as though, if heaven there be, it was irrelevant. His whole book is about the re-establishment of the rule of heaven on earth itself. As with all radical regime changes, those who profit from the present one will need dire warnings if they are to realize the seriousness of their plight.

REVELATION 9.1–12

Locust Attack

[1]Then the fifth angel blew his trumpet. I saw a star falling from heaven to earth, and it was given the key to the shaft which leads down to the Abyss. [2]The shaft of the Abyss was opened, and smoke came out of the pit like the smoke from a great furnace. The sun and the air became dark with the smoke from the pit. [3]Then, out of that smoke, there appeared locusts on the earth, and they were given authority like the authority of scorpions on the earth. [4]They were told not to harm the grass on the earth, nor any plant or tree, but only those people who did not have the seal of God on their foreheads. [5]They were given instructions not to kill them, but to torture them for five months, and their torture was like the torture inflicted when a scorpion stings someone. [6]In those days people will look for death, and won't find it. They will long to die, and death will run away from them.

[7]In appearance, the locusts looked like horses prepared for battle. They had what seemed to be crowns of gold on their heads, and their faces were like human faces. [8]They had hair

like women's hair, and their teeth were like lions' teeth. ⁹They had breastplates like iron breastplates, and the sound of their wings was like the noise of many horse-drawn chariots charging into battle. ¹⁰They have tails like scorpions' tails, and stings as well, and their tails have the power to harm people for five months. ¹¹They have as their king the angel of the Abyss, whose name in Hebrew is Abaddon, and whose name in Greek is Apollyon.

¹²The first Woe has come and gone. The next two Woes are on the way after this.

It is already dark outside, and the wind is getting stronger. You are getting up to close the curtains when all the lights go out: a power failure. As you stumble your way to the cupboard by the back door in search of candles, you sense a cold wind coming at your face: the door is open! What's going on? Then you hear it: a low, growling, grinding sound, not far away. Grabbing a candle, you strike a match. The wind blows it out, but not before you catch a glimpse of Something just outside the door. Like a large dog, but . . . another match, you get the candle lit, but you wish you hadn't. It isn't a dog. It's – you don't know what it is. It's a monster! It's getting bigger! It's got huge teeth, enormous black wings, a long, spiky tail! You try to slam the door, but it's too late . . .

The stuff of horror movies, or nightmares, or both. We can only assume, when John wrote down this vision of the locusts, that he was intending to produce a similar effect. He lavishes more detailed description on these super-locusts than on any other creature in this vivid book. So much so, in fact, that many modern readers, struck by the almost mechanical appearance of the creatures in verses 7–10, have tried to identify them as this or that kind of modern military machine: an attack helicopter, for instance. This seems a typical case of trying to tie down John's symbolism and thereby almost to domesticate it (though a defenceless peasant, seeing an attack helicopter coming his way, might not see it like that).

The point is the nightmare: all your worst dreams realized in an instant. The fifth angel has unleashed something truly monstrous, truly hellish.

Which is not surprising, because the fifth trumpet has allowed another falling star to play a particular role. Normally, it seems, the ultimate source of evil and terror is kept firmly locked up. John's conception of the present creation includes a bottomless pit which, like a black hole in modern astrophysics, is a place of anti-creation, anti-matter, of destruction and chaos. (I don't of course mean that John thinks there is an actual hole in the ground somewhere answering to this description, though some have thought that. Once again we must insist on reading symbols as symbols.) Jesus spoke of the way in which all kinds of wickedness – sexual immorality, theft, murder, adultery, greed, wickedness, treachery, debauchery, envy, slander, pride, stupidity – come bubbling up out of the depths of the human heart, to the surprise and horror of would-be pure persons who are doing their best to keep 'clean' by washing their hands (Mark 7.1–23). That is the black hole inside us all.

Humans were made to reflect their wise, loving creator, but somehow their hearts have become full of rebellion, filth and wickedness. Now it appears that the same is true at a cosmic level. The world, though made by God and loved by God, has come to harbour within it such rebellion, such anti-creation destructiveness, that, though God normally requires it to be restrained, if it is to be dealt with it must, sooner or later, be allowed to come out, to show itself in its true colours.

The monsters – locusts they may be, in a sense, in parallel with the plague of locusts in Egypt and the terrible army of locusts in the book of Joel, but these are man-eating, or rather man-torturing, locusts, with heavy equipment and armour to make them impregnable and irresistible – the monsters are to act under a strict and limiting instruction. They are to harm neither the vegetation (as locusts normally would) nor the people sealed with God's seal, but simply everyone else. The 'locusts' come up under cover of the dark, smoke-filled air (another echo of Exodus, in this case from 9.8–9 when Moses tosses dust from a furnace into the air and it turns into boils) that emerges from the pit whose king is Abaddon or Apollyon. The Hebrew word means 'the place of destruction', and the Greek word means 'destroyer', indicating well enough the anti-creation energy here displayed. The locusts' mission, though, is not simply instant destruction. That would, it seems, be too kind. They are to torture people until they long to die but are unable to do so (verse 6).

As with the plagues of Egypt, so we must assume that the aim here is to challenge the inhabitants of the earth to repent. This point eventually emerges in verses 20 and 21, which function somewhat like the comments in Exodus about Pharaoh and his court: though they saw the plagues, they hardened their hearts, until eventually the writer declares that God himself had hardened their hearts, to make them all the more ready for the judgment when it finally came.

Once more the mystery of iniquity, and of God's dealing with it, leaves us breathless and perhaps dismayed. But the biblical writers, and Jesus himself, would warn us against dismissing such ideas. To do so might well be to make the same mistake as the impenitent people here. We, too, have seen terrible things in our day: monsters, whether helicopters or other military equipment, designed simply to kill and destroy, made to strike terror into human hearts for the sake of human power and empire. Who is to say that such machines do not ultimately come, like these insects-on-steroids in John's vision, from the bottomless pit, under the direction of Apollyon? The 'five months' for which the torture is to last probably reflects John's awareness that this was the normal life cycle, or at least period of activity, of a locust. But the underlying point is that their work here, though horrible, is limited. Throughout the vision John wants his readers to know that God and the lamb remain sovereign, even though for evil to be finally conquered it has to be allowed to come out into the open and do its worst.

REVELATION 9.13–21

The Fiery Riders

[13]Then the sixth angel blew his trumpet. I heard a lone voice from the four horns of the golden altar in front of God, [14]addressing the sixth angel, who had the trumpet.

'Release the four angels,' said the voice, 'the ones who are tied up by the Great River, the Euphrates.' [15]So the four angels were released. They had been prepared for this hour, day, month and year, so that they would kill a third of the human race. [16]The number of the troops and horsemen was two hundred million. (I heard the number.) [17]As I looked, this is how the horses and their riders appeared. They had breastplates made of fire, sapphire and sulphur. Their heads were like lions' heads, and fire, smoke and brimstone came out of their mouths. [18]One-third of the human race was killed by these three plagues, by the fire, smoke and sulphur that came out of their mouths. [19]The power of the horses, you see, is in their mouths and their tails, since their tails are like serpents with heads. That is how they do their damage.

[20]All the other people, the ones who had not been killed in these plagues, did not repent of the things they had made. They did not stop worshipping demons – idols made of gold, silver, bronze, stone and wood, which cannot see, hear or walk. [21]Nor did they repent of their murders, or their magic, or their fornication, or their stealing.

The monster in the dark outside the back door is one kind of nightmare. Quite a different kind, but no less terrifying, is the thought that your country might suddenly be under threat from a fierce and ruthless enemy, whose army is even now massing on the frontier, ready to advance and swallow up defenceless towns and cities in its path.

That political and military nightmare has haunted Western Europe, and now in our own time the entire Western world, since some while before the time of Jesus. When an American president referred to an 'axis of evil', referring to several countries in the Arab world of the Middle East and beyond, he was not only playing on the fears of people most of whom could not have identified those countries on a map. He was awakening much older echoes. For half of the twentieth century, Western Europe and North America looked at the 'iron curtain' across Europe and imagined uncountable armies waiting on the other side, ready to invade in the cause of Communism. Once the Berlin Wall fell, it was not difficult to replace the traditional enemy (Russia) with the new one (the largely Muslim Arab countries), or to portray the supposedly 'Christian' Western countries as the guardians of the **faith** against atheism on the one hand and infidel religion on the other. (The multiple mistakes both of this analysis and of the conduct to which it led are a topic for another occasion.)

But the cold war fears, too, were echoes of much earlier nightmares. In the fifteenth and sixteenth century, Central Europe was gripped by a fear that 'the Turk', in other words the armies of the Turkish empire, would continue what had seemed a relentless advance. In the end they stopped just short of Austria. But, while the Western churches were struggling over the questions of the Protestant Reformation, many of Europe's rulers kept one eye on the eastern horizon as well. Internal religious revolt was one thing, but attack from the east would be far worse.

So it was, too, in the days of the Roman empire. The ancient north-eastern frontier of the land of Israel had notionally been the great river Euphrates (actually, of course, Israel's borders never went anything like that far north; but the biblical mandate was remembered, as in Exodus 23.31, Psalm 72.8 and elsewhere). When the Romans swept through the Middle East, sixty years or so before the birth of Jesus, the upper reaches of the Euphrates became their border, too, against the legendary empire of Parthia, which stretched at its height across modern Iraq, Iran and Afghanistan as far as the Indus river in modern Pakistan.

So when John sees in his vision four angels tied up by the great river Euphrates, ready to be released and to lead their massive armies into battle, everyone from Jerusalem to Rome and beyond knew what this meant. Their worst political and military nightmares. The fact that this vision follows immediately the horrible sight of the massive, torturing locusts reminds us again, if we needed it, that these are symbolic visions, drawing now on one lurid horror-fantasy, now on another, to present the image of escalating terror and torture. All of this was to be unleashed so that – and this is the point of it all – humans might be challenged to repent (verses 20, 21).

Well, one might say, but it didn't work, did it? All those threats, all that torture, all that death (unlike the locusts, the horsemen from beyond the Euphrates are allowed to kill people, as in verse 18), and still people didn't repent. But that is a common enough observation, both in the Old Testament and in the New (e.g. Romans 2.1–11). For many Jewish and early Christian thinkers, the sequence of thought goes like this. Granted the deep-rooted and destructive wickedness which emerges from the depth not only of the individual human heart but even more so from the systems of domination and oppression that humans together create, what is God to do? As we have seen before, if he were simply to wipe out his creation, the whole thing would be a massive failure. But if he allows people space to repent, to come to their senses, to worship him as the source of **life** rather than **demons** and idols which are the source of death (verses 20, 21), then that patient mercy always risks the possibility that people will use the breathing space to make matters worse. The result is that the human systems and individuals that continue to rebel will simply make themselves all the more ripe for eventual judgment, which will at least in part consist of evil bringing about its own downfall, as we shall see in 16.5–6.

If the locusts and the fiery riders are symbols, then, what are they symbols *of*? What does John suppose will be the reality, on earth, which corresponds to these lurid visions? Here we must be cautious. There is a whole spectrum of speculation at this point, ranging from those who see these passages as prophecies of actual warfare in the Middle East (if the locusts can be seen as helicopters, the horses of verses 17–19 could be seen as armoured vehicles or tanks) right through to those who stress that the true reality to which these images point is entirely 'spiritual', with the torture and threat being carried out in the hearts, minds, imaginations and consciences of rebellious and sinful humans.

One possible key to the right answer is to remember that John is writing these visions as a prophetic letter to the churches, to encourage them when they face persecution. He has already warned them, in the visions of the first four of the seven seals, about humanly made disasters which are going to come upon the world. Now, with the seven trumpets, he seems to envisage, to begin with at least, what we call 'natural disasters', plagues which like those of Egypt will do their work without human intervention. But with the fifth and sixth plagues – and again we should not think of them all as separate, distinct events, but as different dimensions of the same terrible overall reality – he is warning his hearers that the plagues to come will, from one point of view, consist of foul, hellish, destructive forces, and, from another point of view, of massive, terrifying armies charging against defenceless people. Thus, in a sense, the sixth trumpet corresponds to the first seal: the rider on the white horse, going off to conquer, has become an army the size of the entire population of Britain three times over, or of two-thirds of the population of the United States. It is as though John is systematically saying, 'Think of your worst nightmares; now double them; and then imagine them coming true all at once, together. That's what it's going to be like. This is God's way of letting evil do its worst, so that it may eventually fall under its own weight.'

The final verses of chapter 9 indicate well enough the shape of John's understanding of the basic human plight. Like all mainline Jews of his day, he believed that human evil emerged from idolatry. You become like what you worship: so, if you worship that which is not God, you become something other than the image-bearing human being you were meant and made to be. Thus verses 20 and 21 stand in parallel. Worship idols – blind, deaf, lifeless things – and you become blind, deaf and lifeless yourself. Murder, magic, fornication and theft are all forms of blindness, deafness and deadliness, snatching at the quick fix for gain, power or pleasure while forfeiting another bit of genuine humanness. **Repentance** is more than just expressing regret for a few peccadilloes. It is a radical, heartfelt, gut-wrenching turning away from the idols which promise delight but provide death. God longs for that kind of repentance. He will do anything, it seems, to coax it out of his rebellious but still image-bearing creatures.

Six trumpets later, though, it still hasn't happened. What about the seventh? Once more, John makes us wait.

REVELATION 10.1–11

A Little Scroll

[1]Then I saw another strong angel coming down from heaven, dressed in a cloud. Over his head was a rainbow; his face was like the sun, and his feet were like fiery pillars. [2]He was holding a small scroll, open, in his hand. Placing his right foot on the sea, and his left on the land, [3]he shouted in a loud voice like a lion roaring. When he shouted, the seven thunders answered with their own voices. [4]When the seven thunders spoke, I was about to write, but I heard a voice from heaven. 'Seal up what the seven thunders said,' instructed the voice. 'Don't write it down.'

⁵Then the angel whom I had seen standing on the sea and the land raised his right hand towards heaven ⁶and swore an oath by the One who lives for ever and ever, who made heaven and what it contains, the earth and what it contains, and the sea and what it contains. This was the oath: that there would be no more time, ⁷but that God's mystery would be completed in the days of the voice of the seventh angel, who was going to blow his trumpet. That is what he had announced to his servants the prophets.

⁸The voice I had heard from heaven spoke to me again. 'Go,' it said, 'and take the open scroll from the hand of the angel who is standing on the sea and on the land.' ⁹So I went up to the angel.

'Give me the little scroll,' I said.

'Take it,' he said to me, 'and eat it. It will be bitter in your stomach, but sweet as honey in your mouth.' ¹⁰So I took the little scroll from the angel's hand, and I ate it. It tasted like sweet honey in my mouth, but when I had eaten it my stomach felt bitter. ¹¹'You must prophesy again', he said to me, 'about many peoples, nations, languages and kingdoms.'

One of the most famous baseball umpires of all time, Bill Klem, earned his reputation by insisting that the umpire's word was not only final, but in a sense creative. On one celebrated occasion, he waited a long time to call a particular pitch. Some umpires would say that the ball was, in its own right, either a 'ball' or a 'strike', so that the umpire would merely be acknowledging the facts of the case. Klem was made of sterner stuff. 'Well,' asked the player, 'is it a ball or a strike?' 'Sonny,' replied Klem, 'it ain't nothing 'til I call it.'

Klem's belief in the power of his words may have annoyed both batters and pitchers in his time, but the idea of speaking words which create a new reality is an ancient one, finding classic expression in the great prophets. They are not only given visions or revelations of things that are to come. They are to speak words which somehow generate that new situation. The words, like God's own words (which the prophet believes is exactly what they are), perform actions; they do things. 'By the **word** of the Lord the heavens were made, and all their host by the breath of his mouth . . . he spoke, and it came to be; he commanded, and it stood firm' (Psalm 33.4, 9). And when God puts words into the mouth of prophets, the same thing happens. The prophet doesn't just describe what is going to happen, like (as it were) a newsreader in reverse. By saying it, the prophet brings it to pass. Prophecy makes things happen.

This now puts John in the hot seat. There are new things yet to happen as part of God's purpose, *and John's words will bring them to pass.* This is the meaning of the angel bringing him the little scroll from **heaven**, which though 'little scroll' is not the same word as the 'scroll' of chapter 5, seems to be the same reality. The lamb has removed the seals; now the scroll can be read, and John is to be the one to do it. This, it seems, is the reason why he was invited into the heavenly throne room.

This is how prophecy works. God's words are to become John's words in order that they may become reality. This is part of what it means to say, as in Daniel 7.14, 22 and 27, that God's people will share his rule over the world. He rules by his word, as the lamb will do in the final judgment (19.15); but here his word is the word given to the prophet to eat, to digest and then to speak.

Like every gift of God, the scroll is sweet as honey to the taste (Psalm 19.10; 119.103). But once John has digested the scroll, he discovers that its **message** is bitter. More dire warnings are to follow, as there were when Ezekiel (2.8; 3.1–3) was commanded, in the same way, to eat the scroll of God's prophecies.

'Eating the scroll' is a vivid metaphor for the way in which the prophet, then or indeed today, can only speak God's word insofar as it has become part of the prophet's own life. It may be nourishing; it may be bitter; it may be both. This is part of what it means to say that God desires to act in the world through obedient human beings. Prophecy – speaking words which bring God's fresh order to the world – is one specialist aspect of the larger human vocation, and here John shoulders that responsibility. What will follow, not least in chapters 12—20, will be God's word, spoken through him, bringing about the terrible judgment and the glorious, victorious mercy in which 'God's mystery would be completed'.

This gift of the little scroll, and the vocation to turn its words into prophecy which will bring God's purposes into reality, all takes place as we are waiting with bated breath for the seventh trumpet to sound. Yes, says the angel, it is coming soon, and when it comes it will complete 'God's mystery' (verse 7). There will be no more time (verse 6): not, I think, in the sense that 'time shall be no more', leaving everything in the timeless 'eternity' beloved of some non-biblical philosophies, but rather that 'time will have run out' for all those who are presuming on God's patience. This time things will reach their goal. This reminds us that the sequence of the seven trumpets is not meant to stand chronologically between the other 'seven' sequences – the letters, the seals and the bowls – but is one key dimension of the same basic sequence. We are building up, at the end of chapter 11, to what could be the final climax of the book – except for the fact that we still have the entire second half of the book to come, in which the same story is approached from a radically different angle, spelling out in depth all sorts of aspects of the story which cannot be told until these preliminary tellings have done their work.

The angel described at the start of the chapter bursts onto the scene in a blaze of light, all the more welcome after the gloom and horror of the previous section. He comes from heaven with God's word for the earth, dressed in a cloud which, we may suppose, is the sign that God himself is present but hidden in this message. The rainbow over his head reminds us of the throne-vision of chapter 4, and of the ancient biblical echoes awoken there. His face is like the sun, as was that of the

son of man in the first chapter, and his feet, like fiery pillars, remind us of the pillar of fire in the desert, the flaming sign of God's personal presence. This is no ordinary angel, and when he speaks we know why: his voice is like a lion roaring. He comes with the words of the lion-lamb, the **Messiah**. He embodies the sovereignty of the creator God over the whole creation: the sea and the land (verses 2, 5) are the two spheres of 'earth', as heaven and earth are the two spheres of the whole creation and male and female are the two spheres, as it were, of the animal world. It could hardly be made clearer that the message he brings is from the creator, since in verse 6 he swears an oath by the one who made heaven, earth and sea and all that they contain. Any suggestion, then, that the message he brings will collude with the forces of destruction and declare that the present world is a piece of trash, to be thrown away and replaced with something completely different, is ruled out. When God's mystery is complete, it will be the fulfilment of creation, not its abolition.

We brace ourselves once more for the seventh trumpet. But before it sounds the churches for whom John is writing need to know where they stand in this great cosmic scenario. Are they after all just spectators, or do they themselves have a particular role to play?

REVELATION 11.1–14

Two Witnesses

[1]Then a measuring rod like a staff was given to me. 'Get up,' said a voice, 'and measure God's temple, and the altar, and those who are worshipping in it. [2]But leave out the outer court of the temple. Don't measure it. It is given to the nations, and they will trample the holy city for forty-two months. [3]I will give my two witnesses the task of prophesying, clothed in sackcloth, for those one thousand two hundred and sixty days. [4]These two are the two olive trees, the two lampstands, which

stand before the Lord of the earth. [5]If anyone wants to harm them, fire comes out of their mouths and devours their enemies. So if anyone wants to harm them, that is how such a person must be killed. [6]These two have authority to shut up the sky, so that it will not rain during the days of their prophecy. They have authority over the waters, to turn them into blood, and to strike the earth with any plague, as often as they see fit. [7]When they have completed their testimony, the monster that comes up from the Abyss will make war on them, and will defeat and kill them. [8]Their bodies will lie in the street of the great city, which is spiritually called Sodom and Egypt, where their Lord was crucified. [9]Their bodies will be seen by the peoples, tribes, languages and nations for three and a half days. They will not allow their bodies to be buried in a tomb. [10]The inhabitants of the earth will celebrate over them, and make merry, and send presents to one another, because these two prophets tormented those who live on earth.'

[11]After the three and a half days the spirit of life from God came in to them, and they stood up on their feet, and great fear fell on all who saw them. [12]Then they heard a loud voice from heaven. 'Come up here!' it said. And they went up to heaven on a cloud, with their enemies looking on. [13]At that moment there was a huge earthquake, and a tenth of the city fell, and seven thousand of the people were killed by the earthquake. The rest were very much afraid, and glorified the God of heaven.

[14]The second Woe has passed. The third Woe is coming very soon.

People find many books puzzling, but the Bible is often the most puzzling of all. People find many parts of the Bible puzzling, but Revelation is often seen as the most puzzling book of all. And people find Revelation puzzling, but the first half of chapter 11 – the passage now before us – is, for many, the most puzzling part of all. (There are some other strong contenders for this dubious distinction, but chapter 11 can hold its own.) What is it about?

At one level it's clear what it's about. John is told to measure the temple. Then two 'witnesses' emerge, doing great and strange deeds before being killed, lying unburied, and then being raised to new life and exalted to heaven. The tone of voice of the passage is quite different from much of the surrounding material. Instead of the big-picture scenes of terrifying horsemen, man-eating locusts and all the rest, we seem to have a short story, albeit a very strange one, about two specific individuals, their work and their fate.

But what does it all *mean*? And how does it fit with the rest of the book? How does it take John's vision forward?

Not surprisingly, readers of Revelation have disagreed as to what it all means. But I am inclined to agree with those who have taken, broadly, the following line.

First, John's 'measuring of the temple' (which echoes similar prophetic actions in Ezekiel 40 and Zechariah 2) has nothing to do with the Jerusalem Temple, or with the heavenly temple/ throne room of chapters 4 and 5. By the time John was writing – indeed, this was true from very early on in the Christian movement – the followers of Jesus had come to see themselves as the true temple, the place where God now lived through his powerful **spirit**. John is commanded to mark out this community so that, as in chapter 7, it may be protected against ultimate harm. However, there is another sense in which the community – seen here in terms of the 'outer court' – is to be left vulnerable. The pagan nations will trample it for three and a half years (a symbolic number, half of the 'seven' which stands for completeness, here broken down into 42 months or 1260 days). Just as Ezekiel's measuring of his visionary temple was a way of marking out the place where God was going to come to dwell, so John's marking out of this human temple, this community, is a way of signalling God's solemn intention to honour and bless this people with his presence.

But what is the task and role of this people? Throughout the book of Revelation, the call of God's people is to bear faithful witness to Jesus, even though it will mean suffering, and quite possibly a shameful death. The seven letters of chapters 2 and 3 continually promised special rewards to those who 'conquered'. This, as we saw, meant the people who, following Jesus who himself achieved victory through his death, were prepared to face martyrdom rather than compromise. Now – this is the part which many find particularly difficult – it appears that the 'two witnesses' of verses 3–13 *are a symbol for the whole church in its prophetic witness, its faithful death, and its vindication by God.* The church as a whole is symbolized by the 'lampstands', as in 1.20. The church is to prophesy, 'clothed in sackcloth' as a sign of mourning for the wickedness of the world and the evil that it will bring on to itself.

Why two witnesses, then? Partly, I think, because John has two great biblical stories in mind as the backdrop. First, there is the story of Moses, who stood up to Pharaoh, the pagan king of Egypt, and demonstrated God's power by the plagues which, as we have seen, are already echoed in chapters 8 and 9. Second, there is the story of Elijah, who stood up to Ahab, the paganizing king of Israel, and demonstrated God's power by successfully praying for a drought and then by calling down fire from heaven. John doesn't mean, though some have thought this, that Moses and Elijah would literally return to earth and carry out what chapter 11 says. That is to mistake the sort of writing this is. What John is saying is that the prophetic witness of the church, in the great tradition of Moses and Elijah, will perform powerful signs and thereby torment the surrounding unbelievers, but that the climax of their work will be their martyr-death at the hands of 'the monster that comes up from the Abyss'.

We haven't met this 'monster' yet. Nor have we yet discovered 'the great city, which is spiritually called Sodom and Egypt, where their lord was crucified'. John will make all this clear in the several chapters that follow, where we learn that the 'monster' is the might of pagan empire, presently embodied by

Rome, and that the 'city' is Rome itself, or maybe in this case the public world of the entire Roman empire. And the point – the point which John is determined his readers will grasp – is this. The God-given and God-protected vocation to bear faithful prophetic witness will not mean that one will be spared from suffering and death, but rather that this suffering and death itself, like that of the Jesus whom the church worships and follows, will be the ultimate prophetic sign through which the world will be brought to glorify God.

How does this work? For three and a half days (there we have the half-of-seven symbol again) the world will celebrate a victory over the church. But suddenly God will act in a new way. The vision of Ezekiel 37, of God's breath coming into the dead corpses, will come into reality. And the vision of Daniel 7, of God's people coming on a cloud to heaven, will also come to pass. The vindication of the church after its martyrdom will complete the prophetic witness.

The result will be that the world, looking on, will at last be converted. That is the meaning of the powerful language at the end of verse 13. Elsewhere, both in Revelation and other biblical books, the idea of people coming in fear and trembling to 'glorify the God of heaven' is an indication not of a temporary or grudging acknowledgement of God's sovereignty, but of a true and penitent turning to God. *The martyr-witness of the church*, in other words, *will succeed where the plagues have failed*. This is how the nations will come to glorify their creator. This is how 'the kingdom of the world' will become the **kingdom** of 'our Lord and his **Messiah**' – which is precisely the point that follows immediately in verse 15.

This most puzzling passage in this most puzzling book, then, turns out to be one of the most important and central statements of what John wants to say to the churches to whom he is writing. The lamb has opened the seals on the scroll, and all kinds of terrifying things have happened as he has done so. The trumpets have blown; terrors of a different sort have come to pass; but now the scroll has been handed to John, and John prophesies in symbolic action (measuring the temple) and parabolic story (the two witnesses). And this is how the kingdom of God, already spoken of in chapters 4 and 5, is to become a reality on earth as in heaven.

We should not mistake the powerful impact of the symbolism in verse 13. When God judged Sodom and Gomorrah, he might have spared it if ten righteous persons were found there (Genesis 18.32). Now, however, only one-tenth of the wicked city is to fall, and nine-tenths is to be saved. When God was judging Israel through Elijah, only seven thousand were left who had not bowed the knee to the pagan god Baal. Now, however, it is only seven thousand who are killed, and the great majority are to be rescued. Suddenly, out of the smoke and fire of the earlier chapters, a vision is emerging: a vision of the creator God as the God of mercy, grieving over the rebellion and corruption of the world but determined to rescue and restore it, and doing so through the faithful death of the lamb and, now, through the faithful death of the lamb's prophetic followers. The way stands clear for the glorious celebration at the end of the chapter, which rounds off the first half of this very carefully structured book.

REVELATION 11.15–19

The Song of Triumph

[15]The seventh angel blew his trumpet, and loud voices were heard from heaven. 'Now the kingdom of the world has passed to our Lord and his Messiah,' said the voices, 'and he will reign for ever and ever.' [16]The twenty-four elders sitting on their thrones in God's presence fell on their faces and worshipped God.

[17]This is what they said:

'Almighty Lord God, we give you our thanks,
Who Is and Who Was,

because you have taken your power, your great power,
and begun to reign.
[18]The nations were raging; your anger came down
and with it the time for judging the dead
to give the reward to your servants the prophets,
the holy ones, too, and the small and the great –
those who fear your name.
It is time to destroy the destroyers of earth.'

[19]God's temple in heaven was opened, and the ark of his covenant appeared inside his temple. There were flashes of lightning,
rumblings, thunderclaps, an earthquake, and heavy hail.

Inscribed over the high altar in Westminster Abbey, one of the
most famous churches in the world, is the King James Version
translation of verse 15, which reads, 'The kingdoms of this
world are become the kingdoms of our Lord, and of his Christ.'
It is an impressive text for an impressive location, looking
down as it does not only on the altar and its magnificent
surroundings but on the Cosmati pavement in front of it,
where for a thousand years kings and queens have been
crowned. The text is designed as a solemn reminder to these
monarchs, and to their subjects, that their crowns are at best
temporary and in any case borrowed. The sovereignty, the
kingdom, belongs to the one true God and to his **Messiah**.

However, the Greek text which King James's translators
were using was wrong. As virtually all other Greek manuscripts
of the New Testament indicate, the word 'kingdom' should be
singular, not plural. In any case, as the translators knew, it only
occurs once in the verse; they put the second 'kingdoms' in
italics, to show that they were adding it to help the sentence to
make, in English, the sense it clearly made in the Greek.

My point in drawing attention to this curiosity is not simply
the mild frustration that Westminster Abbey should have
a wrong reading in such a prominent and powerful place. It
is, rather, that it matters quite a lot that 'kingdom' here is

singular. The vision which John is passing on is a cosmic, global vision, and the 'kingdom' which God has established through his Messiah is not simply a collection of kingdoms, ruling over this nation and that. It is his universal rule, scooping up 'the kingdom of the world' as a single entity and claiming it back as his own rightful property.

This climactic and decisive moment could well have come, one might suppose, towards the very end of the book. Indeed, parts of chapter 19 resemble what we have here. But this reminds us that we are not dealing, in Revelation, with a single sequence of events, in which the seals come first, then the trumpets, then all the material in chapters 12—14, culminating in the bowls of wrath, and so on. What we are dealing with is several different angles of vision on the one single great reality: that through the awful turmoil and trouble of the world, God is establishing through Jesus a people who, following the lamb, are to bear witness to God's kingdom through their own suffering, through which the world will be brought to **repentance** and **faith**, so that ultimately God will be king over all.

There are, no doubt, a thousand different ways to say this; John has chosen three or four. Here we have the climax of one of them, which also functions (because John is writing at several different levels at once) as the climax to the whole of the first half of the book. Verse 19, which finishes this passage, also prepares the way for the very different scene in chapters 12 and 13, where the story as it were begins all over again so that, from quite a new angle, we may see the same drama acted out, and with the same eventual result.

Revelation, like its main biblical prototype (the book of Daniel), is all about the kingdom of God – which is, in my experience, one of the most misunderstood themes in the whole Bible. Far too many Christians have understood 'the kingdom' simply in terms of 'God's kingdom in **heaven**', meaning by that that God is in charge in a place called 'heaven' (as opposed to this messy place called 'earth', from which God wants to rescue us), and that the main aim of life is to 'enter the kingdom of heaven' in the sense of 'going to heaven when you die'. Perhaps one of the many reasons why Revelation has been literally a closed book for so many, and for so much of the church, is that it powerfully and dramatically contradicts this popular view. God's kingdom is *not* simply designed for 'heaven', because God is the creator of the whole world, and his entire purpose is to reclaim that whole world as his own and to set it on the way to become the place he always intended it to be, before human rebellion pulled it so disastrously off track. That, in fact, is the **message** of the four **gospels**, despite many generations of misunderstanding. This misunderstanding has come about partly because, when Matthew uses the phrase 'kingdom of heaven' (the other gospels mostly have 'kingdom of God'), it has been easy for readers with 'going to heaven' in their minds to suppose that that was what Matthew, and hence Jesus, were talking about.

But here it is quite clear – and quite explicitly political in its implications. Those who designed the present altar and its surrounds in Westminster Abbey may have got the wrong text, but they had the right idea. This is not about a private spirituality in the present, or an escapist '**salvation**' in the future. This is about the living God confronting the powers of the world with the news that he is now in charge, and that the mode of his rule is that which was established by 'his Messiah', the lamb. 'Suffering love conquers all' is the message, as powerful as it is unwelcome (unwelcome, sadly, all too often in the church, as well as in the world). History has, of course, proved the point. The time of the church's greatest expansion was the first three centuries, during which the Roman empire was doing its best, through torture and death, to stamp the movement out. 'The blood of the martyrs', said one of the great early teachers, 'is the seed of the church.' So it has proved again and again.

This, then, is the fulfilment of the Psalm which many early Christians saw as a great, central prophecy of Jesus himself.

Psalm 2 speaks of the nations raging against God, and God acting by establishing his king on his holy hill of Zion. He then promises to give to this king, his 'son', the nations of the world as his inheritance. No more will Israel's 'inheritance' be merely the land which God promised to Abraham, a small strip of territory in the Middle East, but rather the entire world and all its kingdoms. The Messiah, God's son-king, will overthrow the nations as they rage and fight. Their best course, says the Psalmist, is to submit, to sue for peace.

In John's vision, here in this chapter, *it has already happened.* Notice the difference between verse 17 and passages like 1.4. There John spoke of God as the one 'Who Was, and Is, and Is To Come'. Here he simply describes God as 'Who Is and Who Was', *because the future has now arrived in the present.* The 'is to come' has become reality. The suffering witness of the martyr-church has faithfully demonstrated to the world that God is God, that Jesus is Lord and King, and the world has responded by glorifying the God of heaven.

What remains now is 'to destroy the destroyers of earth'. This is the ultimate meaning of God's judgment. So often that judgment is seen as negative, 'destructive', thwarting the things which humans really enjoy and want to do. This is one of the biggest lies there is. God's judgment is the judgment of the creator on all that spoils his creation. His purposes, deep-rooted in the vision of chapters 4 and 5, are for his wonderful creation to be rescued from the forces of anti-matter, of anti-creation, of anti-life. It is time for death to die.

The song of the elders evokes another moment like that of 4.5 and 8.5, with lightning, thunder and the rest. These are the moments of transition, the moments when earth itself trembles at the power of the heavenly revelation. In addition, for the only time in the book, John says that as God's **temple** in heaven was opened, revealing his throne room with its song of triumph, so 'the ark of his **covenant**' appeared inside. There had been much speculation in Jewish circles about whether the ark – the box containing the Ten Commandments and other key symbols of the ancient covenant – would be restored in the new temple. Here its appearance seems to signify that God has at last been true to his covenant promises. What he said he would do, he has now done. He has taken his power and begun to reign.

REVELATION 12.1–6

The Woman and the Dragon

¹Then a great sign appeared in heaven: a woman clothed with the sun, with the moon under her feet, and a crown of twelve stars on her head. ²She was expecting a child, and she cried out in pain, in the agony of giving birth. ³Then another sign appeared in heaven: a great fiery-red dragon with seven heads and ten horns. On its heads were seven coronets, ⁴and its tail swept a third of the stars out of heaven and threw them down to the earth. The dragon stood opposite the woman who was about to give birth, so that he could devour her child when it was born. ⁵She gave birth to a male child, who is going to rule all the nations with a rod of iron. And the child was snatched away to God and to his throne. ⁶The woman, meanwhile, fled into the desert, where a place has been prepared for her by God, so that she could be looked after there for one thousand two hundred and sixty days.

I once attended a memorial service for a famous sportsman, a cricketer who had been a boyhood hero for me and for many others. The church was packed, and a special place was reserved for other cricketers who had played with or against the great man and who had come to pay their respects. I was standing near the door when these other cricketers, a few dozen of them, walked in – and it was a very frustrating moment. Most of them, without a doubt, had also been household names. But for me and many others who were there, it was impossible to identify most of them. We remembered how they looked in their sporting prime, in their teens, twenties and thirties. Now, in their sixties, seventies and in some case eighties, they were unrecognizable. Several of us agreed afterwards that we wished they could have worn little labels with their names on, so that the rest of us would know who we were looking at. We might even have asked for their autographs.

That problem of identification is, of course, the problem which we face in chapter after chapter of Revelation. We see these characters come and go across the pages. We know that there's a high probability that John intends them to represent, symbolically, some biblical theme or person, or (as in chapter 11) the corporate identity of God's people. But we wish he could have given them at least a little label, now and then, to give us a clue.

In the present chapter, there is one clue in particular which John has let slip, just in case we might have missed the point completely. The child whom the woman bears is the boy 'who is going to rule all the nations with a rod of iron' (verse 5). That is an obvious reference to Psalm 2.9. As we saw in the previous passage (11.18), John is applying that Psalm explicitly, as many other early Christians had done, to Jesus himself. He is the **Messiah**, the one whom God calls to bring the nations into line (even though we, with chapter 5 behind us, know that Jesus' own way of accomplishing that end is very different to that imagined by the violent Jewish nationalist movements of the time).

This small but vital clue has led some to suggest that the woman in the story is Mary, the mother of Jesus. But this is too hasty by far. That's not how this kind of symbolism works, and John tells us explicitly that she is a 'sign', not a literal mother. It is far more likely that two figures stand behind her. First, there is Israel herself, frequently in scripture referred to as 'daughter Israel', the bride of YHWH. She is here seen not as the faithless Israel rebuked so often by the prophets, but as the true, faithful Israel, the nation that had struggled to stay in God's path and follow his vocation. It is from this faithful Israel, admittedly ultimately through the 'virgin daughter of Israel', Mary herself, that the Messiah is born. But this woman, who now takes centre stage in God's purposes for his world, is the 'priestly **kingdom**, holy nation' of Exodus 19.6. She represents the entire story of God's people, chosen to carry forward his plans for the nations and indeed for the whole creation. That is why the sun, moon and stars form her robe, her footstool and her crown.

That is why, too, the forces that range themselves against the creator God are determined to strike at her, and at her child. Finally, with a swish of his majestic tail, the villain appears on stage – the villain who, we quickly learn, stands behind all the trouble that we have seen in the earlier chapters. The dark secret is revealed; the real problem is identified; the curtain has risen on the drama-within-the-drama, the central action which forms, now, the central scene in the whole book. The woman and her child are carrying the purposes of God for the world. The dragon is doing his best to snuff out those purposes before they can get under way. With the unveiling of the **gospel** of the lion-lamb there goes, as well, the unveiling of the ultimate mystery of evil.

The second image behind the woman in this passage may well be Eve, the original mother of all human **life**. It is Eve, after all, who is told that her 'seed' will crush the serpent's head (Genesis 3.15). The two identities go together. If the woman is 'Israel', she is for that reason the one in whom God's purposes for humanity are to be realized. And that purpose includes, as a central and necessary part of the agenda, the crushing of the ultimate power of evil. The destroyer is to be destroyed.

The dragon himself will be more fully revealed later on, when the mystery of his seven heads and ten horns (imagery popular in Jewish thought from at least as far back as the book of Daniel) will be made clearer. But already we see that he is a figure of considerable power. He is himself, after all, 'in **heaven**' (verse 3). As in the Old Testament, 'the Adversary', the '**satan**' (for this is who he is, as we see in verse 9), is part of the heavenly court, who rebels against the creator's plans for his world. This is, to be sure, another great mystery. But the results of this rebellion are not in doubt: attacks from all sides on the people of God, in the years leading up to the birth of the Messiah, are followed, at that birth itself, by an attempted attack from the would-be 'king of the Jews', Herod (Matthew 2). The dragon is thwarted in his attempt to devour the child at birth. He is then further thwarted because, in a remarkable compression of the entire story of Jesus' life, the child is snatched away to God and his throne (verse 5). In other words, Jesus himself wins the victory through his death, **resurrection** and **ascension**, and is therefore no longer vulnerable to anything the dragon can do.

The woman, meanwhile – the faithful people of God – remains in danger. This, again, can scarcely refer to Mary, and at this point it can't refer, either, to the ethnic people of Israel. As is true all through the book, John believes that since Jesus is Israel's Messiah, Israel is redefined around him, so that the woman who flees to the desert to be looked after by God for a temporary period (three and a half years: 1,260 days) must be the church itself. Once more, John is telling a story in which his readers discover that they are not merely spectators but actually participants. They are part of the 'woman', part of the family who are to be looked after even though, as we shall see, the dragon is now pursuing them (12.13). The idea of the woman fleeing into the 'desert' is probably yet another reference to the **Exodus** story, where the people of Israel escape from the tyrant Pharaoh by going off into the wilderness, even though they have fresh challenges to face once they get there.

The stage is set. The Woman will be with us, in one way or another, right through to the end of the book, though there will be another Woman, a horrible caricature of this one, who will occupy plenty of attention along the way. The Dragon, too, will be with us much of the way, and part of the whole point of chapters 12—20 is to enable the church for whom John is writing to understand how he operates and how, therefore, his power must be overthrown. The church needs to know that its present struggles and sufferings are not a sign that God has gone to sleep on the job. They are the sign that a great, cosmic drama is being staged, in which they are being given a vital though terrible role to play.

REVELATION 12.7–18

The Dragon Is Angry

[7]Then war broke out in heaven, with Michael and his angels fighting against the dragon, and the dragon and his angels fighting back. [8]But they could not win, and there was no longer any place for them in heaven. [9]So the great dragon was thrown down to the earth – the ancient serpent who is called the devil and the satan, who deceives the whole world. His angels were thrown down with him. [10]Then I heard a loud voice in heaven saying, 'Now at last has come salvation and power: the kingdom of our God and the authority of his Messiah! The accuser of our family has been thrown down, the one who accuses them before God day and night. [11]They conquered him by the blood of the lamb and by the word of their testimony, because they did not love their lives unto death. [12]So rejoice, you heavens and all who live there! But woe to the earth and the sea, because the devil has come down to you in great anger, knowing that he only has a short time.'

[13]When the dragon saw that he had been cast down to the earth, he set off in pursuit of the woman who had borne the baby boy. [14]The woman, however, was given a pair of wings from a great eagle, so that she could fly away from the presence of the serpent into the desert, to the place where she is looked after for a time, two times and half a time. [15]The serpent, for its part, spat out of its mouth a jet of water like a river after the woman, to carry her off with the force of the water. [16]But the earth helped the woman by opening its mouth and swallowing up the river which the dragon had spat out of his mouth. [17]Then the dragon was angry with the woman, and went off to wage war against the rest of her children, those who keep God's commands and the testimony of Jesus. [18]And he stood on the sand beside the sea.

A happy argument took place in the changing-room after the end of the match. Who had scored the winning goal? There had been a big scramble in the goalmouth; the ball was bouncing to and fro; two of the attacking players had both swung a foot at it simultaneously. Both were aware of boot on ball, and the next second the ball was in the net and the match won. So who scored the goal?

The manager overheard the discussion and came in with a different spin. 'Actually,' he said, 'I scored the goal.' They rounded on him. 'What d'you mean?'

'Think about it,' he said. 'I chose you both to play today. I taught the others how to get the ball up front in just that situation, and I taught you both how to get past the defenders and be there at the right moment. Without that, the goal wouldn't have happened. I scored that goal.'

Eventually it went down on the sheet as credited to both the players, but the manager had made his point and they knew it. There are more levels than at first appear to the question of who won the decisive victory.

That's the puzzle in this passage, because a decisive victory has been won, but it seems that two quite different groups of people have been involved in winning it. There is 'war in heaven' – an alarming enough concept; Michael, the great archangel of Daniel 10, summons all his angels to fight against the dragon and his angels. If we are able to give this any meaning in our imaginations, it must be that the moral and political struggles of which we are aware, the battles between good and evil, between justice and injustice, which go on in this life, reflect a more primeval battle which has taken place in the spiritual sphere. Michael has won, and the dragon has lost. This loss means that he is thrown down to the earth, ejected from heaven altogether.

But wait a minute. The song of victory which follows this great event gives credit for the victory, not to Michael, but to God's people on earth. 'They conquered him', says the loud voice from heaven, 'by the blood of the lamb and by the word of their testimony, because they did not love their lives unto death' (verse 11). So who defeated the dragon? Was it Michael, or was it the martyrs?

Well, in a sense it was both. The heavenly reality of the victorious battle is umbilically joined to the earthly reality of the martyrs' deaths. As followers of the lamb, they believe that they have already been saved by his blood, and that his self-giving to death is the pattern which they must now follow. And that is what wins the battle.

The dragon is, after all, 'the **accuser**'. The early church learned to see this supernatural 'accusing' activity standing not far behind all the 'accusations' that were levelled against them. Such accusations included both the informal ones, whispered by their critical neighbours, wondering why these people weren't joining in with the usual pagan festivities, especially the imperial religion; and the more formal ones, brought by the authorities, and carrying an official penalty, often death. All sorts of slanders and lies were told about the early church. The Christians learned to see them for what they were: accusations from 'the father of lies' (John 8.44).

Once again John is positioning his hearers on the map of the great cosmic drama. They are to know, and celebrate, the great victory which has already been won: 'the accuser' has no place any more in heaven, because the death of Jesus (who claimed in Luke 10.18 that he had seen the **satan** fall like lightning from heaven) has nullified the charges which the celestial Director of Prosecutions would otherwise bring. But he will do his best, in the time remaining, to attack the woman who has fled to the wilderness, even though, as in Exodus 19.4, God has given her eagles' wings so that she could fly away.

What follows only just avoids descending into a comic-strip cosmic car chase. The dragon spits out a jet of water like a river to carry the woman off; the earth opens its mouth to swallow up the river; the woman escapes; and the dragon, angry, turns his attention elsewhere – precisely to the woman's 'children', further defined as 'those who keep God's commands and the testimony of Jesus'. In other words, once again, you too (John is saying to his readers) are part of this drama. Don't be surprised that the dragon is out to get you, with more of his foul but powerful accusations, spat out like a flood. Trust that the God of creation will look after you. (It's fascinating that it is the *earth* that comes to the woman's rescue; creation itself is shown to be on the side of God and his people, rather than working alongside the dragon.)

You must expect, though, that more is to come: more persecution, more attacks, more false accusations. 'Woe to the earth and the sea' (verse 12) 'because the devil has come down to you in great anger, knowing that he only has a short time.' The decisive battle has been won, and the devil knows it; but his basic nature of 'accuser' is now driving him, more and more frantically, to the attack, to accuse where it's justified and where it isn't, to drag down, to slander, to vilify, to deny the truth of what the creator God and his son, the lamb, have accomplished and are accomplishing. This is the ongoing battle in which all Christians are engaged, whether they know it or not.

The picture John has sketched in this chapter, to encourage and warn his readers and all those who, even today, read his book, is just the opening scene. More is to come. The dragon ends up standing on the sand beside the sea. And the sea, as all ancient Jews knew, was the dark place out of which monsters might emerge.

REVELATION 13.1–10

A First Monster

[1]Then I saw a monster coming up out of the sea. It had ten horns and seven heads. Each of the ten horns was wearing a coronet, and blasphemous names were written on the heads.

113

²The monster I saw was like a leopard, with bear's feet and a lion's mouth. And the dragon gave the monster its power and its throne and great authority. ³One of the heads appeared to have been slaughtered and killed, but its fatal wound had been healed. The whole earth was awed and astonished by the monster, ⁴and worshipped the dragon because it had given the monster its authority. They worshipped the monster too. 'Who is like the monster?' they were saying. 'Who can fight against it?' ⁵And the monster was given a mouth that speaks great, blasphemous words, and was given authority for forty-two months. ⁶It opened its mouth to utter blasphemies against God, to curse his name and his dwelling place – that is, those who dwell in heaven. ⁷It was granted the right to make war against God's holy people and to defeat them, and it was given authority over every tribe and people and language and nation. ⁸So everyone who lived on earth worshipped it – everyone, that is, whose name has not been written from the foundation of the world in the book of life belonging to the lamb who was slaughtered.

⁹If anyone has ears, let them hear!

¹⁰If anyone is to be taken captive, into captivity they will go. If anyone is to be killed with the sword, with the sword they will be killed. This is a summons for God's holy people to be patient and have faith.

He wasn't acting alone. That was the conclusion the enquiry reached after a long investigation into the background of a strange murder in a city street. A foreign diplomat had been stabbed by a young man who ran away, but was caught. At his trial he appeared to be confused, distracted, unsure of himself. He didn't give anything away; but the more the court heard the barrister questioning him, the more they all reached the same conclusion. This wasn't just a crazy man doing something wicked on a whim. There was more to it than that. There were dark forces behind it all. The only question was, 'Which forces?' Which country had hired, or bribed, this young man to kill the diplomat? How might you tell?

As often in the world of realpolitik, or underworld dealings, so in the world of spiritual warfare: the ultimate powers prefer not to show themselves, but to act through others. They choose secondary or tertiary intermediaries; they give them some of their power; they back them up where necessary. We are today perhaps more aware than some of our forebears of how what we call 'dark forces' go to work.

It is, of course, easy to invent conspiracy theories about everything, to see hidden influences at work in what are in fact random events. But it is just as easy, and dangerous, to imagine that events are proceeding in a purely random fashion, when in fact there are powers, forces, energies propelling them in one particular direction.

We talk about 'forces' or 'powers' ('economic forces', 'cultural pressures', and so on); ancient Jews used more vivid language. The present section draws heavily on a biblical passage that was hugely popular in the first century, namely Daniel 7. Many believed that this chapter, together with chapters 2 and 9, predicted the overthrow of pagan empire and the ascent to power of God's people, Israel (or at least the righteous within Israel). The chapter was therefore studied intensely in the hope of finding a clue to what exactly was going on. Fresh expositions of it were offered (perhaps the best known is in the book called 4 Ezra or 2 Esdras, written after the fall of Jerusalem towards the end of the first century). Jesus himself made this chapter one of the key themes in his understanding of his own role in God's purposes.

In Daniel 7, there are four monsters that come up out of the sea. They are, like so much in this kind of writing, the stuff of nightmares. The first is a winged lion. The second is a bear with three tusks in its mouth. The third is a leopard with four wings and four heads. Then comes the fourth beast, greater and more terrible, with iron teeth and bronze claws. It has ten horns, with a further little horn growing up beside them.

The interpretation is quite clear. These monsters represent four kingdoms, the fourth of which in particular will become a great and brutal world empire. The horns represent different kings, the last one of whom will make war against God's people and blaspheme God himself. Then comes the great reversal: 'the Ancient of Days' takes his seat for a court hearing, sitting in condemnation over the last great monster and destroying his power, giving it instead to the 'one like a **son of man**' who comes to be presented before the Ancient of Days and to receive an everlasting, universal sovereignty.

There is no question but that John has this passage of Daniel firmly in mind. No question, either, how he and many in his day were reading it. They are not interested in actual monsters, great Day-of-the-Triffids creatures crawling up out of the Mediterranean Sea to attack the holy land. They are interested in the earthly reality which these monsters represent. And in the first century the identification was not difficult. John's single monster has telescoped Daniel's four into one, part leopard, part bear, part lion, with ten horns and seven heads. The monster is Rome.

Or rather, as we shall see, the monster is the dark power of pagan empire, straddling the earth, crushing everything in its path, blaspheming other gods who get in the way so that it alone (and the dragon who has given it its power) may be properly worshipped. This, perhaps, explains why Pergamum was described in 2.13 as 'where the **satan** has his throne': it was a centre of imperial rule and cult, and John sees behind the pomp and the purple to the dark spiritual reality of satanic rule which has enabled the empire to impose itself across so much of the world. Rome is the obvious and only 'monster' candidate in the first century. But the phenomenon of heartless, dehumanized pagan empire, sadly, did not end with the decline and demise of Rome. That is why the sharp relevance of all this for John's own readers remains, in a different guise, for other readers to this day.

Verse 3 draws attention to a particular feature of Roman rule in the second half of the first century. The ancient Roman republic had become an 'empire' under Augustus, a hundred years or so before, after the murder of his adopted father Julius Caesar (44 BC) and the ensuing civil wars. But with the reign, and then the death, of Nero one might have thought that the precarious, self-glorifying, top-heavy empire would come crashing down under its own weight. Certainly the year after Nero's death (AD 69) must have looked like a mortal wound to the whole monstrous system, with four would-be emperors in quick succession marching on Rome, killing their enemies, claiming the crown, and then – except for the last one – being killed in turn by the next army to arrive. Galba, Otho and Vitellius came and went; Vespasian came, and stayed. Within months his son and heir, Titus, completed the military task on which Vespasian had been engaged before his troops encouraged him to go for the big prize. Titus's legions destroyed Jerusalem, burning the **Temple** to the ground. To many observers, it must have seemed like the end of the world.

Meanwhile, rumours went around that Nero hadn't died after all – or that he had indeed died, but had then come back to **life**. Several would-be 'Nero-alive-again' leaders emerged, and, though none lasted long, the rumour persisted. He was, is not, but is to come, they said (17.8). This may be what John is referring to when he says that one of the monster's heads appeared to have been killed, but its fatal wound had been healed (verse 3). But the central and important feature, which all his readers would have recognized at once, is that the monster claimed worship, and shared that worship with the dark pagan gods that stood behind it. A glance at Roman coins of the period tells its own story, as one emperor after another not only claimed to be 'son of god' but to dress up in the garb traditionally associated with this or that ancient pagan divinity.

And of course, once the emperor becomes a god, there is no room for other gods. It's all right if local and tribal deities are still worshipped, so long as one worships the new god, Rome and the emperor. But if one refuses – as the Christians knew they were bound to refuse – then a collision course is set. Like

Daniel and his friends in the early chapters of the book from which John drew so richly, all the world seemed to be worshipping the monster. Only the faithful few, here described in terms of their names being in the lamb's book of life, refuse to do so.

The last verse of this section may reflect John's sober realism when contemplating the scene he has now drawn. Some people are going to be taken captive. Others are going to be killed with the sword. That's just the way it is. The proper response is not to kick and scream, but to hold firm to patience and **faith**. Chapter 11 meant what it said. It is through the faithful witness unto death that the lamb wins the victory, that God's **kingdom** replaces the kingdom of the monster, that the dragon himself is to lose the last remains of his power. How this is to be worked out we have yet to see. But what John is doing at this point is sketching the larger, darker picture within which the little local struggles of the churches must be seen if they are to make sense, and if the challenge to uncompromising witness is to make sense. Only when we remember the dragon and the monster do we realize what a deadly serious thing Christian faith, patience and holiness really is.

REVELATION 13.11–18

A Second Monster

[11]Then I saw another monster coming up from the earth. It had two horns like those of a lamb, and it spoke like a dragon. [12]It acts in the presence of the first monster, and with its full authority, and it makes the earth and those who live on it worship the first monster, whose fatal wound had been healed. [13]It performs great signs, so that it even makes fire come down from heaven on the earth in the sight of people, [14]and it deceives the people who live on earth by the signs which it has been allowed to perform in front of the monster, instructing the earth's inhabitants to make an image of the monster who had the sword-wound but was alive. [15]It was allowed to give

breath to the monster's image, so that the monster's image could speak, and it could kill anyone who didn't worship the monster's image. [16]It makes everyone, small and great, rich and poor, free and slaves, receive a sign from it, marked on their right hands and on their foreheads, [17]so that nobody can buy or sell unless they have the mark of the name of the monster or the number of its name.

[18]This calls for wisdom. Anyone with a good head on their shoulders should work out the monster's number, because it's the number of a human being. Its number is Six Hundred and Sixty-Six.

I sat in the room, surrounded by shelf after shelf of old books. It felt good. When we took a break from the seminar (it was in a hotel in a large American city), I got up and walked over to the nearest bookcase to inspect what treats it might hold in store. A rude shock awaited me. It wasn't a bookcase; it was a fake. What seemed to be shelves were less than an inch deep. Worse, what looked like books were indeed books – or rather, parts of books. Hundred and hundreds of lovely old leather-bound books had had their spines, and the first half-inch of the book, cut off in order then to be glued to a back wall to make it look as though the room was a genuine library. It would have been easier, actually, to create the real thing with the same books. From then on I found the place creepy, and was glad to escape at the end of the day. It wasn't the real thing; it was a parody.

A parody is what you get when someone produces a fake which looks real but isn't. Sometimes this is done deliberately, for comic effect, as when people turn a Shakespeare tragedy like *Hamlet* into a short, funny skit, or play a Mozart symphony on kazoos and mouth organs. Sometimes it is done with the intent to deceive. And if you deceive enough people your parody becomes a new reality. That is what had happened across the ancient Near East in John's day.

The reality, as John and his readers knew not least from his vision in the throne room (chapters 4 and 5), was that the one

119

sitting on the throne was the all-powerful, sovereign lord of all creation; that the lamb, his son, was the one whose death had conquered the world and rescued people from their slavery to sin in order to appoint them as rulers and priests in God's new creation; and that the **spirit** of God was at work in and through these people to accomplish God's work. The parody, though, which was gaining ground all the time in western Turkey through the first century, was that the Roman empire, gaining its ultimate authority from the satanic dragon, was putting itself about as the world ruler. That was the first monster. And the second, like it but subordinate, seems to be the local elites, in city after city and province after province, who do their best not only to copy the monster at a local level but insist, in order to keep the monster's favour, that everybody in their domain should worship the monster. This was going on all over the place, and John's hearers would have been quite familiar with it. City after city vied with one another to be allowed to build yet another new temple to Rome, to the emperor, or to a member of the emperor's family. These local power-brokers are the second monster, 'coming up from the earth', arising (that is) locally rather than coming across the sea. They complete the Unholy Trinity: the dragon, the first monster, and the second monster, the ghastly combined parody of God, Jesus and the spirit.

Part of the parody of the truth is that the local elites ('horns like those of a lamb', says John: trying to look like what they're not!) even parade the fact of how nearly the monster seemed to have come to being killed, and yet there it is, alive again! Rome had recovered from the apparent death-blow. The Christians, of course, heralded Jesus as the true lamb, and his actual death and **resurrection** was the basis of their allegiance to him, their belief that he had defeated the dragon himself. But the parody was powerful. There were several tricks commonly employed to enable the statues of various gods to move about, to breathe, weep and even speak. Sophisticated pagan writers of the time mention many such devices, pouring scorn on their trickery.

But people were taken in, and more and more people, through the work of the local 'monsters', came to worship the first monster itself. And, through that means, the dragon itself.

What's more, worshipping or nor worshipping was quickly becoming the dividing line between people who were acceptable in the community and people who weren't. Not long after this time, some local officials introduced a formal requirement that unless you had offered the required **sacrifices** you weren't allowed in the market. There were various kinds of marks and visible signs which were used to set people apart either as 'able to trade' or as 'not able to trade'. From quite early on the Christians were faced with a stark alternative: stay true to the lamb and risk losing your livelihood, the ability to sell or buy; or capitulate to the monster, sacrifice to Caesar at the behest of the local officials, and then everything will be all right – except your integrity as one of the lamb's followers.

We can understand the dilemma faced by those Christians back then. We like to think that we would always choose the reality and reject the parody. But would we? When we ask ourselves where similar key issues emerge and challenge us today, it may not be as clear-cut as we like to think – and it's quite possible that many Christians in the first century felt like that too. Does it count as a compromise if I use Caesar's coinage, even though it has words like 'son of god' stamped on it? Is it a compromise if I put my stall out by the side of the road during one of the great imperial festivals, to catch the crowds as they are going to the temple, even if I don't go myself? Will it matter if I buy a slab of beef in the market, even though I know it will have been offered in sacrifice in Caesar's temple just up the road? For us, does it matter if we buy a newspaper which openly mocks the Christian **faith** and promotes every other way of life imaginable except the Christian one – even if all I'm going to read is the sports news? Does it matter if I work for a company that, through one of its other offshoots, is cheerfully polluting lakes and rivers and destroying their wildlife? Should I be worried that my bank is a major investor in companies that work in parts of Latin America where labour laws are practically non-existent, allowing them to get away with virtual enslavement of local populations?

These are not the only, nor even perhaps the most important, questions we face. But it's important to recognize that we, too, face choices which may well not be so clear-cut as we would like. We need to pray for discernment to distinguish the reality from the parody, and to act accordingly.

The final verse of the chapter is one of the most famous in the whole book. It offers the greatest parody of all. It is more or less certain that the number 666 represents, by one of many formulae well known at the time, the name NERO CAESAR when written in Hebrew characters. (Many peoples, and many languages, used letters as numbers, as we would if we devised a system where A=1, B=2 and so on.) The monster who was, is not, and is to come looks pretty certainly to be Nero.

But the number 666 isn't just a cryptogram. It's also a parody. The number of perfection, not least for John, would be, we assume, 777. Some have even suggested that the name JESUS comes out, in some systems, as 888 – a kind of super-perfection. But for John there is little doubt. Nero, and the system he represented and embodied, was but a parody of the real thing, one short of the right number three times over. Jesus was the reality; Nero, just a dangerous, blasphemous copy. We do well to recognize this, but we also do well to search our consciences and our own societies and enquire to what extent we, too, have been deceived by fakes posing as the real thing.

REVELATION 14.1–5

The Lamb's Elite Warriors

[1]As I watched, there was the lamb standing on Mount Zion, and with him were a hundred and forty-four thousand who had his name, and the name of his father, written on their

foreheads. [2]I heard a voice from heaven, like the sound of many waters, and like the sound of mighty thunder, and the voice I heard was like harpists playing on their harps. [3]And they are singing a new song before the throne, and before the four creatures and the elders. Nobody can learn that song except for the hundred and forty-four thousand who have been redeemed from the earth. [4]These are the ones who have never polluted themselves with women; they are celibate. They follow the lamb wherever he goes. They have been redeemed from the human race as first fruits for God and the lamb, [5]and no lie has been found in their mouths. They are without blemish.

On the hill in the distance I could see the little procession, tiny but silhouetted against the sky in the bright Middle-Eastern evening. In my country the sheep are brought from one field to another by people with sticks and dogs. In the Middle East, to this day, the shepherd goes on ahead and the sheep follow him or her. They know the shepherd's voice, but they also know that they can trust him or her to lead them to pasture, to water, to safety. No sticks, or dogs, are required.

Jesus himself, of course, used this image of the shepherd in the tenth chapter of John's **gospel**. And his call to people to 'follow him' is one of the most persistent commands he ever issued. One might almost say that, in the gospels, 'following Jesus' is the basic phrase which describes someone who belongs to Jesus, who believes in him (e.g. Matthew 4.19; 8.22; 9.9; etc.). But, in John's gospel particularly, we find some poignant and striking passages on this theme. 'Whoever serves me must follow me,' he said (John 12.26). Peter insists that he will follow Jesus absolutely anywhere, to prison or even to death (John 13.37; Luke 22.33), but Jesus solemnly warns him that he will in fact deny that he even knows him.

It is in that light that we read the immensely powerful passage in John 21 where Peter, after Jesus' resurrection, tells Jesus three times that he loves him, and Jesus' ultimate response is 'Follow me!' (21.19). Even then Peter has some questions:

'Lord,' he says, looking at the Beloved Disciple following them, 'what about this man?' Jesus' reply is one of the most famous one-liners in all the gospel, echoing through the hearts and minds of all who have struggled with vocation and wondered why things were working out the way they did. 'If it is my will', he replies, 'that he remain until I come, what is that to you? *Follow me!*' Don't ask silly questions; just follow. Don't worry about the others; you follow me. Don't look back (Luke 9.62); follow me.

All that is in the background as we find, in this definition of the lamb's elite warriors, the sentence: 'They follow the lamb wherever he goes' (verse 4). There is a sense in which nothing more needs to be said. The lamb has won the victory over the dragon and his sidekicks, through his own sacrificial death. Now he calls his people to put that victory into practice, by following him down the same path. Jesus had stressed this during his public ministry: if anyone wanted to come after him, they should deny themselves, take up their cross, and follow him. Somehow, the way to victory is the way of the cross. It was strange and challenging then, and it is just as strange and challenging today.

Who then are these 'elite warriors', as I've called them? What purpose is there in them suddenly being revealed at this point in the story? The answer is that John is once again working with Psalm 2. The nations rage, the peoples imagine foolish things, but God's answer is to set his king, his son, 'upon my holy hill of Zion'. Hence the mention of the lamb standing on Mount Zion in verse 1. We have seen the dragon becoming furious with the woman and her offspring, the younger brothers of the child who has been snatched up to **heaven** (12.5). We have seen the two monsters, the great imperial monster who comes from the sea and the local, secondary monster who emerges from the immediate community. They are the ones who, in Psalm 2, are raging and fuming, threatening and blaspheming. But now God is revealing his chosen king, and his chosen king is not alone. He is surrounded by his crack troops, his elite warriors. There is no doubt of their victory.

It is because they are elite warriors that (strictly within the bounds of the symbolism John is using) he speaks of them as 'celibate' or 'virgins'. Ancient Israel had a clear policy about going to war; if war was justified, war was also holy, and those who fought in it had to obey special rules of purity, including abstention (for the time) from sexual relations (e.g. Deuteronomy 23.9–10; 1 Samuel 21.5). As usual, we need to be clear about the symbol and the reality to which it points. In the symbol, this body consists of a hundred and forty-four thousand (we have met them before, of course, in chapter 7); they sing a new song; they have abstained from sexual relations. They are, in other words, the ideal representatives of the people of God, permanently ready for battle. In the reality to which this symbol points, they are in fact a great company which nobody could count; the chances are that they sing songs which all Christians would know; and some of them may be married and some single – but *all are permanently ready for the real battle*, which is the engagement with the monsters and their demands, an engagement which may mean at any moment that they will be required to suffer or even to die.

These elite warriors serve, then, to encourage the small Christian groups who, faced with the monstrous might of Rome and its local supporters, would probably feel powerless and helpless. Not a bit of it, says John: the lamb has been enthroned, just as God promised, and his elite stand around him, ready for the battle in which, following the lamb himself, they are going to win the victory. They will be the conquerors. These are the ones who, instead of the brand of the monster, receive (not a mark, but actually) the name of God and the lamb on their foreheads. This will mark them out in pagan society, of course, once it is known that they are loyal to this name rather than to that of Caesar. But it will also mark them out in God's presence as those whom the **Messiah** will acknowledge to be his (Matthew 10.32).

This great crowd, surrounding the lamb, is not the sum total of all believers. It is the beginning, the great advance sign of an even greater harvest to come. That is the point of the 'first fruits' image in verse 4. At the ancient Jewish harvest-time, the first sheaf of wheat (or whichever crop it might be) was offered to God as the 'first fruits', signifying the expectation and prayer that there would be much more on the way. Even so, these one hundred and forty-four thousand are to be an encouragement to the churches. Already there is a great multitude! The lamb is winning the victory! We can carry on patiently.

And the way they must do so is by following him, especially, in holiness of life. For John, one of the major features of the dragon's whole system is the lie: he creates a world of untruth, a fake world, a sham system from top to bottom. But for the elite, no lie is 'found in their mouths'. Like the lamb himself (Isaiah 53.9), they are without blemish in this respect, as in everything else. This remains a challenge to all those who claim to follow Jesus. Truth and lies may sometimes be hard to tell apart, but this is where we stand at the watershed. God's victory is about the real world, the whole creation. The closer we are to God and to his lamb, the more we see everything clearly and should speak everything truthfully. The **satan** does his best work by keeping things out of people's minds altogether. Where that fails, he persuades them to believe, and to pass on, lies. 'It doesn't matter; it's only a little thing; God wouldn't mind, really; those are only silly, narrow rules; don't you know that God wants you to enjoy yourself?' and so on. Following the lamb means rejecting the lie. Always and for ever.

REVELATION 14.6–13

A Call for Endurance

⁶Then I saw another angel flying in mid-heaven, carrying an eternal gospel to announce to those who live on earth, to every nation and tribe and language and people. ⁷He spoke with a

loud voice, and this is what he said: 'Fear God! Give him glory! The time has come for his judgment! Worship the one who made heaven and earth and the sea and the springs of water!'

[8]He was followed by another angel, and this is what he said: 'Babylon the great has fallen! She has fallen! She is the one who made all the nations drink the wine of the anger that comes upon her fornication.'

[9]They were followed by a third angel, who also spoke in a loud voice: 'If anyone worships the monster and its image, or receives its mark on their forehead or their hand, [10]that person will drink the wine of God's anger, poured neat into the cup of his anger, and they will be tortured in fire and sulphur before the holy angels and before the lamb. [11]The smoke of their torture goes up for ever and ever. Those who worship the monster and its image, and those who receive the mark of its name, will have no respite, day or night.'

[12]This demands patience from God's holy people, who keep God's commands and the faith of Jesus.

[13]Then I heard a loud voice from heaven saying, 'Write this: God's blessing on the dead who from this time onward die in the Lord.'

'Yes,' says the spirit, 'so that they may rest from their works, for the deeds they have done follow after them.'

I had a long email the other day from someone eager to know whether **hell** is really going to be eternal. *Really* 'eternal'. The message was full of detailed references to passages from all over the Bible. The arguments were listed, this way and that. My correspondent had, he said, asked several other church leaders the same question, and he'd never received a satisfactory answer. What did I think?

The first (and the main) thing I thought, and said, was that it was interesting just how obsessed he seemed to be with the question. Most Christians I know, from a wide variety of traditions, probably are not universalists – that is, people who believe that eventually every single human being who has ever lived will enjoy the bliss of God's new world. But most don't find the question of 'hell' (or whatever we're going to call it) among the more pressing questions in their day-to-day pilgrimage.

Perhaps they should. Perhaps this is a sign that many of us have 'gone soft' on something which the Bible clearly teaches. Perhaps we should return to the preaching habits of former generations, warning people to repent in case they end up frying in hell for ever.

Or perhaps we should recognize that in passages like this, as we have seen so often throughout this book, John is working with symbols, and that it's important not only to feel the force of them but also to probe through, to enquire about the reality to which they point.

To get the force of the symbols here, we have to think back to Babylon. Babylon, the capital of the great empire that swallowed up the remaining Israelite tribes in 597 BC, was the city that remained ever after in the Jewish memory as the paradigm of wickedness, of idolatry, immorality and sheer cruelty. Anyone who knows anything about the book of Revelation knows that 'Babylon' is used as a symbol later in the book, in chapters 16, 17 and 18, where John without a shadow of doubt means 'Rome'. But he means 'Rome-seen-as-Babylon', and he is seeing Babylon through the lens, in particular, of two of the greatest Old Testament prophetic books. (We might include a further ancient image: the Tower of Babel in Genesis 11. But that would take us too far away from our main purpose.)

The first is Isaiah. The great central section of the book, chapters 40—55, is addressed to the Israelites in **exile** who have almost given up hope. Babylon, where they have been taken in exile, seems so great and all-powerful. Babylon's gods appear to have won, and YHWH, Israel's God, appears to be just another god, and now a failed one at that. In poetry that has scarcely ever been equalled for its combination of power and tenderness, the prophet expounds the greatness and the **covenant** faithfulness of YHWH. He is the creator of **heaven** and earth; he is not about to be worsted by the puny fake gods of Babylon. He will rescue his people, re-establish the covenant, and renew the whole creation.

And he will do all this through the work of the 'servant'. Four sub-poems emerge from the flow of prophecy. These poems highlight, first, the servant's mission to rescue Israel and bring justice to the world; then his hard and apparently unfruitful work which will yet reveal YHWH to the nations; then his readiness to hear YHWH's voice and his consequent suffering and patience; and finally his shameful death, bearing the sins of his people, leading to his restoration and vindication (42.1–9; 49.1–7; 50.4–9; 52.13—53.12).

Around these poems are oracles of doom on Babylon. She has made her captives drink 'the cup of wrath' to the dregs, but God will take it from them and give it to Babylon instead (51.17–23). The oppressors will fall victim to the wicked systems they have devised. Evil will bring its own reward.

It is in that context that, by way of introduction to the fourth 'servant' poem, the prophet annouces the arrival of a herald with '**good news**' (52.7) – just as John tells us here that he sees an angel carrying 'an eternal **gospel**'. What is this 'good news'?

For many today, the Christian 'good news' or 'gospel' is a **message** about them: God loves them, God forgives them, God promises them a blissful place in 'heaven'. But, without diminishing the personal meaning, most of the summaries of the 'good news' in the Bible are much larger in scope. Paul summarizes the 'good news' in terms of the saving events of Jesus' scripture-fulfilling death and **resurrection** (1 Corinthians 15.3–8), or of Jesus' Davidic descent, his public recognition as '**son of God**' through the resurrection, and his universal lordship (Romans 1.3–5). For Isaiah, there are three elements immediately mentioned, with a further immediate consequence. John seems to be aware of all of this.

First, 'Your God reigns!' This message, announced to the exiles in Babylon, can mean only one thing: your God, YHWH, has won the victory over Babylon, and you are now free to go home. Jerusalem will be rebuilt (52.7, 9).

Second, 'Your God is coming back!' God had, it seemed, abandoned the Temple in Jerusalem when the Babylonians closed in to attack. But now he would return, publicly and visibly (52.8; 40.5).

Third, 'God is doing a powerful and public work of rescue!' (52.10). All the nations would see that Israel's God had saved his people from their plight.

So Babylon fell, the exiles went back home . . . but nobody ever said that YHWH had finally come back. But the early Christians believed, and they believed that Jesus believed, that YHWH had come back, in and as Jesus himself. They believed that his glory was fully and finally revealed when Jesus died on the cross as the innocent lamb (Isaiah 53.7). All this is vital as the complex scriptural background to Revelation 14.

The other passage is Jeremiah. Jeremiah seems to have spent most of his life in the terror and horror of the Babylonian invasion and its aftermath, the sorrow of exile. He has seen some appalling sights and experienced just how atrocious human behaviour can be. And, at the end of his book, he solemnly pronounces God's judgment on the wicked nations that have brought such terrible things to pass. He has oracles against Egypt, the Philistines, Moab, the Ammonites, and Damascus. But then, in chapter 50, he reaches Babylon. Two long chapters of sustained condemnation show where the book's emphasis lies. Perhaps only those who have lived for a generation under a desperately cruel and inhumane regime can even begin to understand why those chapters needed to be written. But perhaps those who think hard about the justice of God, and about the urgent necessity that a good God should not turn a blind eye to injustice and oppression, may glimpse part of the answer too.

And now at last we can, perhaps, begin to understand also why Revelation 14 says what it does. This is 'the gospel', the 'good news', for those who live under 'Babylonian', monstrous, rule. First, God the creator is at last going to sort everything out (verse 7). Second, Babylon is fallen, after all her efforts to make the nations drunk with her own immoral wine (verse 8: this is an image we shall look at more fully a bit later). Third, God's judgment will be just, thorough and complete (verses 9–11).

All this is, in this sense, 'good news' for those who have lived in a world of horror, torture and squalor. God is going to sort it all out! That's what the Psalmist, too, thought of as good news (Psalms 96.10–13; 98.7–9).

What we are not allowed to conclude from all this is that either John, or we, or anybody else, know who if anyone comes into the category described in verses 9–11. These things – which are themselves symbolic, evoking yet more biblical passages, and not literal descriptions – can only be heard with awe, and with the recognition that the deep seduction of evil really can swallow people up whole. John is eager, anxiously eager, to prevent any of Jesus' followers being sucked down into that dark whirlpool of wrath. Their part is to be patient, obedient and faithful, knowing that death itself has been defeated, so as to become now a source, not of curse but of blessing. Their labours in the present, as Paul says in 1 Corinthians 15.58, are not in vain (verse 13).

REVELATION 14.14–20

Reaping the Harvest

¹⁴Then I looked, and there was a white cloud, and sitting on the cloud one like a son of man. He had a gold crown on his head, and a sharp sickle in his hand. ¹⁵And another angel came out of the temple, shouting in a loud voice to the one who was sitting on the cloud, 'It's harvest time! Put in your sickle and reap: the harvest of the earth is ripe!' ¹⁶So the one sitting on the cloud applied his sickle to the earth, and reaped the harvest of the earth.

> [17]Then another angel came out of the temple in heaven. He, too, had a sharp sickle. [18]Yet another angel came from the altar; he had authority over fire, and he spoke with a loud voice to the one who had the sharp sickle. 'Go to work with your sharp sickle,' he said, 'and gather the clusters of fruit from the vine of the earth; the grapes are there in ripe bunches!' [19]So the angel went to work with his sickle on the earth, and gathered the fruit from the vine of the earth, and threw it into the great winepress of God's anger. [20]The winepress was trodden outside the city, and blood came out of the winepress, as high as a horse's bridle, for about two hundred miles.

We watched, last summer, as the reapers went to and fro across the fields. Gradually the landscape changed from golden to brown, with the rich grain being replaced by the earth that would then wait for the next sowing. I was put to shame, one night, when I thought I'd been working late, only to discover when I came out of my study that there were still lights on, away out in the fields, as the reapers continued their urgent labour. We became used to the cartloads coming up the narrow country lane. There was a sense of satisfaction, of a job well done, of the proper cycle of work being completed. Then there was the harvest festival, still an important moment in the life of a rural community.

Someone was complaining on the radio recently that people nowadays didn't celebrate harvest the way they used to. The First World War, they said, had sent so many country workers to their deaths that many centuries-old traditions of country life had died out. People today don't have the same instinctive feel for the joy of harvest as once they did. That certainly wouldn't have been true for a first-century audience reading about harvest-time, on the one hand, and vintage-time on the other. This is what you work for! This is the moment of joy when the long months of sowing, tending, watering, pruning, protecting are at last complete. Now it's time for celebration. Even if many of John's readers lived within cities, nobody in those days and those cultures was far from the land and its regular ways.

Granted that, there should be no doubt that this passage, describing the harvest and the vintage, is meant to be an occasion of great, uninhibited joy. We would need a huge amount of evidence to force us to say anything else.

The passage is often read, of course, the other way: as the story of great and terrifying judgment, with the **son of man**, Jesus himself, executing God's wrath with his sickle (verses 14–16), and an angel from **heaven** gathering up the 'grapes of wrath', understood as the wicked nations who are about to suffer God's eternal anger. But the harvest imagery, and the natural implications it would carry, tell strongly against this. The previous chapter has warned God's people against worshipping the monster; the next chapter will see those same people, with victory won, singing the new song by the sea of glass. How have they come from the one place to the other? By, it seems, being themselves the harvest, the vintage, of the Lord. These are images of **salvation**, not of condemnation.

But it is a salvation-through-suffering. As always in Revelation, John is encouraging his readers to face the prospect of persecution in **faith** and patience. When 'one like a son of man' (an obvious allusion to Daniel 7) is encouraged by the angel to 'put in your sickle and reap' (an obvious allusion to Joel 3), we should see this in terms of the faithful people who are, as Jesus himself said of people, 'white for harvest', ready to be saved (John 4.35). If persecution and martyrdom are to come, they are to be understood not simply as the random and vicious attacks of a brutal regime, but as Jesus himself using human wickedness as his means of bringing in the harvest.

This is particularly striking in the image of the vineyard. Vines, grapes, and the wine which they produce, are regularly seen in scripture as an image of Israel, of God's people. Only when the grapes go wild is there a problem (Isaiah 5). Why then does John speak of the grapes being thrown into the winepress of God's *anger* (verse 19)?

This sends us back to yet another prophetic passage, this time Isaiah 63, where the royal figure who seems to be a development both of the Messiah of Isaiah 9 and 11 and of the Servant of Isaiah 42 and 53 is trampling down the grapes, all by himself, getting his clothes spattered with juice in the process. In that case he is bent on vengeance, on crushing and trampling the peoples who have ruined God's earth and enslaved God's people. By itself that allusion might incline us to suppose that in this picture, too, collecting grapes and throwing them into the winepress might be a sign of the coming judgment.

But when John appeals to Isaiah 63 later in the book, the staining on the clothes of the Messiah is from his own blood (19.13–16). We are told, again and again, that the lamb has conquered through his blood, his sacrificial death, and that his followers are to conquer in the same way. This points us to the strange oxymoron we have already met, 'the anger of the lamb'. Somehow, the way in which God works salvation, and the way he works wrath, are intimately connected – because they meet on the cross; and because they meet, too, in the martyrdom of Jesus' followers. The winepress is where God's wrath is being prepared, for Babylon and all monster-worshippers to drink. But the wine itself is the lifeblood of the martyrs who are being harvested.

That this is what John has in mind is all the clearer when we consider that the winepress is being trodden 'outside the city' (verse 20). Had this been a picture of God's judgment on impenitent Babylon, or any other city, one would expect the winepress to be at the heart of the city; or perhaps, even, that the whole city would *become* a great winepress for the avenging angel, or even the Messiah himself, to trample. But 'outside the city', as we know from Hebrews 13.11–14, was already well known as a summary statement of where Jesus himself was taken to be crucified. It may not be coincidental that the first martyr, Stephen, was himself hustled 'outside the city' in order to be stoned (Acts 7.58).

What then are we to make of the horrible sight of blood flowing out of the winepress, 'as high as a horse's bridle, for about two hundred miles' (verse 20)? There have been, of course, many great battles and massacres in history after which horrified onlookers have reported rivers of blood, birds and animals choking in blood, and so on. But we must once again remind ourselves that we are reading a symbolic prophecy, not a literal one. The idea of something flowing away from a city, and being measured for depth, carries a distant memory of the water of life which flows from the city at the end of Ezekiel. It may be that John, with his visionary imagination working overtime, sees the swelling river of blood as playing a similar role, though whether it will be to effect a further work of grace or a further work of judgment we cannot easily say.

The whole passage is designed to convey a powerful **message** which we need today as much as ever. God's time will come; God will bring his people safely home; God will take even the wickedness and rebellion of the world and make it turn to his praise and to the salvation of his people. And in the meantime his people are to be encouraged in their suffering. Martyrdom itself will be part of God's purpose to bring his wise, healing order – which includes his relentless judgment on relentless sinners – to bear upon the world. As with the **Exodus** from Egypt, the plagues which were inflicted merely served to heighten the glory of God's eventual redeeming act. But that takes us into the next chapter.

REVELATION 15.1–8

Preparing the Final Plagues

[1]Then I saw another sign – a great, amazing sight in heaven: seven angels who were bringing the seven last plagues. With

135

them God's anger is completed. [2]And I saw what looked like a sea of glass, mixed with fire. There, by that glassy sea, stood the people who had won the victory over the monster and over its image, and over the number of its name. They were holding harps of God, [3]and they were singing the song of Moses the servant of God, and the song of the lamb. This is how it went:

Great and amazing are your works,
O Lord God, the Almighty one.
Just and true are your ways,
O King of the nations.
[4]Who will not fear you, Lord,
and glorify your name?
For you alone are holy.
For all nations shall come
and worship before you,
because your judgments have been revealed.

[5]After this I looked, and the temple of the 'tabernacle of witness' was opened in heaven. [6]The seven angels who had the seven plagues came out of the temple, clothed in clean, shining linen, wearing golden belts across their chests. [7]Then one of the four living creatures gave the seven angels seven golden bowls filled with the anger of the God who lives for ever and ever. [8]The temple was filled with smoke from the glory of God and his power. Nobody was able to go into the temple until the seven plagues of the seven angels had been completed.

What is it that attracts people to the Christian **message**? What is it that draws them to worship the God whom Christians call 'father'? If you went round your local church and asked people that, you would (I suspect) get a wide variety of answers. Some will have been drawn in by the kindness and gentleness of a pastor, whether ordained or lay, who looked after them at a moment of crisis. Some will have gone to a meeting where they were able to express all kinds of questions and doubts and where they were received with courtesy and respect, and given such answers as were available – but it will be the courtesy and the respect that has done the trick. Others again may have found themselves at a major turning point in their lives and, not knowing where else to go for guidance, may have come to the church and found more than they expected.

This short but powerful song gives a quite different sort of reason why not only individuals but nations will come and worship the true and living God: 'your judgments have been revealed'. Since Revelation doesn't often talk about all the nations coming to worship (though ancient Jewish traditions about such things were well known, and the early Christians picked up on them to explain the arrival of so many non-Jews within the people of the **Messiah**), when it does it is worth pondering closely what it means. What are the 'judgments' of God? How have they been 'revealed'? And how has this brought the nations to worship?

When the Bible speaks about God 'judging', or putting into effect his 'judgments', it is just as much a cause for celebration as for anxiety. We have already referred to the famous passages at the end of Psalms 96 and 98, where the whole of creation, animal and vegetable as well as human, sings for joy because YHWH is coming 'to judge the earth'. Why? Why is that **good news**?

Imagine a village in the outlying countryside of Judaea. It's a long way from the city, and even traders don't come there that often, far less government officials. A circuit judge comes to the neighbouring small town once every few months if they're lucky. But that doesn't mean that nothing needs doing. A builder is cheated by a customer, who refuses to admit his fault. A widow has her small purse stolen, and since she has nobody to plead for her she can do nothing. A family is evicted from their home by a landlord who thinks he can get more rent from someone else. And a fraudster with his eye on the main chance has accused a work colleague of cheating him, and though nothing has been done about it the other colleagues seem inclined to believe the charge. And so on. Nobody can do anything about any of these – until the judge comes.

When he comes, expectations will be massive. Months of pent-up frustrations will boil over. The judge will have to keep order, to calm down accusation and defence alike. He will have to hear each case properly and fairly, taking especial care for those with nobody to speak up for them. He will steadfastly refuse all bribes. And then he will *decide*. Judgment will be done. Chaos will be averted and order will be restored. The cheats will be put in their place, the thief punished and made to restore the purse. The grasping landlord will have to give way, and the false accuser will suffer the punishment he hoped to inflict. And the village as a whole will heave a sigh of relief. Justice has been done. The world has returned into balance. A grateful community will thank the judge from the bottom of its collective heart.

Now magnify the village concerns up to the global level. The wicked empire, and its local henchmen, have become more and more powerful, taking money, lives and pleasure as and when they please. It's no use appealing to the authorities, because it's the authorities who are doing the wrong. So the cry goes up to God, as it did to the God of Israel when the Egyptians were making their lives more and more miserable. And God's action on behalf of Israel is therefore a great act of liberating, healing, sigh-of-relief *judgment*. Things are put right at last.

We would expect, of course, that Israel itself would thank God for his rescue operation, his great act of 'judgment' which has set his people free. But the story of the **Exodus**, which is once again dominating John's horizon, goes further than that. It isn't only Israel that will see what God has done and give him thanks. The nations will look on and say to themselves, 'There really is a God in Israel; there really is a God who puts things right, who judges the earth' (see Psalm 58.11). And, saying that, they will come to worship him.

For John, as for all the early Christians, there was one great act of judgment above all others which was already compelling people from many nations to worship Israel's God. God had raised Jesus from the dead, after his condemnation as a false Messiah. God had reversed the verdict of the human court! He had done the unthinkable, and had demonstrated Jesus to be Messiah after all! What's more, the **resurrection** proved that the cross itself had been the great, spectacular act of judgment, in which sin and death were themselves being condemned and executed.

Now, having done all that in Jesus the Messiah, Israel's God was demonstrating that the followers of Jesus were his true people, not least through their faithful testimony to Jesus, even on peril of their own death. This is the further 'judgment' which flows from the 'judgment' revealed in the lamb.

It is therefore the martyrs, those who have 'won the victory over the monster and over its image, and over the number of its name', who have discovered that they have come through death, as the Israelites had come through the Red Sea, and are now standing, like Moses and Miriam in Exodus 15, singing a new song of praise for the fresh act of judgment which God had performed. (The song in this passage owes something to Deuteronomy 32 as well, but the focus of the passage is then on a different part of the Exodus story.) The plagues in Egypt have reached a crescendo, and Pharaoh and his people have consented to let the Israelites go. They have gone through the Red Sea, sung the song, and arrived at Mount Sinai. There, with the fire and smoke of divine revelation, God gives Moses the instructions not only about the **law** itself but also about the Tabernacle, the place of 'witness' or meeting, where God himself would come to meet with his people. It was the forerunner of the **Temple** in Jerusalem.

Now, in a fresh visionary twist, John sees that the heavenly throne room which is also the heart of the heavenly temple has a 'tabernacle of witness' within it. This 'tabernacle' has been opened, not to let Moses or anyone else in, but to let out the angels who were carrying the seven last plagues, not for Egypt but for Babylon and for the world that had fallen for her seductions.

As with the Tabernacle in Exodus, as with Isaiah's vision in the Temple (Isaiah 6), and as with Solomon's dedication of the Temple (1 Kings 8), the presence of God is shrouded in smoke, making it impossible for ordinary comings and goings. This is a solemn moment. The new song is exuberant, and heartfelt. Deliverance has occurred. But now we are homing in on the greatest showdown of them all. We left the dragon and the two monsters behind, two chapters ago. They have drawn many into their destructive ways. It is time, now, for the destroyers to be destroyed. This is the purpose of the seven last plagues, and of the cataclysmic judgments which follow them.

REVELATION 16.1–9

The First Four Plagues

[1]Then I heard a loud voice coming from the temple, addressing the seven angels. 'Off you go,' said the voice, 'and pour out on the earth the seven bowls of God's anger.' [2]So the first one went off and poured out his bowl on the earth, and foul, painful sores came on the people who had the mark of the monster, and those who worshipped its image. [3]The second one poured his bowl on the sea, and it turned into blood like that from a corpse. Every living thing in the sea died. [4]The third one poured his bowl on the rivers and the springs of water, and they turned into blood. [5]Then I heard the angel of the waters saying,

'You are the one Who Is and Who Was,
you are the holy one, and you are just!
You have passed the righteous sentence:
[6]they spilt the blood of saints and prophets
and you have given them blood to drink.
They deserve it.'

140

⁷And I heard the altar respond, 'Yes, Lord God Almighty, your judgments are true and just.'

⁸Then the fourth angel poured his bowl upon the sun, and it was allowed to burn people with its fire. ⁹People were burned up by its great heat, and they cursed the name of the God who had authority over these plagues. They did not repent or give him glory.

I was cycling down the road one day when I came up beside my former tutor. I had studied the New Testament with him some years before, and was now engaged on some early work towards my doctorate.

'How are you getting on?' he asked. 'How's it going?'

At that stage I was up to my neck in Romans 1.18—3.20. Readers of Paul will know that this passage is mostly about God's wrath against all human wickedness – in other words, against all of us.

'Actually,' I confessed, 'I'm having a hard time with wrath.'

'Aren't we all!' he replied cheerfully, and cycled off.

I think I know what he meant. We would all much rather live in a world without wrath. We would all much rather imagine a God without wrath. In fact, a substantial part of mainstream Western Christianity has imagined just that – and has followed through on the consequences. H. Richard Niebuhr, one of America's most famous twentieth-century theologians (and brother of the even more famous Reinhold Niebuhr), once memorably described the **message** of much ultra-liberal Christianity: 'A God without wrath brought men without sin into a **kingdom** without judgment through the ministrations of a **Christ** without a cross.' Pretty damning, that. We might have preferred a '**gospel**' like that, but it certainly isn't the one we've got.

And it certainly doesn't match the world we've got. That's the problem. In any family, school, business, country – in any organization or system of whatever sort – there will be deep problems. Things will go wrong. Human pride, greed, fear or suspicion will take over. Unless it is spotted, named and dealt with, it will only get worse. If it is allowed to flourish unchecked, it can even be hailed as a new way of living. The story of the twentieth century was in part the story of just that, as new ways of being – Communism, Fascism and Apartheid being the three most obvious – reared their ugly heads and did untold damage to people and societies, until eventually they collapsed under their own weight, not least the weight of the lies which were needed to sustain them. It was partly because H. Richard Niebuhr could see this going on that he warned against a wrathless, sinless, crossless message. It might lull us to sleep just when we needed to be wide awake.

The 'wrath' of the creator God consists of two things, principally. First, he allows human wickedness to work itself out, to reap its own destruction. Second, he steps in more directly to stop it, to call 'time' on it, when it's got out of hand. If we knew our business, we would thank God for both of these, even though both can appear harsh. They need to be. If they were any less than harsh, the wickedness in question would merely pause, furrow its brow for a moment, and then carry on as before. What we see here, in the first four plagues, is a mixture of both types of 'wrath'.

We remind ourselves yet once more that this is deeply and powerfully symbolic language. This is obvious when it comes to angels 'pouring bowls of wrath' this way and that, but people often forget the lesson when they read the symbolic consequences. The point at issue in these first four plagues is fairly simple. God will allow natural elements themselves (earth, sea, rivers and sun) to pass judgment on the human beings who have so grievously abused their position as God's image-bearers within creation. They are supposed to be looking after God's world, and caring for one another as fellow humans. But God will call the natural elements themselves to turn on them and judge them for their wickedness.

These judgments are total. Before, with the seals and the trumpets, only a part of the world was harmed or destroyed (remember, again, that all this is symbolic), sending a warning signal to those who need to repent. Here that note is absent. This time, everything in the sea dies. All the rivers turn to blood (again, John is drawing on the plagues of Egypt). There is no more space for **repentance**. These plagues are the beginning of that long process, which will end in chapter 20, by which God will rid his beautiful world, first (in this chapter) of those who have assisted in its destruction and decay, then (in chapters 17 and 18) of the great imperial systems that have set up massive structures of injustice, and finally (chapters 19 and 20) of the dark powers that lie behind those systems themselves, ending (as in 1 Corinthians 15.26–28) with Death and Hades themselves.

This long, powerful sequence of thought tells us as clearly as anything could that what we are faced with is neither a capricious or ill-tempered divine being nor a careless, laissez-faire world ruler. We are faced with the God who made the world, and whose generous love is seen most clearly in the **sacrifice** of his own son, the lamb, the one who shares his very throne. If this God (to look no further than our own recent history) does not hate the wickedness of the communist and fascist systems that devastated so much of Europe, he is not a good or loving God. If he does not hate Apartheid, with its systematic dehumanization of half the human race, he is not a good God. And if he does not finally do something about these and similar systems, he is not a loving God.

Because of the nature of his love, he will not always be stepping in and calling 'time' before the appointed moment. If he did, too many, who might yet repent and be rescued, would be caught in the middle. But he will let evil take its course and bring its own nemesis; and, at a moment which only he is in any position to judge, he will bring the necessary closure on the world's wrongs. This he must do if he is, indeed, the father

143

of Jesus the **Messiah**. This is what it means that the angels pour out the bowls of his wrath upon the earth, the sea, the rivers and the sun.

REVELATION 16.10–21

The Last Three Plagues

[10]Then the fifth angel poured his bowl upon the throne of the monster. Its kingdom was plunged into darkness, and people chewed their tongues because of the pain [11]and cursed the God of heaven because of their agonies and their terrible sores. They did not repent of what they had been doing.

[12]Then the sixth angel poured his bowl on the great river Euphrates, and its water was dried up in order to prepare the way for the kings from the rising sun. [13]Then I saw three unclean spirits coming out of the mouth of the dragon, out of the mouth of the monster, and out of the mouth of the false prophet. They were like frogs. [14]These are the spirits of demons, who perform signs and go off to the kings of the whole earth, to gather them together for war on the great day of Almighty God. [15](Look – I am coming like a thief! God's blessing on the one who stays awake, and on those who keep their robes about them, so as not to go around naked and have their shame exposed!) [16]And they gathered the kings together at the place which in Hebrew is called Mount Megiddo.

[17]Then the seventh angel poured his bowl on the air, and a loud voice came out of the temple from the throne. 'It is done!' said the voice. [18]And there were lightnings and rumblings, and thunderclaps and a great earthquake, such as there had never been before, no, not such a great earthquake since the time that humans came on the earth. [19]The great city was split into three parts, and the cities of the nations collapsed. Then Babylon the Great was recalled in the presence of God, so that he could give her the cup of the wine of his anger. [20]Every island fled away, and the mountains disappeared. [21]Enormous hailstones, each weighing a hundred pounds,

fell from the sky on people. They cursed God because of the plague of the hail, because its plague was terrible.

The lunch had been substantial, the meeting was tedious, the room was warm, and the speakers droned on and on. The chairman noticed that one of his colleagues was finally subsiding into slumber. With cruel timing, he waited until the poor man's head had come to rest on his arms, folded on the table in front of him. Then, interrupting the speaker, he said, 'Perhaps Dr Johnson would like to give us his opinion on this matter?'

We all looked at our colleague, by now happily asleep. His neighbour dug him in the ribs. Pulled back out of his dream, he had no idea that he had been asked a question, let alone what it was about. The rest of us hid our smirks, propped open our own eyes as best we could, and tried to concentrate.

That's the kind of shock that John administers to his hearers in verse 15. Suddenly, in the midst of the terrible last three plague-oracles, he turns to them and says, 'Hey! Stay awake at the back, there! Jesus is on the way, and you don't want to be caught half naked, do you?'

This is so surprising that some modern readers of Revelation have imagined that a later copyist has placed verse 15 here by accident. But a very odd accident it would be: why this, why here? It's much more likely, I suggest, that John is aware, as the plagues become more terrible, that some of his hearers might nod off, not physically but spiritually. How easy to think, 'Oh, yes, those people have got it coming to them – they are wicked and they deserve it; but we're all right, we can just relax. Let's sit back and enjoy the movie.' No, you can't, John is saying. I'm talking about the serious danger of deceitful spirits let loose into the world. Many of you have a poor track record at recognizing deceit when it stares you in the face. You need to keep awake, otherwise Jesus might arrive and find your head just coming to rest on your arms . . .

That would be the wrong mistake to make. These final three plagues, which complete the sequence of the seven bowls, are terrible indeed, and part of their terror is the sense of how easy it is to give allegiance to the systems that are here under judgment. As with the seals and the trumpets, the first four seem to belong to one set, and the last three to another. Unlike the seals and the trumpets, however, there is no gap, no pause, between the sixth and the seventh, just as there is no chance, now, of further time for **repentance**.

We should not make the mistake, once more, of thinking that this chapter describes things that must happen *before* the events of chapters 17—20 take place. As with the three sequences of seven, so with the final scene of judgment upon Babylon, the monsters and the dragon: these are different angles of vision on the same ultimate reality. As the voice from the **temple** declares in verse 17: 'It is done!' It's happened. It's been completed. Those who fall under judgment here are those who have been given every chance to repent, and have refused. They have chosen to go down with the monsters rather than to suffer and be vindicated with the lamb. In the language of chapters 17—22, they have chosen the way of the harlot rather than the way of the bride.

The fifth plague, then, is a direct attack on the monster's throne – not, presumably, one particular geographical location, but rather a strike at the very heart of the monstrous imperial system, making it collapse under its own weight (as we saw in 1989 with the fall of Eastern European Communism). The 'darkness' evokes, once more, the plagues of Egypt, reminding us yet again that the point of the plagues is the destruction of the oppressors in order that the oppressed might escape.

The sixth plague awakens again, as in chapter 9, the deep-seated fear in Western Europe about the great enemy to the east, in their case Parthia. The Euphrates river formed the boundary; like the river Rhine in Europe, it was a natural barrier, relatively easy to defend. But the sixth angel's bowl, when poured out, dries up the river, so as to prepare the way for a very different kind of '**Exodus**': instead of the children of Israel going dry shod through the Red Sea, the kings from the east can now charge with their armies across the river, ready to attack.

But why would the rulers of the west be drawn into such a foolish confrontation? The answer is that the dragon, the monster from the sea, and the monster from the land – who now, we discover, is also described as a 'false prophet' (verse 13) – will deceive the kings of the earth, and lure them to this great and disastrous battle. Again there is an echo of the plagues of Egypt, since the 'unclean spirits' that come out of the mouths of the Unholy Trinity appear like frogs, able to hop to and fro with their specious stories and plausible arguments, persuading the great and powerful to commit themselves to a hopeless cause.

No wonder John tells his readers that they need to keep awake. This is very, very dangerous territory. Anyone who has lived through the build-up to a war, where suddenly all the newspapers and television stations seem to be pushing one way, and the frog-like, hopping-to-and-fro thing called 'public opinion' happens to go along with the prevailing mood, will know what John is talking about, and why he issues this warning.

What then about 'Mount Megiddo' (the word in the original is Harmagedon, sometimes spelled without the initial 'H')? Literally it is a place, some way inland from Mount Carmel in the north of Palestine, where several major battles took place in ancient times, and though no 'Mount Megiddo' as such is known in ancient Israel the area was a well-known battlefield, and the town of Megiddo was close to mountains where, in prophetic symbolism, such conflicts might occur. It would, in any case, be most unusual for John suddenly to use a place name literally, and we should not suppose he has done so here. His point is simply that all the powers of evil must be brought to one place, so that they can be dealt with there. This is why the three frogs are allowed to perform their deceits. We should no more try to locate John's Mount Megiddo on a map than we should try to produce an exact sequential chronology of all the events he describes, here and in the rest of the book.

And then the seventh bowl. Into the 'air' it goes – the space between **heaven** and earth, the sphere of spirits and powers and ideas and influences. And this will finish it all. This brings the whole work to completion. As in 8.5 and 11.19, which likewise round off a sequence of judgments, the collision between heaven and earth results in thunder, lightning and earthquakes. (Remember, once more, that this is symbolic!) As in Zechariah 12, where Jerusalem is split apart by an earthquake, 'the great city' (Rome?) is split into three, and the other cities collapse as well, like Jericho before the trumpets of Joshua. Islands flee away, mountains disappear.

John's hearers would have no difficulty in getting the point. This is not the collapse of the physical earth. This is the only way to describe the collapse of the entire social and political system *on* the earth. Terrible things will happen in human society, for which the only fitting metaphor will be earthquakes and huge hailstones. God will allow the lie at the heart of pagan society, like a crack in the earth's crust, finally to be exposed. The tectonic plates of different idolatrous human systems will move against one another one more time, and nothing will ever be the same again.

And, in the middle of it all, God will remember Babylon (verse 19b). Chapters 17 and 18, in other words, belong at this point. Part of the final judgment of the last bowl of wrath is the judgment on the city that has become the world's whore. Only when her ghastly parody has been unveiled and destroyed can we appreciate what it means to belong to the people John calls the bride.

REVELATION 17.1–8

Babylon the Great

[1]Then one of the seven angels who had the seven bowls came over and spoke to me. 'Come with me,' he said, 'and I will show you the judgment of the great whore who sits on many waters. [2]She is the one with whom the kings of the earth committed fornication; she is the one whose fornication has been the wine that has made all the earth-dwellers drunk.'

[3]So he took me away, in the spirit, to the desert. There I saw a woman sitting on a scarlet monster. It was full of blasphemous names, and had seven heads and ten horns. [4]The woman was wearing purple and scarlet, and was decked out with gold, precious stones and pearls. In her hand she was holding a golden goblet, full of abominations and the impurities of her fornications. [5]On her forehead was written a name: 'Mystery! Babylon the Great, Mother of Whores and of Earth's Abominations!' [6]I saw that the woman was drunk with the blood of God's holy people, and with the blood of the witnesses of Jesus. When I saw her, I was very greatly astonished.

[7]'Why are you so astonished?' asked the angel. 'I will explain to you the secret of the woman, and of the monster that is carrying her, the one which has the seven heads and the ten horns. [8]The monster you saw was, and is not, and is due to come up from the Abyss and go to destruction. All the inhabitants of the earth will be amazed – all, that is, whose names are not written in the book of life from the foundation of the world – when they see the monster that was and is not and is to come.

They are brought in vans, they are brought in cars with blackened windows, they are brought across the sea, either captured by force or lured with the promise of a better life. They arrive in countries of the West, knowing no one except their captors, possessing nothing except what little they are given. They are beaten, threatened and raped. Then they are sent out onto the streets. They are the new slaves: frightened, shocked, horribly abused, their physical bruises only a pale indication of the mental and emotional bruising building up inside. They are the new prostitutes, today's new breed of whore.

There were, of course, plenty like them in the ancient world, too: plenty of girls and boys with no other means of livelihood, enslaved whether literally or virtually. The world of vice is like a lobster pot: easy to get in, very difficult to get out, and all you can do is wait for death.

But there were then, and there are today, whores of a different kind, and this is the kind that John sees in his vision. (I say all this because it's easy for comfortable Western moralists to use words like 'whore', 'harlot' and the rest, waving a well-dressed hand at such riff-raff, ignoring or even colluding with the social realities which have pushed the majority of such people to this level of despair and degradation.) There were then, and there are now, young men and women who have no need to sell themselves, but who have discovered that it's a quick way to make quite a lot of money, and that if you play your cards right you can maintain a high social status, with fancy clothes, glittering jewels and the finest pearls. Throughout history, there have been some who have lived very well (in the world's eyes) by this means, maintaining a discreet clientele among the rich and famous, a business-and-pleasure arrangement of mutual satisfaction . . .

. . . and mutual destruction. Everything John now says by way of metaphor – because 'Babylon the whore' is a metaphor, as we shall see – depends on his perception, rooted in his Jewish and Christian belief in the goodness and God-givenness of the created order, that men and women are called either to celibacy or to married fidelity, and that this is one of the central motifs within the creator's purposes for his whole world. That is why, of course, the final great image in the book is the marriage of the lamb and his bride in the garden city, echoing but far transcending the union of Adam and Eve in the original garden. The rich whore who's in it of her own volition can dress up fine, can put on a great show, and (not least) can hold out a wonderful golden goblet as though she's inviting you to a rich banquet. But the eye of faith, not merely of cynicism, recognizes that the goblet is full of urine, dung and blood. Sorry about the nasty words; but perhaps I should have used even nastier ones. The phrase 'abominations and the impurities of her fornications' (verse 4) doesn't quite catch, for most of us, the full force of what John is saying. His point is that the outward appearance of the whore is magnificent, but the inner reality is disgusting, stomach-churning filth.

Why, then, does John use the image of the whore to display Babylon in all its horrible reality? First, because his whole book is about the creator and his creation, which reaches its full glory in the coming together of the lamb and the bride, the husband and wife, in loyal and loving faithfulness, and what he sees in Babylon is the deepest and darkest parody, the thing (like the monster's 666 as opposed to the perfect 777 or the lamb's 888) which is so near to the truth and yet so far. The best and most successful lies are those that are so like the truth that it only takes a little blink to be deceived.

Second, because one of the great images of Israel and YHWH in the Old Testament is that of Israel as YHWH's bride, and one of the saddest prophetic images for when that relationship goes wrong is Hosea's picture, based on his own tragic experience of marriage, of Israel playing the whore and going off after idols. This is probably the root of John's particular vision. The point about Babylon is that it has worshipped idols: the quick-fix pseudo-divinities that promise the earth, take all you have to give, and then leave you with nothing. Babylon, in fact, has become such a pseudo-divinity in itself.

Third, because, like all great imperial systems ever recorded, the Roman world which John knew thrived on sexual irregularity. Whoredom was not simply a metaphor for Rome's idolatry and social and economic oppression, but also metonymy: illicit sex was a further symptom of the problem. When you have power and money, why not? John, like Paul, and like Jesus himself in Mark 7 and 10, sees this behaviour, and the corruption of God's ideal of male–female marriage, as an accurate telltale sign of the corruption of the human heart which, springing from the worship of idols, can only be cured by the heart-changing operation which results in worshipping the true God.

Fourth, and finally, John uses the image of whoredom as an appropriate metaphor for Babylon's oppression because there is something uncannily like prostitution going on when the rich empire lures others into its den. Here, says the great empire, is luxury beyond your wildest dreams! Here all your fantasies can be fulfilled! You don't have to work hard for them, you don't have to organize your own country wisely, justly or humanely to achieve them; all you have to do is to come to me, and I'll share them with you. Oh, yes, of course, there's a price, but you won't mind paying that, will you? And the rulers of the world, captains, merchant bankers, eminent men of letters, distinguished civil servants, chairmen of many committees, industrial lords and petty contractors, queue up eagerly, not knowing that they are all going into the dark. By the time the folly is exposed for what it is, it is too late. Once you take the golden cup offered by Babylon, you have to drink it.

Babylon, in every sense ancient and modern, gets her power from the monster on which she sits – the monster which we recognize from chapter 13 as the one that has come up out of the sea (verses 3, 7–8). The monster still amazes people with its new life after its apparent demise. John sees that the monster (inhuman, idolatrous empire) sustains and supports the particular system he presently sees in Rome, whose golden goblet of economic and military power hides so much misery, squalor and suffering. The monster, well capable of luring the whole world with its deceits, is for the moment content to have that world running after the whore. That suits its purposes fine. The only thing in the way is those wretched people who will not worship it, and insist instead on worshipping this new, crazy god, the one they know as Jesus. Hence Babylon the whore is drunk with the blood of God's people. Witness to Jesus, and Babylon knows what to do. The whore can turn violent when necessary. John's readers knew that well. Some would come to know it better.

This terrifying, multi-layered denunciation of the outwardly delightful and inwardly deceitful city ought to give pause for serious thought to all those of us who live within today's glossy Western culture – and all others who look on and see our glitzy world from afar. Where are we in this picture?

REVELATION 17.9–18

The Monster and the Whore

[9]"This is a moment for a wise and discerning mind. The seven heads are seven hills, on which the woman sits. And there are seven kings; [10]five have fallen, one is still there, and the other has not yet arrived, and when he does come he is destined to remain for only a short time. [11]And the monster, which was and is not, he is the eighth king. He is also one of the seven, and he goes to destruction. [12]The ten horns that you saw are ten kings who have not yet received their kingdom, but will receive their authority as kings with the monster for a single hour. [13]All of these are of one mind: they give their power and authority to the monster. [14]They will make war with the lamb, and the lamb will conquer them, because he is Lord of lords and King of kings. Those with him are called and chosen and faithful.

[15]'As for the waters you saw,' he continued, 'where the whore was sitting, these are peoples and multitudes and nations and languages. [16]The ten horns you saw, and the monster, will hate the whore and will make her desolate and naked, and will eat her flesh and then burn her in the fire. [17]God has put it into their hearts to do his will and, with a single purpose, to give their kingdom to the monster, until God's words are

completed. [18]The woman which you saw is the great city that has royal dominion over the kings of the earth.'

I remember my excitement when, as a boy, I learned to read a map. Someone had given me a 'maps made easy' sort of book, which explained how all the symbols worked. I remember being especially fascinated by the contour lines. Growing up as I did in a part of the country with plenty of hills to climb, I loved to imagine the gentle slopes with spaced-out contours and the steep or even sheer sides of the hill where the contours were so close together that there seemed no space, and sometimes indeed was no space, between them. And then there were the forests, the churches, the post offices, and so on, all picked out with their own little symbols. Now, of course, you can go online and switch to and fro from a traditional style of map to an aerial photograph, and back again. That makes it easy, though no less fun. But the need for symbolic designs has not gone away. And the need to be able to interpret them remains.

Of course, if someone climbing a hill were to object that there were no contour lines on the hill itself, we would explain that these were merely map-makers' symbols to tell you something about the reality, not actual representations of what you'd find when you got there. I doubt if anyone actually does make that mistake, but people frequently make the equivalent mistake when faced with a bit of apocalyptic 'decoding' such as we find in the present passage. John has already given us a symbolic picture of the monster and the whore. Now he's going to tell us – unusually for him – what it all means, step by step. But will it work? Will we be able to see, as it were, the contour lines when we get to them?

Probably not – though many have tried. John's first clue is straightforward: 'The seven heads are seven hills, on which the woman sits.' No problem: there really are seven hills in Rome (I've been up them), and everybody in the ancient world who knew anything about Rome knew that this was so. But the seven kings, broken up into five who have come and gone, one who is there, another who is about to arrive but only for a short time, and another who is an eighth and yet one of the five . . . who are they?

From one point of view we might be able to identify them, though it would mean a much earlier date for the book than most people now reckon. If we start a list of Roman emperors with Augustus, we then add Tiberius, Gaius, Claudius and Nero, to make five. That takes us up to Nero's death in AD 68 – and remember that many people around the empire believed either that Nero didn't really die or that he did die but would come to life again and lead an army against Rome, perhaps from Parthia, in order to take back his throne. After Nero came Galba, who lasted into 69 but not for long, and then Otho, who snatched the throne but again didn't keep it for long. That makes seven, and it is just possible that this is the moment when John is writing, speaking about Otho as the seventh, short-lived emperor, who is about to be ousted by the returning Nero, the monster who was and is not and is to come: the eighth, though one of the seven.

If your head is spinning at this point, it may not be because you are slow on the uptake about either ancient history or first-century symbolic writing, but because John wasn't expecting you to make that sort of identification. The numbers, too, may well be symbolic. The seven kings stand for the apparent perfection of the monstrous kingdom, with the eighth (though one of the seven) a king who will appear to take the kingdom forward into a new day, but who will instead lead it to its destruction. In other words, don't try to match up the emperors precisely. What matters is that the monster's kingdom looks perfect and impregnable, but forces from within its own ranks will destroy it.

But then there come ten more kings. This is another clue to indicate that John is not expecting us to work our way through lists of emperors. However late we date Revelation, it cannot be as late as the end of the second century, which is what we would have to say if we were to add another ten emperors to the seven (or eight) already listed. It is far more likely that the 'ten kings' who are part of the monstrous system, and who eventually round on the whore herself and destroy her, are different ruling elites within the larger Roman empire – kings and princes from the far-flung corners of the Western world – who will finally tire of Mistress Rome herself, and will use the bestial, monstrous power of Rome's own empire to attack the city that has for so long scooped up and sucked in all the wealth and glory that was going.

These rebel forces are every bit as much part of the monster's rule as was the whore herself. They, like the whore, will persecute the followers of Jesus (verse 14); they are bound to, because the monster's rule depends on being absolute, and allows no space for any rivals, especially a rival who claims absolute and unique allegiance and worship. But – here it is again, another reference to John's own readers in their situation – the lamb will conquer them, because he is 'King of kings and Lord of lords', and those with him are called, chosen and faithful. The lamb will conquer them, of course, by the same method by which he has always conquered: by his own blood, and by the blood of his own, the martyrs who remain faithful.

Meanwhile, the ten kings, who will receive their authority collectively for a short but vital period (verse 12) will be God's instruments, it seems, of bringing all the evil of the monster's domain to its head. Finally, as we have seen before, evil will turn on evil and destroy itself in the process. The brief description of the fall of Babylon, drawn partly from the biblical prescription for the punishment of a whore (Leviticus 21.9), and partly from Isaiah's description of the fall of the original Babylon (Isaiah 47), anticipates the terrible chapter that is to come, where the judgment of Babylon is spelled out in far more detail.

All this may seem to be complex beyond the point of comprehensibility. But the abiding and overriding lesson for the church, then and now, should nevertheless be clear. The brutal but seductive 'civilizations' and national empires, which ensnare the world by promising luxury and delivering slavery, gain their power from the monster, the System of Imperial Power. Some have called this 'the domination system', a system which transcends geographical and historical limitations and reappears again and again in every century. John's readers already know that this system itself gains its power from the dragon, the **accuser**, the **satan**. Those who are caught up in the resultant battles need not feel that they are merely part of a dangerous confusion, of ignorant armies clashing by night. They are part of the lamb's victorious army, who will conquer the monster in the usual way, by his blood and by the **word** of their faithful testimony. Thus it has been, and thus it will be.

REVELATION 18.1–8

Babylon's Plagues

[1]After this I saw another angel coming down from heaven with great authority; the earth was flooded with the light of his glory. [2]He shouted out in a strong voice, and this is what he said: 'Babylon the great has fallen! She has fallen! She has become a place for demons to live, a refuge for every unclean spirit, a refuge for every unclean bird, a refuge for every unclean, hateful monster. [3]All the nations drank from the wine of the wrath of her fornication; the kings of the earth committed fornication with her, and the traders of the earth became rich from the power of her luxury.'

[4]Then I heard another voice from heaven, and this is what it said: 'Come out of her, my people, so that you don't become embroiled in her sins, and so that you don't receive any of her plagues. [5]Her sins are piled up to the sky, and God has remembered her wickedness. [6]Pay her back as she has paid others; give her double again for all her deeds. Mix her a double dose

in her own cup – the cup in which she mixed her poisons. [7]She made herself glorious and lived in luxury; balance that by giving her torture and sorrow! She said in her heart, "I'm the queen! I'm on the throne! I'm not a widow! I'm never going to be a mourner!" [8]Therefore her plagues will come in a single day, death, mourning and famine, and she will be burned with fire, because God the Lord, who judges her, is strong.'

One of the constant problems in a small country like mine is the challenge of where everyone is going to live. Despite government regulations which, in theory, protect what is called 'green belt', one hears almost every day of this developer, that local council, or even the national government itself, deciding that, no matter what had been said before, this particular piece of land needs, alas, to be paved over with concrete, to make a car park, a new supermarket, a fresh bit of line for a high-speed train, or yet another city bypass.

No doubt, case by case, the argument can often be made – though sometimes it appears that the power exercised by special interests, such as the big supermarket chains, may tip the scales in ways that shouldn't be allowed. But we live in a world where the danger seems to be that the city will encroach upon the wild, open spaces.

John, and many of his readers, lived in a world where the danger seemed to go the other way. The open spaces were often deserted and wild, not in a positive sense ('Oh, look, there's some nice countryside for us to go and enjoy') but in a negative sense: the wilderness became a haunt of wild animals, the desert offered criminals a place to hide and plot, and open spaces between towns and cities were lawless, dangerous places from which travellers would be eager to escape by scurrying into the next built-up area.

Cities, in short, were often seen as the result of humans extending their civilizing reach into previously uncharted territory. John would have understood this from a biblical perspective:

the garden of Eden was the start of a project in which the humans were commanded to bring God's fruitful rule to bear upon the world. Creation was designed to be a garden city, a place where the delights of human community and the delights of glorious countryside were somehow combined – a balance that has proved harder and harder to maintain.

We shall see John's own vision of this ideal city at the end of the book. But for the moment we are shown its opposite: the city which tried, like Babel of old, to make itself The Place, the summit of human achievement, by its own efforts and to its own glory – and which ends up shrinking to a shell, with the wild desert creeping back into its palaces, its temples, its fine streets and shops and courtyards. Creation will reclaim what arrogant humans had thought to construct. Babylon will become a place for **demons**, for unclean spirits, for birds and monsters of all the wrong kinds.

And this, John says, is **good news** – just as the destruction of Babel, and the confusion of tongues (Genesis 11) was good news. The angel who shouts out that Babylon has fallen (echoing Isaiah 21.9 and Jeremiah 51.8) is bringing the news that human arrogance and oppression, and the wanton luxury and vice to which they lead, will not have the last word. God will have the last **word**, and creation itself will hear this word as a word of freedom, a sigh of relief, a flood of glorious light (verse 1) let in upon a darkened dungeon.

The judgments articulated in verses 6–8 are carefully structured so as to emphasize that what happens to the wicked city is what she has brought upon herself. These are not arbitrary. Nor will the vengeance be brought about through the agency of God's people; vengeance is too dangerous a weapon to be handled by the followers of the lamb (Romans 12.19, quoting Deuteronomy 32.35). It is God's own work, turning wickedness back on itself, allowing arrogance to reach a giddy height from which it can only crash helpless to earth (verse 7, echoing Isaiah 47.8–9). Babylon is to be given the only medicine she knows, the medicine she mixed for others; she has been using her cup to brew a potion for those she wanted to poison, and she will now have to drink it herself (verse 6).

The command is therefore given that God's people should 'come out of her'. That, clearly, echoes the summons of Isaiah 48.20 and 52.11–12, and particularly Jeremiah 51.45. But how should John's hearers apply this **message** to themselves? The faithful among them have not compromised with Babylon. The unfaithful or compromised (as in the seven letters) have already received stern warnings about the persecution that is to come, and the urgent need to 'conquer'. Maybe John directs this summons to the latter group. Or maybe, as well or instead, he is hoping that this voice from **heaven** will be heard by yet others, who at the moment are still firmly in the grip of Babylonian captivity, and who might just, even at this last hour, recognize the hollowness of it all, the way in which the entire system is riddled with deceit, based on lies, and heading for disaster. Are such people 'God's people'? Well, John believes in the God who delights in calling 'my people' those who were 'not my people'. Perhaps there is yet hope – for those who will renounce Babylon, and run from it as from a great fire.

It is perhaps important to say at this stage that, though Rome went through all kinds of internal troubles during the first century, of which we have mentioned one in particular (the 'year of the four emperors' in AD 69) and might have mentioned others such as the great fire of Rome in 64, for which Nero blamed the Christians, John's picture of the fall of Babylon has a wider reference than this. Nor is it simply a long-range prophecy of the eventual sack of Rome, centuries later, by invading hordes from the north (in 410, by the Visigoths; in 455, by the Vandals; in 546, by the Ostrogoths). Rome has after all been rebuilt, and some, however misguidedly, still refer to it as the 'eternal city'.

No. John's vision is of that which Rome in his day was the obvious and classic example: the city which sits in luxury at the heart of empire, dispensing favours upon fawning (and fee-paying) visitors, giving royal treatment to those who can be useful, or who have substantial bank balances, and tossing aside as so much trash those who can't and haven't. Empires come and empires go; it is cold comfort to be told that this or that great system will eventually fall by its own weight, to be replaced by another which may be still worse. What matters is that God's purposes of judgment and mercy will be worked out, not necessarily as we might like but as God sees best. Hence the stress on angels with great authority, and voices coming from heaven itself.

It isn't enough merely to topple tyrants. The difficulty is that God does not want anarchy either. Human rulers are there because that is how God wants to run the world; structures of authority are part of the good creation (Colossians 1.15–16). The problem comes when those structures arrogate to themselves powers beyond those of being humble servants of God's good purposes for his world and his image-bearing creatures. The part of God's faithful people has always been to discern the point at which the one passes into the other, and to have no hesitation, when that happens, in leaving, either physically or spiritually. Like Lot, pleading to be allowed to stay in the vicinity of Sodom (Genesis 18.16, 18, 20), it is all too easy even for the followers of the lamb to become embroiled in the imperial sins, and to run the risk of sharing the plagues (verse 4).

REVELATION 18.9–24

Babylon's Judgment

[9]The kings of the earth who committed fornication with her and shared her luxury will weep and lament over her when they see the smoke from her fire. [10]They will stand far off, fearful of her tortures. 'Alas, alas,' they will say, 'the great city! Babylon the powerful city! Your judgment has come in a single hour.' [11]The merchants of the earth will weep and mourn over

her, because nobody will buy their cargo any more, [12]their cargo of gold and silver, of precious stones and pearls, fine linen and purple, silk and scarlet, all the sweet-smelling wood, carved ivory, vessels of expensive wood, brass, iron, marble, [13]cinnamon, oriental spice, incense, myrrh, frankincense, wine, olive oil, fine flour, wheat, cattle, sheep, horses, chariots and bodies . . . yes, human lives.

[14]All the fruit for which you longed has gone from you; all your luxuries and sparkling objects have been destroyed; you won't find them any more. [15]The merchants who sold these things, and who made themselves rich from her, will stand a long way off for fear of her tortures. They will weep and mourn, [16]and say, 'Alas, alas! The great city! It was clothed in fine linen, purple and scarlet, decked out in gold, precious stones and pearls – [17]but in a single hour such great wealth has been destroyed!'

All the master mariners, all those who ply their ships to and fro, all sailors, and all who do business on the sea, stood a long way off [18]and shouted out when they saw the smoke of her fire. 'Who is like the great city?' they said. [19]They threw dust on their heads and shouted out, weeping and mourning. 'Alas, alas,' they said, 'the great city! Everyone who had ships on the sea could get rich from her wealth, but in a single hour she has become a desert.'

[20]Celebrate over her, heaven, and you holy ones, apostles and prophets, because God has passed against her the sentence she passed against you.

[21]Then a strong angel picked up a rock like a huge millstone and hurled it into the sea, with these words: 'Babylon the great city will be thrown down like that with a splash, and will never be seen again! [22]Never again will people hear the sound of harps, musicians, flute players and trumpeters in you. Never again will there be any skilled workmen plying their trade in you. Never again will people hear the sound of the mill in you. [23]Never again will anyone see the light of a lamp in you. Never again will anyone hear the voice of bridegroom and bride in you. Your merchants were the mighty ones of the earth; all the nations were deceived by your magic.'

²⁴In her has been found the blood of prophets and God's holy ones, and all those who have been slaughtered on the earth.

We smelt it before we saw it: a sour, bitter stench which seemed to cling to the nostrils. We looked at one another and ran outside. There, about a mile away, but with a gentle wind carrying it in our direction, was a cloud of thick, grey-black smoke, rising above the trees, hanging in mid-air. As we listened, we could even hear the noise of crackling.

Soon a crowd gathered. It was the old mill at the bottom of the road. Still half-full of bales of wool, it had caught light. Soon, on that bright Friday morning, it was beyond rescue. Never again would anyone make anything there. For days afterwards, despite the fire brigade's energetic hosing, there were still smouldering remains, still the sour smell in the air.

Now multiply a building in a country lane by a million; and, instead of an old woollen mill, imagine a city with every kind of building and every kind of trade. Cities develop their own life, as complex as a human body. Every part links up with every other part: an elaborate interlocking network of trade and travel, of manufacture and communication. When you work there, there is so much you take for granted: this shop on this corner, that factory down that street, this temple, that restaurant, these streets leading to those homes, and schools, and markets.

Suddenly, in an hour, it is all gone (verses 10, 17). The long lament of the kings and the merchants, in which John has drawn together material from Isaiah 23 and Ezekiel 27 (though as usual constructing a fresh picture of his own), is as much a lament about the sudden speed of Babylon's downfall as about the lost opportunities for trading, great though that loss is. Those who remember one or other of the great stockmarket crashes will know that sense: systems that you could, literally, bank on have suddenly collapsed. The bottom goes out of the market. Millionaires become paupers overnight. The speed of ruin is crucial to the sense of shock in this haunting description.

John does not say that the gold, silver, precious stones and the rest were bad things which nobody should have celebrated in the first place. Interestingly, many of them find an honoured place in the New Jerusalem of chapter 21. Rome was able to bring all these fine commodities, listed in verses 12–14, from the ends of the earth. Among the things John mentions are goods that would have come from India, China and Africa, as well as Arabia, Armenia and beyond. This was truly a world-wide trade.

But the giveaway point comes at the end of verse 13. John has built up a marvellous catalogue of luxury goods as well as the basics of trade – flour, wheat, cattle and so on. But then, right at the end, we find the horror. Among the goods are *bodies – yes, human lives.* When you worship idols, the idols demand **sacrifices**. When you worship Mammon the money-god (or Mars the war-god; or Aphrodite the sex-goddess), they will demand sacrifices all right. And some of those sacrifices will be human. Here, in the middle of this lament over Babylon, we find one of the many places in the New Testament where a small but significant note of implacable protest is raised against the entire system upon which the ancient world was built. Slavery – the buying, selling, using and abusing of human beings as though they were on a par with gold and silver, ivory and marble (except that you could ill-treat them in a way you would never do with your luxury jewels and furnishings!) – was the dark thread that ran through everything else. Slavery was to the ancient world, more or less, what steam, oil, gas, electricity and nuclear power are to the modern world. Slavery was how things got done. Life was almost literally unthinkable without it.

And yet John believed in the God of the **Exodus**, the God who sets slaves free. A huge amount of his book, as we have seen, was built up on the basis that what God did in Egypt he will do again, this time on a cosmic scale – and that the basic act of slave-freeing has already taken place with the sacrificial death of Jesus. 'With your own blood you purchased a people for God' (5.9). That's Exodus-language, buying-slaves-to-set-them-free language. Now John looks at Rome/Babylon and sees, with his mind's eye, the slave-market. He sees, perhaps, families: captured far away and now auctioned off, the husband to this person, the wife to that, the beautiful daughter to a seedy, smirking old man, the strong son to a mine-owner. The system is rotten, and its rottenness infects everything else that happens in such a city.

John can clearly understand the shock and bemusement of the merchants and mariners, can hear their cries of dismay echoing out across the countryside as they see the plume of smoke and smell the acrid, bitter smell. He can appreciate how great this ruin is. He has written a beautiful and haunting lament over it. But he has no sympathy for Babylon. Babylon, after all, has accused and condemned God's people, and now God is passing that same sentence on her (verse 20). God is (in other words) allowing the ancient law of Deuteronomy 19.16–20 to come into force in this particular case. The false accuser must suffer the penalty he intended to inflict on his victim.

For Babylon has gained her power from the monster, and the monster from the **accuser**, the **satan**, the old dragon who, though out of sight for the moment, is remembered from chapter 12 and will shortly reappear. The whole system is built on lies, on false accusations and false claims. So much of Revelation is about being able to tell the difference between the lie and the truth; and so many of the lies appear as accusations. That is why it is so difficult to overthrow the Babylons of this world, unless it is simply by the force of the new Babylon, whatever that may be. In fact, it is impossible – except through the blood of the lamb, and the faithful witness of his followers.

The scene ends with a prophetic act worthy of Jeremiah, or indeed of Jesus – both of whom spoke of stones being cast into the water. Jeremiah (51.63–64) was commanded to tie the scroll of his own words to a stone, and throw it into the river Euphrates, declaring, 'Thus shall Babylon sink, to rise no more.' Jesus (Mark 9.42) spoke of a millstone around someone's neck, dragging them down into the water, as the punishment for child abuse; and he spoke of 'this mountain', perhaps meaning the **Temple** mount itself, being 'thrown into the sea' (Mark 11.23). Now John sees an angel performing an act of great and powerful prophetic symbolism. Babylon is to be hurled into the sea, never to rise, never again to hear its musicians and workmen, never again to see the lighting of lamps or the making of a marriage. An enormous splash, and Babylon sinks like a stone, never to be seen again.

Once more, in case anyone should feel the last vestiges of sympathy for Babylon and all that it stood for, we have the explanation: Babylon is a city founded on violence, not only the blood of the martyrs. Babylon has been at the centre of a network of violence that spanned the world, and all who have been slaughtered on earth have, in a sense, been slaughtered at the behest of Babylon. The merchants have grown rich on the back of military conquest. Money and power have done their collective worst, and John lumps them together, as we have seen, under the metaphor of fornication. Babylon the whore is gone, and will not return. And we, who live in the shadow of modern Babylons, can and must shudder as we, too, watch the plume of smoke and smell the bitter smell.

REVELATION 19.1–10

God's Victory

[1]After this I heard something like a loud voice coming from a huge crowd in heaven. 'Alleluia!' they were saying. 'Salvation and glory and power belong to our God! [2]His judgments are

true and just! He has judged the great whore who corrupted the earth with her fornication, and he has avenged the blood of his servants for which she was responsible.' ³Once more they said, 'Alleluia! The smoke from her goes up for ever and ever.'

⁴Then the twenty-four elders and the four creatures fell down and worshipped God who is seated on the throne. 'Amen!' they said. 'Alleluia!' ⁵And a voice came from the throne: 'Give praise to our God, all you his servants, and you who fear him, both small and great.' ⁶Then I heard something like the sound of a great crowd, like the sound of many waters, and like the sound of strong thunder, saying, 'Alleluia! The Lord our God, the Almighty, has become king! ⁷Let us celebrate and rejoice and give him the glory, because the marriage of the lamb has come, and his bride has prepared herself. ⁸She has been given shining, pure linen to wear.' (The linen is the righteous deeds of God's holy people.)

⁹'Write this,' he said to me. 'God's blessing on those who are called to the marriage supper of the lamb.' And he added, 'These words are the true words of God.' ¹⁰I fell down at his feet to worship him, but he said to me, 'Look! Don't do that! I am a fellow-servant with you, and with your brothers and sisters who hold on to the testimony of Jesus. Worship God!' (The testimony of Jesus, you see, is the spirit of prophecy.)

In the strange new world of postmodern Britain, weddings are still highly popular, but they are also highly expensive. So much so, in fact, that it is now the norm rather than the exception for couples to live together for some years, intending to get married, but finding that in order to afford the kind of spectacle they have been led to expect they have to save up. Even in areas of relative poverty, people still spend tens of thousands of pounds to stage something that seems appropriate to the occasion.

There is much about this modern custom that I find sad. It feeds commercial interests, and gives to the ceremony itself a flavour which is out of keeping with its real meaning. But at another level I regard it as an affirmation of something profoundly true about what it means to be human. We are, after all, made male and female in God's image, and in Genesis that is the climax of the whole story of creation. For a man and a woman to come together in marriage, whether they know it or not, is to plant a signpost which says: God's creation is wonderful! God's purposes for it are not over! His plan is going ahead, and we are part of it! Theologians down the ages have always seen the promises made at a wedding, promises of faithfulness through thick and thin, as a proper reflection of God's promises to his world, to the human race, and to his own people in particular. A wedding, then, is a glorious symbol. Even when people enter upon it with no thought of God, and with an eye only for the dress, the photographs and the wine, it remains powerful.

All of that is in the background of the great reversal which now takes place in the book of Revelation. The whore has been judged; the bride steps forward. The glossy, glitzy world of Babylon has been overthrown; God's people emerge, with shining, pure linen to wear as God's own gift. The marriage of the lamb and his bride is to be the focal point of the marriage of **heaven** and earth themselves, and Babylon, the symbolic equivalent of the ancient Babel which thought to climb up to heaven by its own energy, is shown up as a futile parody of the real thing, a human attempt to get, by sheer greed, what God proposed to give by sheer grace.

We find ourselves back in the throne room/temple, and once again we see the elders and the living creatures worshipping God on the throne. As in chapter 5 they celebrated the lamb's victory, giving him the right to open the seals so that the scroll could be read, so now they lead the praises of God along with a huge crowd, presumably the same crowd that we heard at the end of chapter 5 and then again in chapter 7.

The praise begins with a word which is so familiar that we are surprised to find that this chapter is the only place it is found in the New Testament. It is the ancient Hebrew celebration, found often enough in the Psalms, of YHWH's glory and sovereignty: Alleluia! Praise to YHWH! Verses 1, 3, 4 and 6 form a crescendo of praise, from giving God thanks for his proper judgment against the whore, to the celebration that her overthrow is final (this is the meaning of the smoke going up for ever; in other words, this is not merely a temporary reversal), to the summons to all peoples, small and great, to praise God, and finally to the celebration which recalls the majestic statement in 11.15: 'Alleluia! The Lord our God, the Almighty, has become king!'

Like the claim of almost incredulous joy in Isaiah 52.7 ('Your God reigns!' It's true! He's done it! He's become king at last!), this is no abstract, theoretical, general statement about the overall providence or sovereignty of God. Discussions about God's sovereignty, in the abstract, can easily turn into displacement activities designed to avoid having to face the challenge of what it means that God *has become king* by overthrowing Babylon the whore, and so preparing the way for that of which Babylon and her pernicious trade was a ghastly parody, namely the marriage of the lamb and his bride.

The idea of such a wedding goes back, of course, to the ancient Jewish tradition of Israel's as YHWH's bride – wooed in the wilderness, married at Sinai, unfaithful for many generations and eventually cast away, but then wooed and won all over again in a covenant renewal that would result in the renewal of the whole creation (Isaiah 54—55). The whole of the Song of Songs, though at one level simply a spectacular poem of erotic love, has been seen by Jewish and Christian commentators alike as an allegory of the love between God and his people (for Christians, Christ and his people). Now this glorious theme comes to a spectacular completion, and is joined with another ancient theme of celebration: God's great feast, the banquet to which he will invite all and sundry (Isaiah 25.6–10).

Jesus himself employed the theme of a king's marriage-supper for his son (Matthew 22.1–14; see too Matthew 25.1–13), and hinted at the further related theme, that of the appropriate clothing for the wedding. Here John's vision, drawing on all of these, focuses on the fact that the great moment has come at last. This is what the world had been waiting for, ever since Genesis 1, ever since the covenant with Abraham (which always envisaged the birth of a family), ever since the covenant with Moses, ever since the renewal of the covenant promised at the time of the exile. Marriage is the ultimate covenant, Jesus is the ultimate bridegroom. And though John uses his imagery freely enough to allow the church to be both the bride and the guests invited to the bride's wedding party (verse 9), this should not distract us from the sense of fulfilment, of excitement, of rightness and fitness, that emerge at last after the sorry tale of human rebellion, wickedness, pride and arrogance has run its course.

John himself is so excited by all this that he begins to worship the angel who is revealing it all to him. (He does it again at the end of the book, in 22.8, with the same result.) But this would be a bad mistake. He must not confuse the messenger with the message. Even John, even at this moment, can slip up, can lapse into idolatry, into worshipping that which is not God. Perhaps he tells us this in order to encourage those of his readers who are battling with the challenge of idolatry themselves: it's been a challenge for me, too, he says. But in saying this he reveals something remarkable. Throughout the book the focus has been on the uninhibited worship offered by the whole creation to 'the One on the throne and the lamb' (5.13). Jesus shares the throne of God; Jesus shares the worship which is due to the one God and him alone. The angel's rebuke highlights the total difference between Jesus himself and all others, no matter how exalted those others may be.

This also reminds us, looking right back to the first verse of John's book, that the central thing about prophetic inspiration is 'the testimony of Jesus', that is, the testimony which Jesus himself bore, faithful to death, and which the church must now bear to Jesus. The **Spirit** is given through the work of Jesus, so that the church may be faithful to Jesus, and him alone.

REVELATION 19.11–21

The Monster Defeated

[11]Then I saw heaven opened, and there was a white horse. The one who was sitting on it is called Faithful and True, and he judges and makes war justly. [12]His eyes are like a flaming fire, and there are many coronets on his head. He has a name written there which nobody knows except himself. [13]He is clothed in a robe dipped in blood, and he is called by the name 'God's Word'. [14]The armies of heaven follow him on white horses, all wearing shining, pure linen. [15]A sharp two-edged sword is coming out of his mouth, so that with it he can strike down the nations. He will rule them with a rod of iron, and he will tread the winepress of the wine of the anger of the wrath of Almighty God. [16]On his robe, and on his thigh, is written a name: King of kings, and Lord of lords.

[17]Then I saw a single angel standing in the sun, and shouting in a loud voice, calling to all the birds that fly in mid-heaven: 'Come here! Gather round! This is God's great feast! [18]Come and eat the flesh of kings, and the flesh of generals, the flesh of the strong, the flesh of horses and their riders, the flesh of all people, free and slave, small and great!' [19]And I saw the monster and the kings of the earth and their armies gathered for war with the one who sits on the horse and with his army. [20]And the monster was captured, and with it the false prophet who had performed the signs in its presence, with which it had deceived those who received the monster's mark and those who worshipped its image. The two of them were thrown alive into the lake of fire which burns with sulphur. [21]All the rest were killed by the sword which came out of the mouth of the one who was sitting on the horse. All the birds feasted on their flesh.

People used to write books and articles about 'the messianic expectation' in the time of Jesus. Ancient Jewish sources were combed and sifted to yield every fragment of information about what Jesus' contemporaries were waiting for when they were waiting for a **Messiah**.

The more this exercise has gone on, the more complicated it has become. Many Jewish texts of the period say nothing about a Messiah. Some (like the **Dead Sea Scrolls**) seem to think there will be two Messiahs, a royal Messiah and a priestly Messiah. Others divide, and go in different directions: some with a wise king like Solomon, some with a warrior king like David, many with a **Temple**-cleansing king like Hezekiah or Josiah. Hardly ever do we find a single text that puts it all together.

And that's just the texts. We don't know how many people read those texts, or would have agreed with them if they had done. What we do know, however, is that there were several would-be royal or 'messianic' movements in the century before and after the time of Jesus, and that these movements attracted a good many people. We can learn a lot from them about what people thought a Messiah ought to do.

One of the central tasks facing a Messiah, it seems, is that he would have to fight the decisive battle against Israel's enemies, both the pagan hordes who were always coming in fresh waves to overwhelm God's people, and the renegades within Israel who were colluding with their pagan masters and corrupting the pure life of God's people. This would then go hand in hand with the task of purifying the people's worship by renewing or restoring the Temple. It is because Jesus showed no sign of being a military leader, and because he showed no interest in cleaning up the Temple, that many said then, and many have said since, that he couldn't have been in any sense thinking of himself as 'Messiah'.

But this is to forget just how radical Jesus' own redefinition of the Jewish expectation seems to have been. Throughout his

172

public career he took as his main theme the belief which John has been celebrating on and off throughout Revelation: the **kingdom of God**. 'The kingdom of the world has passed to our Lord and his Messiah.' 'Alleluia! For the Lord our God, the Almighty, has become king!' These statements are, of course, linked directly to statements about the victory of Jesus.

Jesus himself spoke of victory – but it was not the victory one might expect, over the forces of Rome. Indeed, when others wanted to fight Rome, he hinted strongly if strangely that this was missing the proper target. The true enemy was the dark power that stood behind Rome and all other pagan empires. Jesus spoke about fighting a battle with the real enemy, the **satan**, the one who had led all humanity, Israel included, into rebellion against the creator God. And Jesus seems to have believed that the ultimate way to fight this true battle was by giving up his life.

It is this that explains the military imagery of the present passage. Once more, this is symbolic language, truly pointing to a reality which lies beyond it. It would be as much a mistake to suppose (as some, sadly, have done) that this passage predicts, and legitimates in advance, an actual military battle between followers of Jesus and followers of other gods as it would be to suppose that the reality which corresponds to the monster that comes up from the sea is an actual physical creature with the heads, horns and so on described in chapter 12. The victory here is a victory *over* all pagan power, which means *a victory over violence itself*. The symbolism is appropriate because it is taken directly from the passages which speak most powerfully, and are most regularly referred to in the New Testament, of the triumph of the Messiah: Isaiah 11, where the Messiah will judge the nations with the sword of his mouth; Psalm 2, where he will rule them with a rod of iron; Isaiah 63, where he will tread the winepress of the wrath of God. As John's readers know well by now, the actual weapons which Jesus uses to win the battle are his own blood, his loving self-**sacrifice**:

With tears he fights, and wins the field,
his naked breast stands for a shield.
His battering shot are babish cries,
his arrows made of weeping eyes.
His martial ensigns cold and need,
and feeble flesh his warrior's steed.

Thus the sixteenth-century poet Robert Southwell gloried in the paradox of Jesus and his victory. It is in the light of such imagery that we can make the best sense of the spectacular portrait of Jesus in verses 11–16. This is how the King of kings and Lord of lords comes before the world. The ultimate justice which drives his victorious battle (verse 11) is the justice of God's love, which will not work with anything other than the **Word** (verses 13, 15), and will not be dressed in anything other than purity and holiness (note the 'shining, pure linen' of verse 14, matching the bride's dress in verse 8). Love will win the day, because in the person of Jesus it has trampled the grapes of wrath once and for all (verse 15).

If the military imagery is just that, imagery, so of course is the picture of the birds swooping in, like so many vultures, to gorge themselves on the flesh of those who follow the monster and the false prophet. If the whore has been dealt with in chapters 17 and 18, now it is the turn of these two, the great imperial system and the local elites who promote it and deceive the nations. Here they are for one last battle. (The well-known Narnia story, *The Last Battle*, by C. S. Lewis, owes a good deal to the book of Revelation, not least his brilliant portrayal of the ways in which the monster and the false prophet deceive the people.) Their fate is to be thrown alive 'into the lake of fire which burns with sulphur', an echo of various biblical passages, not least the fate of Sodom and Gomorrah in Genesis 18.

Many in our own day are still oppressed by monstrous forces, and the local propaganda machines that promote their cause. Equally, many otherwise well-intentioned people are taken in by the lies and deceits which these systems continue to put out. Revelation 19 stands as a promise to the first, and a warning to the second. Once you understand who Jesus was and is, and the significance of the victory which he has won in his death, there can be no doubt about the final outcome. Monstrous regimes may come and go. Lies and deceits will continue to be spread. We must be on our guard. But the King of kings and Lord of lords will be victorious. In the meantime, there must be no compromise.

REVELATION 20.1–6

Reigning for a Thousand Years

¹Then I saw an angel coming down from heaven. In his hand he held the key to the Abyss, and a large chain. ²He grabbed hold of the dragon, the ancient serpent, who is the devil and the satan. He tied him up for a thousand years, ³threw him into the Abyss, and locked and sealed it over him, so that he wouldn't be able to deceive the nations any more, until the thousand years were complete. After that he must be let out for a short time.

⁴Then I saw thrones, with people sitting on them, who were given authority to judge. And I saw the souls of those who had had their heads cut off because they had borne witness to Jesus, and because of the word of God; and also those who had not worshipped the monster or its image, and had not received the mark on their foreheads or their hands. They came to life, and reigned with the Messiah for a thousand years. ⁵The rest of the dead did not come back to life until the thousand years were complete. This is the first resurrection. ⁶Blessed and holy is the one who has a share in the first resurrection! The second death has no power over them. They will be priests to God and the Messiah, and they will reign with him for a thousand years.

After I published my book *Surprised by Hope*, I had a number of letters and emails from people telling me their experiences with thinking it through, leading study groups on it, and in some cases preaching in the new way I was recommending.

The central point of the book is that, over against the common Western Christian view that what matters is 'going to heaven when you die', the proper Christian expectation is of a two-stage post-mortem reality. First, those who belong to the Messiah go to be 'with him', as Paul says in Philippians 1.23. Then, at last, Jesus will appear, as heaven and earth come together in a great fresh act of new creation. That will be the moment of resurrection, the moment the dead have been waiting for. Resurrection, the abolition of death itself, giving God's people new bodies to live in God's new world, is the great hope both of ancient Judaism and of classic Christianity.

A lot of my readers took to this like ducks to water, which was of course gratifying. But not all their congregations thought that way. One pastor reported that he had preached enthusiastically on this theme the next Easter Day, only to be confronted after the service by his leading lay people, extremely put out because this wasn't the Easter message they were used to hearing. I suppose that is bound to be the case, granted the way in which so much Western Christianity, 'evangelical' just as much as 'liberal', has slipped its New Testament moorings in this most vital of areas.

But here in Revelation 20 we are faced with a quite different sort of problem. It is hard enough to get people to envisage a two-stage post-mortem reality, with 'resurrection' as the second of two stages. But Revelation 20 seems to envisage a *three*-stage reality: first the souls resting under the altar (6.9); then the resurrection of some, not all, to share a thousand-year reign with Jesus; then, after a further flurry of activity and a second 'last battle', the final resurrection of all people, of the wicked to hear and face their condemnation, and of God's people to hear and receive 'the verdict that leads to life' (Romans 5.18). No other writing, Jewish or Christian, has any mention of this 'double resurrection', let alone of the surrounding events. What are we to make of it all?

There are three interlocking problems which are made considerably more confusing (for us) by John's kaleidoscopic imagery. First, we are naturally puzzled as to why, after the monster and the false prophet have been thrown into the lake of fire, there seems to be not only a delay before the satan joins them there but also a temporary respite in which he is let out of jail one last time to do his worst before being finally overthrown. Why the delay, and why must he again be released?

Second, what is John referring to, in real, historical terms, when he speaks of the thousand years in which these 'first-resurrection' people reign with the Messiah? How does that relate to the subsequent picture of the New Jerusalem in chapters 21 and 22? Is the one a metaphor for the other? Are they describing, or at least denoting, two quite different things? Or what?

Third, how then does this 'first resurrection' relate to the second one (John doesn't call it 'the second resurrection', but his description of this one as the 'first', in verse 6, implies it)? What sort of story can we tell, or should we tell, that will bring out the reference, the meaning and the flavour of these very puzzling six verses?

To begin with, we may note that, just as 1 Thessalonians 4 is the only passage of scripture to describe anything like a 'rapture' (and, as I've argued frequently elsewhere, it doesn't mean 'the rapture' as popularly understood in Dispensationalism), and just as Revelation 16.16 is the only place in scripture to mention a final great battle at 'Armagedon', so Revelation 20 – the passage now before us – is the only passage in scripture where a 'millennium' is even mentioned. Those who go in for speculative prophecy-interpretation have, of course, snapped up these and other snippets, taken them (usually) out of their actual contexts, and constructed a quite different world-view in which they play a far more important role than they do in scripture itself. That alone ought to make us wary of following where such interpreters lead – quite apart from the dualistic framework within which such 'prophecy-interpretation' is regularly set, with the wicked world being thrown away while 'the saints' remain safe in heaven, and without any sense of the renewal of creation, so important in this book, as in the **gospels** and Paul.

But all that is merely ground-clearing. Let us consider the temporary binding of the **satan**. Yes, it would be much tidier if the battle in chapter 19 had seen off all God's adversaries. Nobody would have grumbled, I suspect, if the satan had been part of the defeated host, and the book had proceeded straight to the New Jerusalem. But Revelation is seldom tidy, at least not in the way we might like. And we have noticed, twice already, that the sequence we expect is interrupted. It may help to remind ourselves of those two moments.

First, in the sequence of seals, we had to pause between the sixth and the seventh seals; judgment was suspended while the suffering and martyred people of God were 'sealed' (chapter 7). Then, between the sixth and seventh trumpets, we again had to pause, this time while John was given the scroll from which he prophesied about God's witnessing people. Those people were seen under the image of the two, like Zerubbabel and Joshua, the king and the priest, and like Moses and Elijah, the prophets, through whose death and resurrection the world would come to glorify the true God (chapters 10 and 11).

Those were the two earlier 'unexpected pauses', and now we have another one. Again, we note, it concerns the suffering and martyred people of God, who are again celebrated as the true witnesses, the priest-kings who share the Messiah's rule (verse 6).

This may give us the clue to our first two questions. We must not forget that 'the satan' was initially a member of the heavenly council. Though he has fallen from his position, he may still, by God's permission, play a role. (I am reminded of the role Tolkien gave to Gollum, right up to the climax of *The Lord of the Rings*, and on reflection I guess that Tolkien was aware of exactly this kind of parallel.) The satan's job was always to 'accuse' where accusation was due, to make sure (as a good Director of Public Prosecutions) that nothing reprehensible went unreprehended. Now, one last time, he must play that role, even though as before he will pervert it and try to deceive and accuse in all directions, warranted or not (verse 8). He must ultimately do the worst he can, so that when he is defeated there will be no last tiny remnant of suspicion that anything worthy of 'accusation' has been left unaccounted for. He must be allowed a final moment to flail around with his lies and accusations, so that in his overthrow it will be clear beyond the slightest doubt that 'there is therefore now no condemnation for those in the Messiah Jesus'. Like a boxer staggering to his feet to face the last punch, he must come up one more time, even if only to be knocked out flat on the canvas for ever.

But, before that can happen, the reign of Jesus, with and through his millennial people, must be established by the first resurrection. John itemizes these people not just as martyrs (as opposed to other Christians) but specifically as those who had been beheaded for their witness. We should, I presume, take that symbolically. It may hint at something to do with their true citizenship in Jesus' **kingdom**; it was Roman citizens who were beheaded, a greatly preferable death to many others the Romans devised, not least crucifixion itself. It seems, in any case, contrary to John's normal line to suggest a radical difference between one set of martyrs and another.

But should we take the thousand years symbolically as well? Again, I believe we should. John has used all kinds of symbolic numbers throughout his book. It would be very odd if he were suddenly to throw in a rather obvious round and symbolic number, but expect us to take it literally. There were some, around the year AD 1000, who supposed they were about to see

the end of this 'millennium', but as with other such specula-
tions the date passed without significant eschatological events
taking place. But what is the actual reality to which the symbol
points?

It appears at first sight very difficult to see this millennium as
'the age of the church'. Nobody aware of church history would
suppose that there has been no satanic attack, no deceiving of
the nations (or of the church itself) during that time.

It could be a time still in the future, either the final prelude to
the **second coming** of the Messiah or a period immediately after
that coming – the classic 'post-millennial' and 'pre-millennial'
interpretations. Both of these seem to me to miss the point, for
reasons too numerous to go into here (I have discussed them
elsewhere).

The clue to the passage is, I believe, in the opening line:
'I saw thrones, with people sitting on them, who were given
authority to judge.' This is straight out of Daniel 7, where the
'thrones' were for 'the Ancient of Days' and 'One like a **son
of man**'. But Daniel 7 itself interprets the latter phrase cor-
porately, so that 'the saints of the most high' receive the kingdom and the authority to judge. It looks, then, as though John
is referring not to a thousand-year period *on earth*, but to the
heavenly reality which obtains during a particular period. Jesus,
according to the whole New Testament, is *already* reigning
(Matthew 28.18; 1 Corinthians 15.25–28; etc.); and what John
is saying is that the martyrs *are already reigning with him*. This,
indeed, is more or less what is said, as well, in Ephesians 2.6,
where the church is 'seated in heavenly places in the Messiah
Jesus'. Presumably they aren't just sitting there doing nothing.
Perhaps, after all, John's 'millennium' does correspond to a
more widely known early Christian view – though in Ephesians
there is no sense that this only applies to martyrs.

As to the 'binding' of the satan (verse 2), Jesus declared that
he had already accomplished this, which was why he was able
to perform exorcisms (Matthew 12.29). The satan was, after

all, still able thereafter to work through Judas and others, to accuse Jesus and bring about his death. Perhaps what we are seeing in Revelation 20 is the cosmic version of that story.

Perhaps. At this point above all – above all the rest of the New Testament, in my experience – it doesn't do to be too dogmatic. We must hold on to the central things which John has made crystal clear: the victory of the lamb, and the call to share his victory through **faith** and patience. God will then do what God will then do. Whether we describe the final events as Revelation 20 has done, or as Paul does in Romans 8.18–26 or 1 Corinthians 15.20–28, it is clear that the one who wins the victory is the creator God, who does so to defeat and abolish death itself and so to open the way to the glories of the renewed creation. That is what matters.

REVELATION 20.7–15

Final Judgment

[7]When the thousand years are complete, the satan will be released from his prison. [8]Out he will come to deceive the nations at the four corners of the earth, Gog and Magog. He will summon them for battle, a throng like the sand of the sea in number. [9]They came up over the full width of the earth, and closed in on the place where God's holy people are encamped, and the beloved city. Then fire came down from heaven and burnt them up. [10]And the devil who had deceived them was thrown into the lake of fire and sulphur where the monster and the false prophet had already been thrown. They will be tortured day and night for ever and ever.

[11]Then I saw a large white throne, and the one who was sitting on it. Earth and heaven fled away from his presence, and there was no room left for them. [12]Then I saw the dead, great and small, standing in front of the throne. Books were opened; and another book was opened, which is the book of life. The dead were judged on the basis of what was written in the books, in accordance with what they had done. [13]The sea

gave back the dead that were in it; Death and Hades gave back the dead that were in them; and each was judged in accordance with what they had done. [14]Then Death and Hades were thrown into the lake of fire. This is the second death, the lake of fire. [15]And if anyone was not found written in the book of life, they were thrown into the lake of fire.

John was not the first to suppose that after God's great act of rescue and restoration there might be a further challenge, a final fling of the powers of evil against the already-redeemed people of God. In one of his favourite books of scripture, Ezekiel, he found just such a picture, which had already been explored by other Jewish writers, and would continue to be a matter of speculation and interest for some considerable time after his day.

This picture is found in Ezekiel 38. It is no coincidence that this comes straight after the passage (chapters 34—37) which predicts the work of the divine Good Shepherd, the cleansing of Israel's hearts from sin, and the return from **exile** seen in terms of a **resurrection** of the dead. Ezekiel 38 then focuses attention on the nation of Magog, in the far north, and Gog its king. (Israelite geography, and indeed Greek and Roman geography, was a bit hazy once you got north of the Black Sea.) By the time John gets hold of this tradition he appears to treat 'Gog and Magog' as two nations, symbolically representing 'the four corners of the earth'. Anyway, the point is that Gog/Magog will mount a last, vain attack on God's people, even after their rescue from Babylon. Granted this implicit narrative in Ezekiel, we can perhaps see why, for John, this final episode had to follow the demise of Babylon in chapters 17—19 and the 'first resurrection' of 20.4–6.

Once more we need to say: the release of the **satan**, though unexpected and unwelcome to us, seems to be part of the strange divine plan to ensure that all evil, every trace, is rooted out of the world, allowing the great transformation into 'new

heaven and new earth' to take place. The satan, the **accuser**, must do all he can, and then he too must be destroyed. It is as though, faced with a farmyard full of infected material, one were first to find the ideal broom with which to sweep the yard clean, and then were to throw the broom itself into the fire, its horrible work done. It is, no doubt, difficult for us to hold in our minds the idea of the satan as still, even at this stage, doing work which God requires to be done, and then being punished for it. But that is because our minds slip so easily from metaphor into metonymy, from symbol to actual referent (like someone who hears a friend, late for an appointment, say 'I must fly,' and is then surprised when the friend, rather than taking a helicopter, gets into his car). It is useless, in other words, to stand in judgment over the morality of God's dealings with the satan, or indeed with 'Gog and Magog', as though God were the chief military officer of a United Nations peacekeeping force and these other creatures were leaders of recalcitrant or insurgent forces. The whole thing is a set of pictures, of shifting, kaleidoscopic images, pointing beyond themselves to the deepest and darkest mysteries of iniquity. The same is true for the geographical symbol of the nations surrounding 'the place where God's holy people are encamped, and the beloved city'. This has nothing more to do with a location in the Middle East, or indeed elsewhere, than the thousand years has to do with a precise calendrical period.

The point, yet again, is that evil must be allowed, under certain controls, to do its worst, so that it can at last be defeated. Interestingly, though the satan summons the nations for a battle, no battle takes place. The great battle of chapter 19, in which the rider on the white horse wins the victory by means of the sword of his mouth, is indeed the last battle. On this occasion, in an Elijah-like move, fire comes down from heaven and consumes them. Then, and only then, the devil is thrown into the lake of fire and sulphur, along with the monster and the false prophet. Babylon was overthrown three chapters ago; the two monsters met their doom in chapter 19; now at last the dragon has been overthrown as well, and for good.

There remain the last great powers: Death and Hades. 'Death' is here both the fact and the power of death; 'Hades' is the abode of the dead, the place from which they cannot escape except by a great new act of God. In ancient cosmology, the sea was not thought to be part of Hades, so those who died by drowning in the sea, and were never recovered for burial, formed a separate category of the dead. But they too will now be brought to stand before the great white throne, which seems to have replaced the original throne of chapters 4 and 5. Heaven and earth are being shaken, and the throne room itself seems to be under reconstruction.

The point is then that God, the creator, at last takes his seat for the final judgment. Here, as throughout scripture, this judgment will be in accordance with the totality of the life that each person has lived. That, it seems, is what is written in the 'books'.

Countless anxious protestant teachers, worried that this somehow does away with '**justification** by **faith**', miss the point entirely. We should not necessarily try to fit Paul's way of saying things exactly into John's, but actually things are simpler than that in this case. When Paul speaks of 'justification by faith', he is talking about the present reality according to which all those who believe in Jesus as the risen Lord are already assured of the divine verdict, 'in the right', and are also assured thereby that this same verdict will be issued on the last day. But the way in which the verdict of the last day corresponds to the verdict issued in the present, on the basis of faith alone, is by the work of the **spirit**; and the spirit produces, in the individual Christian, that overall tenor of life (Paul does not suppose that Christians are incapable of sinning) which is 'seeking for glory, honour and immortality' (Romans 2.7).

In any case, the most important book is 'the book of life'. John has mentioned this several times before (3.5; 13.8; 17.8), where it is said to be the lamb's book of life, and to have been written before the foundation of the world. This is a vivid way of safeguarding the truth taught by Jesus in John's **gospel**, 'You did not choose me, but I chose you,' as well as by Paul in Romans 8.28–30 and elsewhere. But this, like justification by faith, is subject to the proviso that if there is choosing being done, it is God who chooses, and the God who chooses is the triune God who works as father, son and spirit, not as a blind watchmaker or a celestial bureaucrat. When God chooses, he also redeems; when God chooses and redeems, he also works in people's lives; and the **miracle** of the divine–human relationship, from the very beginning, has always been that human thought, will and action is somehow enhanced, rather than being cancelled out, by the divine initiative and power. To say less than this would be to leave John's picture of the books as merely a puzzle. To say more would be to wander off into large theological questions to which Revelation gives no attention.

Perhaps the most important thing to note is that, once again, Death itself, along with its home base, Hades, is finally destroyed. John Donne's poem, 'Death, be not proud', ends with the majestic line: 'And Death shall be no more; Death, thou shalt die.' Some writers have tried to suggest that 'resurrection' and 'new creation' are simply a fancy way of talking about what actually happens at or after death: 'thinking of death as resurrection', I remember one such writer saying. Resurrection is then an *interpretation* of death. But that is precisely what John is here denying, much as Paul does in 1 Corinthians 15. Resurrection, in the first-century world, emphatically meant the *undoing* of death, not its reinterpretation. It meant that the processes of bodily corruption and decay were reversed, producing a new 'physical' body with 'immortal' properties. John is nothing if not a creational theologian. He has told us from early on that God is celebrated as the creator of the whole world, and indeed that all creation joins in his praise. If creation is not gloriously reaffirmed at the last, God has been finally defeated: the satan has won. But it is, and he hasn't been. The 'new heaven and new earth' we are about to witness are that glorious reaffirmation.

So why does John say that 'earth and heaven fled away from his presence' (verse 11)? Because, it seems, earth had been corrupted by the evil done within it, and heaven too had been the place from which the satan had conducted his initial rebellion. The first earth and heaven were the pilot project. Now, with all obstacles to the ultimate goal having been removed, they can be dismantled, so that the final reality to which they were advance signposts can at last be revealed. The whore has been overthrown, and it is time for the bride to appear. The dragon, the monster and the false prophet have been destroyed, and it is time for God and the lamb to be revealed, with the spirit enabling the bride to say, 'Come'. The rule of death is at an end; the rule of life is about to begin.

REVELATION 21.1–5

New Heaven, New Earth

[1]Then I saw a new heaven and a new earth. The first heaven and the first earth had passed away, and there was no longer any sea. [2]And I saw the holy city, the new Jerusalem, coming down out of heaven, from God, prepared like a bride dressed up for her husband. [3]I heard a loud voice from the throne, and this is what it said: 'Look! God has come to dwell with humans! He will dwell with them, and they will be his people, and God himself will be with them and will be their God. [4]He will wipe away every tear from their eyes. There will be no more death, or mourning or weeping or pain any more, since the first things have passed away.'

[5]The one who sat on the throne said, 'Look, I am making all things new.' And he said, 'Write, because these words are faithful and true.'

When has there been a moment in your life when you have said to yourself, 'This is new'? I don't just mean a car with a few new gadgets, or a meal with a different combination of sauces and seasonings – though these, too, may point in the right direction. I'm thinking more of major life-experiences in which we think to ourselves, 'Everything is going to be different now. This is quite new. This is a whole new world opening up.'

Such experiences might well include some major life-events: birth, marriage, full recovery from a long and dangerous illness, the experience of someone new coming to live with you. All these, interestingly, feature in the list of images which John uses as he builds up this breathtaking picture of the new **heaven** and new earth. 'I will be his God and he shall be my son' (verse 7): a final new birth. The holy city is like 'a bride dressed up for her husband': a wedding. There will be 'no more death, or mourning or weeping or pain any more': the great recovery. And, central to this whole picture, and indeed explaining what it all means, is the great promise: 'God has come to dwell with humans.' The new, permanent guest.

Putting it like this is in danger of belittling John's picture, trimming it down to our comparatively trivial examples. But, as with all symbolism, these are signposts pointing into the unknown future; and at every point John is saying, 'It's like this, but much, much more so.' The new heaven and new earth will be new in a new way; newness itself will be renewed, so that instead of a mere transition within ongoing human **life**, what God has planned will be the renewal of all things. 'Look,' he said, 'I am making all things new.'

All things: here we have the new heaven, the new earth, the new Jerusalem, the new **Temple** (which is the same thing as the new Jerusalem; as we shall see, there is no temple in the city because the whole city *is* the new temple), and, not least, the new people, people who have woken up to find themselves beyond the reach of death, tears and pain. 'The first things have passed away.'

So many Christians have read John's book expecting that the final scene will be a picture of 'heaven' that they fail completely to see the full glory of what he is saying. Plato was wrong. It isn't a matter – it wasn't ever a matter – of 'heaven' being the perfect world to which we shall (perhaps) go one day, and 'earth' being the shabby, second-rate temporary dwelling from which we shall be glad to depart for good. As we have seen throughout the book, 'earth' is a glorious part of God's glorious creation, and 'heaven', though God's own abode, is also the place where the 'sea' stands as a reminder of the power of evil, so much so that at one point there is 'war in heaven'. God's two-level world needs renewing in both its elements.

But when that is done, we are left not with a new heaven only, but a new heaven and a new earth – and they are joined together completely and for ever. The word 'dwell' in verse 3 is crucial, because the word John uses conjures up the idea of God 'dwelling' in the Temple in Jerusalem, revealing his glory in the midst of his people. This is what John's **gospel** says about Jesus: the **Word** became flesh and lived, 'dwelt', pitched his tent, 'tabernacled', in our midst, and we gazed upon his glory. What God did in Jesus, coming to an unknowing world and an unwelcoming people, he is doing on a cosmic scale. He is coming to live, for ever, in our midst, a healing, comforting, celebrating presence. And the idea of 'incarnation', so long a key topic in our thinking about Jesus, is revealed as the key topic in our thinking about God's future for the world. Heaven and earth were joined together in Jesus; heaven and earth will one day be joined fully and for ever. Paul says exactly the same thing in Ephesians 1.10.

That is why the closing scene in the Bible is not a vision of human beings going up to heaven, as in so much popular imagination, nor even of Jesus himself coming down to earth, but of the new Jerusalem itself coming down from heaven to earth. At first sight, this is a bit of a shock: surely the new Jerusalem, the bride of the lamb, consists of the people of God, and surely they are on earth already! How can they have been in heaven as well?

The clue here is that, as Paul says in Colossians 3.3, 'our life is hidden with the **Messiah** in God'. When somebody belongs to the Messiah, they continue with their life on earth, but they have a secret life as well, a fresh gift from God, which becomes part of the hidden reality that will be 'revealed' at the last day (Colossians 3.4; 1 John 3.2). That is why, in those great scenes in Revelation 5, 7 and 19, there is a great, uncountable number of people standing around God's throne in heaven, singing glad songs and shouting out their praises. This is the heavenly reality which corresponds to the (apparently) weak, feeble praises of the church on earth. *And one day this heavenly reality will be revealed*, revealed as the true partner of the lamb, now transformed, Cinderella-like, from slave-girl to bride.

The newness of this vision is not a matter of God throwing away his first creation and, as it were, trying again, having a second shot to see if he can get it right this time. That is the superficial impression many have received from 20.11, when heaven and earth flee from God's presence, and from the statement in 10.6 that there would be 'no more time' – which, as we have seen, is not saying that time itself will be abolished, but that there will be no more delay. What we have in Revelation 21 and 22, however, is the *utter transformation* of heaven and earth by means of God abolishing, from within both heaven and earth, everything that has to do both with the as-yet incomplete plan for creation and, more particularly, with the horrible, disgusting and tragic effects of human sin.

The new world, in other words, will be like the present one in the sense of its being a world full of beauty, power, delight, tenderness and glory. In this new world, for instance, the temple, which was properly there in heaven as well as on earth (11.19), will be abolished (21.22); not because it was a stupid idea for God to dwell among his people, but because the Temple was the advance model of God's great hidden plan for the whole cosmos, now at last to be realized. The new world will be like the present one, but without all those features, particularly death, tears and everything that causes them, which make the present world what it is.

That is what is meant by there being 'no more sea'. Throughout this book, as in much of the Bible, the sea is the dark force of chaos which threatens God's plans and God's people. It is the element from which the first monster emerged. It is contained in the first heaven, 'contained', that is, both in the sense that it is there as part of the furniture and in the sense that its boundary is strictly limited. Evil is only allowed to do enough to overreach itself and to bring about its own downfall. But in the new creation there will be no more sea, no more chaos, no place from which monsters might again emerge.

The centre of the picture, though, is not, or not yet, the new world itself, but the one true God who made the first creation and loved it so much that he sent the lamb to redeem and renew it. Up to now, 'the one who sits on the throne' has been mentioned only obliquely. He has been there; he has been worshipped; but all the talking has been done by Jesus, or by an angel, or by 'a voice from heaven'. Now, at last, for the first time since the opening statement in 1.8, God himself addresses John, and through him addresses his churches and ours. This personal address by God himself is, it seems, part of the newness, just as in verse 4 God himself 'will wipe away every tear from their eyes', an act of utter gentleness and kindness to be performed not by some junior heavenly official but by God himself. Through this is a revelation of God's eternal character, most of us, contemplating this wonderful prospect, will feel a whole new world opening up before us.

REVELATION 21.6–21

New Jerusalem

⁶Then he said to me, 'It is done! I am the Alpha and the Omega, the beginning and the end. I will freely give water to the thirsty, water from the spring of the water of life. ⁷The one

who conquers will inherit these things. I will be his God and he shall be my son. [8]But as for cowards, faithless people, the unclean, murderers, fornicators, sorcerers, idolaters and all liars – their destiny will be in the lake that burns with fire and sulphur, which is the second death.'

[9]Then one of the seven angels who had the seven bowls filled with the seven last plagues came over and spoke to me. 'Come with me,' he said, 'and I will show you the bride, the wife of the lamb.' [10]Then he took me in the spirit up a great high mountain, and he showed me the holy city, Jerusalem, coming down out of heaven from God. [11]It has the glory of God; it is radiant, like the radiance of a rare and precious jewel, like a jasper stone, crystal-clear. [12]It has a great high wall with twelve gates, and twelve angels at the gates, and names inscribed on the gates, which are the names of the twelve tribes of the children of Israel. [13]There are three gates coming in from the east, three gates from the north, three gates from the south and three gates from the west. [14]And the wall of the city has twelve foundation-stones, and on them are written the twelve names of the twelve apostles of the lamb.

[15]The one who was talking with me had a golden measuring-rod, so that he could measure the city, its gates, and its wall. [16]The city stands foursquare, with the same length and breadth. He measured the city with his rod: it was twelve thousand stadia (that is, fifteen hundred miles), with the length, the breadth and the height being equal. [17]Then he measured its wall, and it was one hundred and forty-four cubits in terms of human measurement (which was what the angel was using). [18]The material of which the wall is built is jasper, and the city itself is pure gold, like pure glass. [19]The foundations of the city wall are decorated with every kind of precious stone: the first foundation is jasper, the second sapphire, the third agate, the fourth emerald, [20]the fifth onyx, the sixth carnelian, the seventh chrysolite, the eighth beryl, the ninth topaz, the tenth chrysoprase, the eleventh jacinth, the twelfth amethyst. [21]The twelve gates are twelve pearls, with each gate consisting of a single pearl. The street of the city is pure gold, clear as glass.

191

When people decide they are going to read the Bible, they often begin, naturally enough, with the book of Genesis. Encouraged by the fast-paced story with its drama, incident and passion, they often move on to the book of Exodus, expecting more of the same. And to begin with they are not disappointed. In fact, the first 20 chapters of that 40-chapter book are just as full of drama, if not more so.

But then the trail appears to go cold. Suddenly we hit a seam of detailed instructions about what to do if you want to sell your daughter as a slave (21.7), what happens when an ox gores someone to death (21.28), what you should do when your enemy's donkey has collapsed (23.5), and so on. Interesting in their way, but not quite what one had expected. Not such fun. And so some give up, and abandon the quest for whole-Bible reading.

Which is a thousand pities; because the rest of the book of Exodus, from chapter 24 onwards, is one long drama about *God dwelling in the midst of his people.* Exodus is all about how the God who rescued his people from Egypt through the great plagues, and brought them to the awesome vision of Sinai and gave them the **Law**, then commanded his own dwelling to be built to specific instructions. And by the end of the book it was done.

But not without a titanic struggle. It always takes an act of enormous grace, overcoming enormous resistance, for God's dwelling to be set up on earth. It is, after all, the **kingdom**-struggle, the agony through which God's kingdom arrives (in other words, God himself arrives as king) on earth as in **heaven**.

In the book of Exodus, Moses is up the mountain, receiving the detailed instructions about the beautiful, spectacular Tabernacle and how to have it made (chapters 25—31), but meanwhile the people down below are getting bored and impatient. And, as often happens when God's people get bored and impatient, they make themselves idols. In this case, they give Aaron gold earrings, and he makes the golden calf (chapter 32). 'These are your gods, O Israel,' he declares, 'who brought you up out of the land of Egypt!' (32.8). As always, the idol is what you get when you snatch at something good, something you are actually promised (in this case, God's powerful presence with his people), but in your own way and without waiting for the right moment. So Moses returns with a word of sorrowful but terrible judgment. And, worse, God threatens to withdraw his presence, to scupper the plan that he would come and live in the midst of his people.

That would be, to put it mildly, a major setback not only for Israel but for the whole world, since the point of there being an Israel in the first place was that through Israel God would bless the whole world. The idea of God dwelling in the midst of his people was always an advance signpost to God's eventual goal, that his presence would flood the whole world (Numbers 14.21). So Moses wrestles with God in prayer; God reveals yet more grace and mercy; and he consents after all to live with his people (chapters 33—34). This means that the Tabernacle can be built at last (chapters 35—39), and as it is erected God comes, in cloud and fire and glory, to live in it (chapter 40). That is how the book of Exodus works.

It is also, in more ways than most people realize, how the book of Revelation works. We have seen the great plagues, like the plagues of Egypt. We have seen the redeemed people standing by the sea, singing the song of Moses and the lamb. We have seen the great deception, the great idolatrous system, the great whore Babylon, clothed in gold and silver and jewels but inside full of vile, unclean and abominable oppression, lust, violence and degradation. Babylon is the parody, the bride is the reality, *as the golden calf was the parody and the Tabernacle the reality*. Now at last, as with the Tabernacle, 'God has come to dwell with humans' (verse 3). The jewels which Babylon wore, like the golden earrings out of which Aaron made the calf, are tawdry and worthless beside the precious stones with which the city's foundations are decorated (verses 19–21).

193

The idea of perfect marital unity between the lamb and his bride is reflected in the very different imagery of the structure of the new Jerusalem. On the one hand, it is designed to reflect the identity of God's people: the twelve tribes of Israel are named on the gates, and the **twelve apostles** on the foundation-stones (verses 12–14). The city wall defines the city, but the gates, as we discover presently, will never be shut. They are for decoration rather than defence.

On the other hand, we have the extraordinary measurements of the city. (The angel measures this heavenly city, as John was told to measure the heavenly **temple** in 11.1; this time, we find out what the measurements were, as in the original vision of Ezekiel 40—48 which lies behind a great deal of John's vision at this point.) As verse 16 makes clear, the city is not only vast in terms of its footprint – fifteen hundred miles each way, roughly the same number of square miles as the Roman empire. (That, of course, may be part of the point.) It is also fifteen hundred miles *high*. John, of course, has no thought of what kind of buildings would occupy this extraordinary structure; he is constructing a symbolic universe, not an architect's design. The city will be an enormous, perfect *cube* . . . because that is the shape of the holy of holies at the heart of the ancient Temple in Jerusalem (1 Kings 6.20). The whole city has become God's dwelling place, God's temple. Or, more exactly, the very centre of God's temple, the holy of holies, the place where God dwells for ever.

That is why the city 'has the glory of God' (verse 11). That doesn't just mean that it's a wonderful thing to look at, though that is clearly true as well. It means that God's glory, God's own glorious presence, is there, gleaming from every stone and jewel and shining from the pure gold of the street. And it is why, too, the city comes 'down out of heaven from God': this great new reality, the place of God's dwelling on earth, can never be something that humans make (that takes us back to Babylon, to Babel!), but remains always and for ever the gift of God's love and grace.

So, when God finally speaks, it is to declare not only that he is making all things new, but, as in 1.8, that he is Alpha and Omega, the beginning and the end. Only in the light of who God is – the sovereign creator, source and goal of all things – can we find the comfort we need, the long-promised water of life of which Jesus himself spoke in John 4 and elsewhere. Only then can we hear the promise, echoing the promises of the letters in chapters 2 and 3, to the one who conquers. And only then, perhaps, can we take with full seriousness the warnings, addressed to the church of the present, that in the church of the future there will simply be no room for the cowards (those who shy away from the conflict and struggle required for this 'conquest') and for 'all liars'.

The other categories are, basically, variations on the lie. The faithless, the unclean, murderers, fornicators, sorcerers and idolaters are all basically people who dislike, or even hate, God's world, and decide that they will live the lie, will act to make the world the way they would want it instead. In the new creation, there is no room for anti-creation. In the world of life, there is no room for death.

The picture we are gazing at in these chapters is certainly a vision of the ultimate future. Yet, as we have seen from the letters at the start of the book, there are signs that this reality keeps peeping through even in the present world of death and tears, of cowards and liars. Just as nothing we do in the present is *merely* relevant to the present, but can carry implications into God's future, so nothing in the vision of the future is *merely* future. Because the central reality of God's future is Jesus himself, and because Jesus is not merely a future reality but the one who lived and died and rose again and even now reigns in glory and holds the seven stars in his hand, the reality of the new city, though still a matter of hope, is something to be glimpsed in the present, especially in the ways sketched throughout this book: worship and witness. The new city is not just a dream, a comforting future fantasy. Those who follow the lamb already belong in that city, and already have the right to walk its streets. God might have abandoned his creation in disgust because of Babylon's wickedness, just as he might have abandoned the Israelites in the wilderness because of the golden calf. But out of sheer mercy he will come to dwell with his people, and that mercy will flow out to flood the whole world. But that takes us into the third and final part of the description of this glorious, unparalleled new city.

REVELATION 21.22—22.7

God and the Lamb Are There

[22]I saw no temple in the city, because the Lord God the Almighty is its temple, together with the lamb. [23]And the city has no need of sun or moon to shine on it, for the glory of God gives it light, and its lamp is the lamb. [24]The nations will walk in its light, and the kings of the earth will bring their glory into it. [25]Its gates will never be shut by day, for there will be no night there. [26]They will bring the glory and the honour of the nations into it. [27]Nothing that has not been made holy will ever come into it, nor will anyone who practises abomination or who tells lies, but only those who are written in the lamb's book of life.

22 [1]Then he showed me the river of the water of life. It was sparkling like crystal, and flowing from the throne of God and of the lamb [2]through the middle of the street of the city. On either bank of the river was growing the tree of life. It produces twelve kinds of fruit, bearing this fruit every month; and the leaves of the tree are for the healing of the nations. [3]Nothing accursed is there any more. Rather, the throne of God and of the lamb are in the city, and his servants will worship him; [4]they will see his face, and his name will be on their foreheads. [5]There will be no more night, and they will not need the light of a lamp or the light of the sun, because the Lord God will shine on them; and they will reign for ever and ever.

> ⁶"These words', he said to me, 'are trustworthy and true. The Lord, the God of the spirits of the prophets, has sent his angel to show his servants what must soon take place. ⁷Look, I am coming soon. God's blessing on the one who keeps the words of the prophecy of this book.'

Earlier today, I came upon some workmen who were putting scaffolding up around an old stone building. Scaffolding is normally extremely functional: it's made to do a job, not to look pretty. But supposing a builder decided to construct a beautiful shell of scaffolding? Supposing he made it so stunning that people came to admire the scaffolding itself, without even realizing that there was something far, far more impressive being built inside it? When the building was finished, some might be sad at the thought that this wonderful sight was to be taken away. But the builder would, of course, insist on removing the scaffolding, however splendid it was. That was the point of it in the first place, to do its job and then be dismantled so that the ultimate reality, the real new building, could be seen in all its glory.

That is the spirit in which we must read verses 22 and 23. We are not surprised, by now, that there is 'no temple' in the new city (as there was both in the earthly Jerusalem and also in its heavenly counterpart, as in 11.19 and 15.5). We have already realized that God's own dwelling in the city, and the shape of the city as a giant cube, are telling us that there cannot be a 'temple' as a specific place within the city where God lives. The Temple in Jerusalem, and also it seems in the first **heaven**, are advance signposts to that great, almost unthinkable reality to which nevertheless so much of the New Testament points, that 'the earth shall be filled with the knowledge of the glory of the Lord as the waters cover the sea' (Habakkuk 2.14). That is the goal towards which so much of scripture is pointing, a goal forgotten by those who imagine that the whole aim is to leave earth behind and go to heaven instead. Heaven

197

has come down to earth; why would we want it otherwise? We have the reality. We don't need the signpost any more.

But in verse 23 we discover that it isn't only the Temple that is no longer needed. Even the sun and the moon, the two great lights that play such an important part in the first creation, and are celebrated as such in many scriptural passages (think of the sun in Psalm 19, where it is an image of God's holy law itself) – even the sun and the moon will become redundant. They are part of the scaffolding, and we must not mistake them for the ultimate reality. They are yet another pair of signposts to the ultimate truth, that God himself is the light of his people, shining and radiant. Slowly we rub our eyes, and discover that even the glorious world of Genesis 1 was the beginning of something, rather than an end in itself. It was itself a great signpost, pointing to the world that God always intended to make out of it.

This will come as news to many, but in fact it should be central to the world-view of the Christian. The whole of Christian theology is based on the goodness of creation, yet the goodness of creation consists partly in this, that it points beyond itself to the new creation. It isn't the case that the new creation was an afterthought, a Plan B once the first creation had gone so badly wrong. Human sin has meant that God's eventual design has had to be arrived at by a long, winding and often tear-stained and blood-spattered route, the most important tears and blood being those of God himself, in the person of the lamb. But, as with the triumphant conclusion of Exodus, so with Revelation, the goal is achieved by the power of sheer mercy and grace, the mercy and grace through which creation is not abolished but fulfilled, not thrown away and replaced but renewed from top to bottom.

The mystery then unfolds a step further. For most of Revelation, 'the nations' and their kings have been hostile. They have shared in the idolatry and economic violence of Babylon; they have oppressed and opposed God, his purposes and his people.

But the earlier hints of God's wider redeeming purpose now come fully into play. The witness of the martyr-church in chapter 11 resulted in the nations, which had been raging against God, coming instead to give him glory (11.13). Now here they come in procession, in the long fulfilment of scriptural prophecies such as Psalm 72.10–11 (note the prayer in 72.19, that God's glory would fill the whole earth!), Isaiah 49.6–7, Zechariah 14.16–17, and above all Isaiah 60, the chapter which anticipates several elements in John's vision. Here they come, bringing their glory into the city through the wide-open gates. The city itself is not a tableau, a static picture with people simply gazing at the glorious golden streets or indeed at God himself and the lamb. It is a bustling community, filled with activity, as the nations come to worship and do homage.

John is careful to add the warning that this inclusivity specifically does not stretch to those who practise abomination or tell lies. This is necessary for the same reason that one does not allow smoking in a library or the playing of radios in a concert hall. That which ruins the beauty and holiness of God's new city is ruled out by definition.

But it isn't just a matter of people coming into the city from outside. **Life**, liquid life, the water of life, is flowing from the city to the world around. God's generous love is the souce and goal of all things. How can the city where he and the lamb are personally present be other than the great wellspring of life, flowing out to those who need it! So, from the ultimate fulfilment of Genesis 1, via Isaiah 60, John turns to the ultimate fulfilment of Genesis 2, via Ezekiel 47.

Once God's glory has returned to the newly built **Temple** in Ezekiel 43, we discover that this temple is actually a kind of new Eden, from which a river will flow out to irrigate the world around. In Genesis, there were four rivers flowing from the garden, but in Ezekiel's new Eden there is only one, and it grows deeper and deeper until it pours itself down the great Judaean escarpment to make even the Dead Sea fresh. Ezekiel saw in his vision fruit trees on either bank of the river (47.12), with their fruit for food and their leaves for healing. John, in one of the most moving reworkings of biblical imagery in his entire book, sees the river of the water of life flowing, sparkling on its way through the city streets and out into the countryside beyond. And though it is clear enough in Ezekiel that this is a rebirth of Genesis 2, in John it is even clearer, and more sharply focused. The tree which grows in profusion on either bank of the river is 'the tree of life', the tree which was forbidden to Adam and Eve as they were expelled from the garden (it would have been utterly disastrous for them to be made immortal in their sinful state). And the 'tree of life' is not merely there to provide healing for this person, or that, for this Adam or this Eve. The vision of John has always concerned the larger realities, the huge and often hard-to-see social, cultural and political pains and puzzles, the ignorant armies clashing by night and the would-be 'world leaders' who turn out to be the blind leading the blind. Now the leaves of the tree are for *the healing of the nations*. The new Jerusalem, too, it seems, is in a sense a project, not a tableau. God establishes the city of his presence in order that the nations may not only come to do homage but may be healed. The city is to be priestly, gathering up the praises of the rest of creation, and royal, the source of that healing, wise order through which God's rule is to be established.

It thus appears that the new Jerusalem, in John's vision, is not the whole of the new creation. It is the centrepiece and glory of it, the fountain from which there flows freely all that the world could need. It is the holy of holies, but actually the whole earth is to be full of God's glory, is to be the ultimate temple. This is what is meant when John describes the servants of God and the lamb not only worshipping (verse 3), not only seeing his face (verse 4), but also reigning 'for ever and ever' (verse 5). From the start of the book we were told that the lamb's followers were to be a royal priesthood, and now we see what this means. It is from the city, the city which is the bride, the bride which is the lamb's followers, that healing, restorative stewardship is to flow. This is how the creator God will show, once and for all, that his creation was good, and that he himself is full of mercy.

John's vision, then, is of a new Eden; but it is a city, not simply a garden. All the elements of the garden are still there, but enshrined and enhanced within and around the city. We know in our bones that we were made for both, though the romantic idyll of the countryside on the one hand and the developers' dream of the city on the other hand both routinely fail to hit the mark. The new creation, drawing the double vision together, transforms and heals both. As heaven and earth come together, as the bride and the lamb come together – both of them signs that the dualities in Genesis are at last united, as was always intended – so the garden and the city come together as well. Humans, in community with one another and with God, are to exercise their delighted and wise stewardship over the earth and its fruits, in the glorious light that comes from the throne.

Like other aspects of this vision of the ultimate future, this, too, is to be anticipated in the present.

REVELATION 22.8–21

'I Am Coming Soon!'

[8]I, John, am the one who heard and saw these things. And when I heard them and saw them, I fell down to worship before the feet of the angel who showed them to me. [9]'Look! Don't do that!' he said to me. 'I am a fellow-servant with you, and with the other members of your prophetic family, and with those who keep the words of this book. Worship God!

[10]'Don't seal up the words of the prophecy of this book,' he added. 'The time is near, you see. [11]Let the unjust go on being unjust, and the filthy go on being filthy – and let the just go on doing justice, and let the holy still be holy.

[12]'Look! I am coming soon. I will bring my reward with me, and I will pay everyone back according to what they have done. [13]I am the Alpha and the Omega, the first and the last, the beginning and the end.'

[14]God's blessing on those who wash their clothes, so that they may have the right to eat from the tree of life and may enter the city by its gates. [15]But the dogs, the sorcerers, the fornicators, the murderers, the idolaters, and everyone who loves to invent lies – they will all be outside.

[16]'I, Jesus, have sent my angel to give you this testimony for the churches. I am David's root and offspring; I am the bright morning star.'

[17]The spirit and the bride say, 'Come!' And let anyone who hears say, 'Come!' Let the thirsty come; let anyone who wants the water of life take it freely.

[18]I testify to everyone who hears the words of the prophecy of this book: if anyone adds to them, God will add to that person the plagues that are written in this book. [19]And if anyone takes away from the words of the book of this prophecy, God will take away that person's share in the tree of life, and in the holy city, which are described in this book.

[20]The one who gives this testimony says, 'Yes, I am coming soon!'

Amen! Come, Lord Jesus.

[21]The grace of the Lord Jesus be with you all.

I stood in the cloister and listened to the bells. To begin with, I could hear each of the ten, clear in the morning air. But gradually, as the order changed and the echoes multiplied in the ancient stone colonnades, they seemed to merge into one: a glorious, wild, ancient sound, awakening not only echoes but memories of years long past and imaginings of years yet to come. Even so, out of the rich confusion of their noise, the lowest two or three notes kept intruding, wherever they were in the constantly changing pattern: dong – dong – *dong*, dong . . . dong . . . *dong*. They were part of the whole music and yet seemed to be saying: Pay attention. This is important. Listen hard. We're telling you something. Keep awake.

Something of that sense comes over us as we reach the end of this most remarkable of books, whose surface we have skimmed in the interests of time and space and yet whose depths we have glimpsed as we have sped by. To begin with, we may have been able to hear most of the notes. But as the pace quickened and the echoes multiplied, the sequence of events – the letters, the seals, the trumpets and the bowls, and all that went with and around them – may have merged into one in our memory, a glorious, wild, ancient sound, pointing us back to the very dawn of time and the most ancient of scriptures, and yet pointing us on through symbolic signposts to things yet to come in God's ultimate future. But, out of this rich confusion of vision and image, two or three notes now stand out, emerging variously from all that has gone before, part of the music and yet with something else to say. Pay attention. Keep these words. I am coming soon. I am coming soon.

Coming soon! That had been the hope of Israel for many a long year, before ever John saw Patmos, indeed before Jesus opened his eyes to the frosty light of a Bethlehem morning. Malachi, four hundred years earlier, had warned the bored and careless priests that 'the Lord whom you seek will suddenly come to his **Temple**'. He will come! Ezekiel had described the glory of the Lord abandoning the Temple to its fate (Ezekiel 10.18–19; 11.22–23), but Ezekiel had also promised that he would come back once the Temple had been properly restored (43.1–5). At no point in the next four hundred years, however, did anyone report the kind of vision Ezekiel had had in mind, or an experience that might correspond to the vision of God's glory in the Temple as in Exodus 40 or Isaiah 6. The Lord had not returned – but he would come. He would come. The hope of God's coming back was at the heart of the hope for the restored Temple, which was itself at the heart of the hope for a restored Israel. The hope within the hope within the hope. Surely, he is coming soon!

The early Christians all believed that this promise had been fulfilled – in Jesus. He had come to Jerusalem, to the Temple, as the solemn judge whose coming they had been promised. But they saw the promise fulfilled even more completely, in the most startling and shocking way, when Jesus was 'lifted up' on the cross, and then raised from the dead. This was the real 'return of the Lord to Zion'. This was the moment when the glory of the Lord was revealed, for all flesh to see it together.

And so they were able, without difficulty and from the very beginning, to translate the much older Jewish hope, for YHWH to come back, into the sure and certain hope that Jesus would come back. The fusion of identity between Jesus and God, sharing the throne and both able to say 'I am the Alpha and the Omega' (21.6 with 22.13), together receiving the worship which must be given to no other (22.9), gave this translation a firm base. And the multiple 'comings' of Jesus which the church experienced in worship, in prayer, in the witness of the martyrs, and not least at the time of their own deaths, meant that the hope was not set in a vacuum, but reinforced daily and weekly. The great bell rings on in these verses. I am coming soon. The time is near. I am coming soon. Yes, I am coming soon!

The note of urgency explains the second bell which we hear in these verses, repeated again and again against the echoes and resonances of all that has gone before. This is a book of urgent prophecy. These words are trustworthy and true (verse 6). God's blessing on the one who keeps the words of the prophecy of this book (verse 7), on those who keep the words of this book (verse 9). Don't seal up the words of the prophecy of this book (verse 10). To everyone who hears the words of the prophecy of this book . . . if anyone takes away from the words of the book of this prophecy . . . which are described in this book (verses 18–19). These words. This prophecy. This book. This book. One might almost hear it as the voice of a very, very old man, slipping in and out of consciousness of the present life but more and more into consciousness of the next life, repeating again and again the thing he is seeing, the thing that really matters. I am coming soon. This book. This prophecy. I am coming soon.

How easy it is to hear the bells and walk away. How easy to dismiss them as a cheerful cacophany. What is Revelation all about? say people. Can't make head or tail of it myself. Happy hunting ground for heretics and fanatics, sneer others. Full of rambling fantasies and dark, sub-Christian threats, say others again. But still the bells ring on. I am coming soon. This book. This prophecy. Coming soon. Listen to this man. He may be old, he may even be rambling, but it's just possible he knows where the treasure is buried. It's just possible he's trying to tell us. These things are trustworthy and true.

And through the echoing bells, we hear another voice, a voice singing within the church. I am the Alpha and the Omega, the first and the last, the beginning and the end. I, Jesus, have sent my angel to give you this testimony. I am David's root and offspring, the bright morning star. The song mingles with the bells, the voice of Jesus clearly audible through the echoing repetitions, the urgings, the warnings. Warnings there are indeed: it's too late to change now; wash your clothes in the lamb's blood, so that you can eat from the tree of life, because those who don't, those who love inventing lies of every kind, will be outside (verse 15). John isn't worried about 'consistency' here; that's not how bells and choirs work. Yes, those people were in the lake of fire before, and now they're outside the city. It's the same picture with another twist of the kaleidoscope, as usual. Stop worrying about that; listen to the music. The words of this book. Coming soon. This prophecy. Yes, I am coming soon.

And, when you are ready, join in. 'The **spirit** and the bride say, "Come!"' The spirit has been a mysterious presence throughout John's book: sometimes sevenfold, sometimes 'the spirit of prophecy'. So much of the focus has been on God and the lamb. We might have thought, if we weren't careful, that John believed in a Binity rather than a Trinity.

How wrong would we have been. It is the spirit that enables the bride to be the bride. It is the spirit that enables the martyrs to keep up their courage and bear true witness. It is the spirit that inspires the great shouts and songs of praise. The spirit goes out from God's throne and, breathing into and then through the hearts, minds and lives of people of every nation, tribe and tongue, returns in praise to the father and the lamb. This is as trinitarian as it gets, and the bride is caught up in that inner-divine life, so that when she says 'Come!' to her beloved we can't tell whether this is the spirit speaking or the bride, because the answer is both. The spirit of the **Messiah** enables his bride to be who she is, lovely in limbs, and lovely in eyes not his.

And the bells find tongue to fling out broad his name, to ring out their praise and their invitation. Come to the waters. There is still time. Come and take the water of life, freely. John's readers may find it hard to see in their neighbours on the street anything but cold, hostile stares and the threat of informing the authorities. They may be so aware of the present rule of the dragon, the monster and the false prophet that all they want is to escape, to be rescued, not to hold out to their neighbours God's repeated and generous invitation. But see they must, because the mercy of God is vast and his invitation wide as the world. Because he has made us as he has, he will not compel except with the appeal of love; only those who tell lies about his love, and about everything else, will resist (verse 15). But because he is who he is, the creator whose purposes are gloriously fulfilled in the slaughtered lamb, he will go on inviting and welcoming and pouring out the water of life for all the thirsty. Listen to the bells. These words. This prophecy. This book. Coming soon. Yes, I am coming soon.

And the spirit awakens in one and another, in the cloister and the church, in the war zone and the throne room, in the island of exile and the house of torment, in the hearts of men and women, in the dreams of little children, even on the bishops' bench and in the scholar's study, the prayer, the cry, the song, the hope, the love: Amen! Come, Lord Jesus.

The letter – it always was a letter, as well as a prophecy and a revelation – ends as it should, with a closing greeting. 'The grace of the Lord Jesus be with you all' (verse 21). But, however conventional, this greeting now carries the freight of the entire book. It is dense with a thousand images of 'grace', pregnant with the power of the word 'Lord' when spoken under the nose of Caesar, sparkling in the still-open invitation to 'you all', and above all delicious with the name, the name that is now exalted high over all, the name of the slaughtered lamb, the name of the one we love and long to see. This book has been a revelation of Jesus, a testimony to Jesus, an act of homage to Jesus. This word. This book. This prophecy. Listen to the bells. Coming soon. This Jesus.

GLOSSARY

accuser, the, *see* **the satan**

age to come, *see* **present age**

apostle, disciple, the Twelve

'Apostle' means 'one who is sent'. It could be used of an ambassador or official delegate. In the New Testament it is sometimes used specifically of Jesus' inner circle of twelve, but Paul sees not only himself but several others outside the Twelve as 'apostles', the criterion being whether the person had personally seen the risen Jesus. Jesus' own choice of twelve close associates symbolized his plan to renew God's people, Israel (who traditionally thought of themselves as having twelve tribes); after the death of Judas Iscariot (Matthew 27.5; Acts 1.18), Matthias was chosen by lot to take his place, preserving the symbolic meaning. During Jesus' lifetime they, and many other followers, were seen as his 'disciples', which means 'pupils' or 'apprentices'.

ascension

At the end of Luke's **gospel** and the start of Acts, Luke describes Jesus 'going up' from earth into **heaven**. To understand this, we have to remember that 'heaven' isn't a 'place' within our own world of space, time and matter, but a different *dimension* of reality – God's dimension, which intersects and interacts with our own (which we call 'earth', meaning both the planet where we live and the entire space–time universe). For Jesus to 'ascend', therefore, doesn't mean that he's a long way away, but rather that he can be, and is, intimately present to all his people all the time. What's more, because in the Bible 'heaven' is (as it were) the control room for 'earth', it means that Jesus is actually in charge of what goes on here and now. The way his sovereign rule works out is of course very different from the way earthly rulers get their way: as in his own life, he accomplishes his saving purposes through faithful obedience, including suffering. The life and witness of the early church, therefore, resulting in the spread of the gospel around the world, shows what it means to say that Jesus has ascended and that he is the world's rightful Lord.

baptism

Literally, 'plunging' people into water. From within a wider Jewish tradition of ritual washings and bathings, **John the Baptist** undertook a vocation of baptizing people in the Jordan, not as one ritual among others but as a unique moment of **repentance**, preparing them for the coming of the **kingdom of God**. Jesus himself was baptized by John, identifying himself with this renewal movement and developing it in his own way. His followers in turn baptized others. After his **resurrection**, and the sending of the **holy spirit**, baptism became the normal sign and means of entry in the community of Jesus' people. As early as Paul, it was aligned both with the **Exodus** from Egypt (1 Corinthians 10.2) and with Jesus' death and resurrection (Romans 6.2–11).

Christ, *see* Messiah

circumcision

The cutting off of the foreskin. Male circumcision was a major mark of identity for Jews, following its initial commandment to Abraham (Genesis 17), reinforced by Joshua (Joshua 5.2–9). Other peoples, e.g. the Egyptians, also circumcised male children. A line of thought from Deuteronomy (e.g. 30.6), through Jeremiah (e.g. 31.33), to the **Dead Sea Scrolls** and the New Testament (e.g. Romans 2.29) speaks of 'circumcision of the heart' as God's real desire, by which one may become inwardly what the male Jew is outwardly, that is, marked out as part of God's people. At periods of Jewish assimilation into the surrounding culture, some Jews tried to remove the marks of circumcision (e.g. 1 Maccabees 1.11–15).

covenant

At the heart of Jewish belief is the conviction that the one God, YHWH, who had made the whole world, had called Abraham and his family to belong to him in a special way. The promises God made to Abraham and his family, and the requirements that were laid on them as a result, came to be seen in terms either of the agreement that a king would make with a subject people, or of the marriage bond between husband and wife. One regular way of describing this relationship was 'covenant', which can thus include both promise and **law**. The covenant was renewed at Mount Sinai with the giving of the **Torah**; in Deuteronomy before the entry to the promised land; and, in a more focused way, with David (e.g. Psalm 89). Jeremiah 31 promised that, after the punishment of **exile**, God would make a 'new covenant' with his people, forgiving them and binding them to him more intimately. Jesus believed that this was coming true through his **kingdom**-proclamation and his death and resurrection. The early Christians developed these ideas in various ways, believing that in Jesus the promises had at last been fulfilled.

Dead Sea Scrolls

A collection of texts, some in remarkably good repair, some extremely fragmentary, found in the late 1940s around Qumran (near the north-west corner of the Dead Sea), and virtually all now edited, translated and in the public domain. They formed all or part of the library of a strict monastic group, most likely **Essenes**, founded in the mid-second century BC and lasting until the Jewish–Roman war of AD 66–70. The scrolls include the earliest existing manuscripts of the Hebrew and Aramaic scriptures, and several other important documents of community regulations, scriptural exegesis, hymns, wisdom writings, and other literature. They shed a flood of light on one small segment within the Judaism of Jesus' day, helping us to understand how some Jews at least were thinking, praying and reading scripture. Despite attempts to prove the contrary, they make no reference to **John the Baptist**, Jesus, Paul, James or early Christianity in general.

demons, *see* **the satan**

devil, *see* **the satan**

disciple, *see* **apostle**

Essenes, *see* **Dead Sea Scrolls**

eternal life, *see* **present age**

exile

Deuteronomy (29—30) warned that if Israel disobeyed YHWH, he would send his people into exile, but that if they then repented he would bring them back. When the Babylonians sacked Jerusalem and took the people into exile, prophets such as Jeremiah interpreted this as the fulfilment of this prophecy, and made further promises about how long exile would last (70 years, according to Jeremiah 25.12; 29.10). Sure enough, exiles began to return in the late sixth century BC (Ezra 1.1). However, the post-exilic period was largely a disappointment, since the people were still enslaved to foreigners (Nehemiah 9.36); and, at the height of persecution by the Syrians, Daniel 9.2, 24 spoke of the 'real' exile lasting not for 70 years but for 70 *weeks* of years, that is, 490 years. Longing for the real 'return from exile', when the prophecies of Isaiah, Jeremiah, etc. would be fulfilled, and **redemption** from pagan oppression accomplished, continued to characterize many Jewish movements, and was a major theme in Jesus' proclamation and his summons to **repentance**.

Exodus

The Exodus from Egypt took place, according to the book of that name, under the leadership of Moses, after long years in which the Israelites had been enslaved there. (According to Genesis 15.13f., this was itself part of God's covenanted promise to Abraham.) It demonstrated, to them and to Pharaoh, King of Egypt, that Israel was God's special child (Exodus 4.22). They then wandered through the Sinai wilderness for 40 years, led by God in a pillar of cloud and fire; early on in this time they were given the **Torah** on Mount Sinai itself. Finally, after the death of Moses and under the leadership of Joshua, they crossed the Jordan and entered, and eventually conquered, the promised land of Canaan. This event, commemorated annually in the Passover and other Jewish festivals, gave the Israelites not only a powerful memory of what had made them a people, but also a particular shape and content to their **faith** in YHWH as not only creator but also redeemer; and in subsequent enslavements, particularly the **exile,** they looked for a further **redemption** which would be, in effect, a new Exodus. Probably no other past event so dominated the imagination of first-century Jews; among them the early Christians, following the lead of Jesus himself, continually referred back to the Exodus to give meaning and shape to their own critical events, most particularly Jesus' death and **resurrection.**

faith

Faith in the New Testament covers a wide area of human trust and trustworthiness, merging into love at one end of the scale and loyalty at the other. Within Jewish and Christian thinking, faith in God also includes *belief,* accepting certain things as true about God, and what he has done in the world (e.g. bringing Israel out of Egypt; raising Jesus from the dead). For Jesus, 'faith' often seems to mean 'recognizing that God is decisively at work to bring the **kingdom** through Jesus'. For Paul, 'faith' is both the specific belief that Jesus is Lord and that God raised him from the dead (Romans 10.9) and the response of grateful human love to sovereign divine love (Galatians 2.20). This faith is, for Paul, the solitary badge of membership in God's people in **Christ,** marking them out in a way that **Torah,** and the works it prescribes, can never do.

fellowship

The word we often translate 'fellowship' can mean a business partnership (in the ancient world, businesses were often run by families, so there's a sense of family loyalty as well), or it can mean a sense of mutual belonging and sharing in some other corporate enterprise. Within early Christianity, 'fellowship' acquired the sense not just of belonging to one another as Christians, but of a shared belonging to Jesus **Christ,** and a participation in his life through the **spirit,** expressed in such actions as the 'breaking of bread' and the sharing of property with those in need.

forgiveness

Jesus made forgiveness central to his **message** and ministry, not least because he was claiming to be launching God's long-awaited 'new **covenant**' (Jeremiah 31.31–34) in which sins would at last be forgiven (Matthew 26.28). Forgiveness doesn't mean God, or someone else, saying, of some particular fault or sin, 'it didn't really matter' or 'I didn't really mind'. The point of forgiveness is that it *did* matter, God (and/or other people) really *did* mind, but they are not going to hold it against the offender. It isn't, in other words, the same thing as 'tolerance': to forgive is not to tolerate sin, but to see clearly that it was wrong and then to treat the offender as though it hadn't happened. The early Christian answer to the obvious question, 'How could a holy and righteous God do that?' is 'Through the death of Jesus'. What's more, Jesus commanded his followers to extend the same forgiveness to one another (Matthew 6.12). Not to do so is to shut up the same door through which forgiveness is received for oneself (Matthew 18.21–35).

Gehenna, hell

Gehenna is, literally, the valley of Hinnom, on the south-west slopes of Jerusalem. From ancient times it was used as a garbage dump, smouldering with a continual fire. Already by the time of Jesus some Jews used it as an image for the place of punishment after death. Jesus' own usage blends the two meanings in his warnings both to Jerusalem itself (unless it repents, the whole city will become a smouldering heap of garbage) and to people in general (to beware of God's final judgment).

Gentiles

The Jews divided the world into Jews and non-Jews. The Hebrew word for non-Jews, *goyim*, carries overtones both of family identity (i.e. not of Jewish ancestry) and of worship (i.e. of idols, not of the one true God YHWH). Though many Jews established good relations with Gentiles, not least in the Jewish Diaspora (the dispersion of Jews away from Palestine), officially there were taboos against the contact such as intermarriage. In the New Testament the Greek word *ethne*, 'nations', carries the same meanings as *goyim*. Part of Paul's overmastering agenda was to insist that Gentiles who believed in

Jesus had full rights in the Christian community alongside believing Jews, without having to become circumcised.

good news, gospel, message, word

The idea of 'good news', for which an older English word is 'gospel', had two principal meanings for first-century Jews. First, with roots in Isaiah, it meant the news of YHWH's long-awaited victory over evil and rescue of his people. Second, it was used in the Roman world of the accession, or birthday, of the emperor. Since for Jesus and Paul the announcement of God's inbreaking **kingdom** was both the fulfilment of prophecy and a challenge to the world's present rulers, 'gospel' became an important shorthand for both the message of Jesus himself and the apostolic message about him. Paul saw this message as itself the vehicle of God's saving power (Romans 1.16; 1 Thessalonians 2.13).

gospel, *see* good news

heaven

Heaven is God's dimension of the created order (Genesis 1.1; Psalm 115.16; Matthew 6.9), whereas 'earth' is the world of space, time and matter that we know. 'Heaven' thus sometimes stands, reverentially, for 'God' (as in Matthew's regular '**kingdom** of heaven'). Normally hidden from human sight, heaven is occasionally revealed or unveiled so that people can see God's dimension of ordinary life (e.g. 2 Kings 6.17; Revelation 1, 4—5). Heaven in the New Testament is thus not usually seen as the place where God's people go after death; at the end, the new Jerusalem descends *from* heaven *to* earth, joining the two dimensions for ever. 'Entering the kingdom of heaven' does not mean 'going to heaven after death', but belonging in the present to the people who steer their earthly course by the standards and purposes of heaven (cf. the Lord's Prayer; 'on earth as in heaven', Matthew 6.10), and who are assured of membership in the **age to come.**

hell, *see* Gehenna

high priest, *see* priests

holy spirit

In Genesis 1.2, the spirit is God's presence and power *within* creation, without God being identified with creation. The same spirit entered people, notably the prophets, enabling them to speak and act for God. At his **baptism** by **John**, Jesus was specially equipped with the spirit, resulting in his remarkable public career (Acts 10.38). After his **resurrection**, his followers were themselves filled (Acts 2) by the same spirit, now identified as Jesus' own spirit; the creator God was acting afresh, remaking the world and them too. The spirit enabled them to live out a holiness which the **Torah** could not, producing 'fruit' in their lives, giving them 'gifts' with which to serve God, the world and the church, and assuring them of future resurrection (Romans 8; Galatians 4—5; 1 Corinthians 12—14). From very early in Christianity (e.g. Galatians 4.1–7), the spirit became part of the new revolutionary definition of God himself: 'the one who sends the son and the spirit of the son'.

John (the Baptist)

Jesus' cousin on his mother's side, born a few months before Jesus; his father was a **priest**. He acted as a prophet, baptizing in the Jordan – dramatically re-enacting the **Exodus** from Egypt – to prepare people, by **repentance**, for God's coming judgment. He may have had some contact with the **Essenes**, though his eventual public message was different from theirs. Jesus' own vocation was decisively confirmed at his **baptism** by John. As part of John's message of the **kingdom**, he outspokenly criticized Herod Antipas for marrying his brother's wife. Herod had him imprisoned, and then beheaded him at his wife's request (Mark 6.14–29). Groups of John's disciples continued a separate existence, without merging into Christianity, for some time afterwards (e.g. Acts 19.1–7).

jubilee

The ancient Israelites were commanded to keep a 'jubilee' every fiftieth year (i.e. following the sequence of seven 'sabbatical' years). Leviticus 25 provides the basic rules, which were expanded by later teachers: land was to be restored to its original owners or their heirs, and any fellow Jews who had been enslaved because of debt were to be set free. It was also to be a year without sowing, reaping or harvesting. The point was that YHWH owned the land, and that the Israelites were to see it not as a private possession but as something held in trust. People debate whether the jubilee principle was ever put into practice as thoroughly as Leviticus demands, but the underlying promise of a great remission of debts was repeated by Isaiah (61.1–2) and then decisively by Jesus (Luke 4.16–21). It is likely that this underlies the action of the first Christians in sharing property and giving to those in need (Acts 4.32–35, etc.).

justification

God's declaration, from his position as judge of all the world, that someone is in the right, despite universal sin. This declaration will be made on the last day on the basis of an entire life (Romans 2.1–16), but is brought forward into the present on the basis of Jesus' achievement, because sin has been dealt with through his cross (Romans 3.21—4.25); the means of this present justification is simply **faith**. This means, particularly, that Jews and **Gentiles** alike are full members of the family promised by God to Abraham (Galatians 3; Romans 4).

kingdom of God, kingdom of heaven

Best understood as the king*ship*, or sovereign and saving rule, of Israel's God YHWH as celebrated in several psalms (e.g. 99.1) and prophecies (e.g. Daniel 6.26f.). Because YHWH was the creator God, when he finally became king in the way he intended this would involve setting the world to right, and particularly rescuing Israel from its enemies. 'Kingdom of God' and various equivalents (e.g. 'No king but God!') became a revolutionary slogan around the time of Jesus. Jesus' own announcement of God's kingdom redefined these expectations around his own very different plan and vocation. His invitation to people to 'enter' the kingdom was a way of summoning them to allegiance to himself and his programme, seen as the start of God's long-awaited saving reign. For Jesus, the kingdom was coming not in a single move, but in stages, of which his own public career was one, his death and **resurrection** another, and a still future consummation another. Note that 'kingdom of heaven' is Matthew's preferred form for the same phrase, following a regular Jewish practice of saying 'heaven' rather than 'God'. It does not refer to a place ('heaven'), but to the fact of God's becoming king in and through Jesus and his achievement. Paul speaks of Jesus as **Messiah**, already in possession of his kingdom, waiting to hand it over finally to the father (1 Corinthians 15.23–28; cf. Ephesians 5.5).

last days

Ancient Jews thought of world history as divided into two periods: 'the **present age**' and 'the **age to come**'. The present age was a time when evil was still at large in its many forms; the age to come would usher in God's final reign of justice, peace, joy and love. Ancient prophets had spoken of the transition from the one age to the other in terms of the 'last days', meaning either the final moments of the 'present age' or the eventual dawning of the 'age to come'. When Peter quotes Joel in Acts 2.17, he perhaps means both: the two ages have overlapped, so that Christians live in the 'last days', the time between God's **kingdom** being launched in and through Jesus and it being completed at Jesus' return. The New Testament gives no encouragement to the idea that we can calculate a precise timetable for the latter event, or that the period of history immediately before Jesus' return will be significantly different (e.g. more violent) than any other (see Matthew 24.36–39).

law, *see* Torah

life, soul, spirit

Ancient people held many different views about what made human beings the special creatures they are. Some, including many Jews, believed that to be complete, humans needed bodies as well as inner selves. Others, including many influenced by the philosophy of Plato (fourth century BC), believed that the important part of a human was the 'soul' (Gk: *psyche*), which at death would be happily freed from its bodily prison. Confusingly for us, the same word psyche is often used in the New Testament within a Jewish framework where it clearly means 'life' or 'true self', without implying a body/soul dualism that devalues the body. Human inwardness of experience and understanding can also be referred to as 'spirit'. See also **holy spirit; resurrection.**

message, *see* **good news**

Messiah, messianic, Christ

The Hebrew word means literally 'anointed one', hence in theory either a prophet, **priest** or king. In Greek this translates as *Christos*; 'Christ' in early Christianity was a title, and only gradually became an alternative proper name for Jesus. In practice, 'Messiah' is mostly restricted to the notion, which took various forms in ancient Judaism, of the coming king who would be David's true heir, through whom YHWH would bring judgment to the world, and in particular would rescue Israel from pagan enemies. There was no single template of expectations. Scriptural stories and promises contributed to different ideals and movements, often focused on (a) decisive military defeat of Israel's enemies and (b) rebuilding or cleansing the **Temple.** The **Dead Sea Scrolls** speak of two 'Messiahs', one a priest and the other a king. The universal early Christian belief that Jesus was Messiah is only explicable, granted his crucifixion by the Romans (which would have been seen as a clear sign that he was not the Messiah), by their belief that God had raised him from the dead, so vindicating the implicit messianic claims of his earlier ministry.

miracles

Like some of the old prophets, notably Elijah and Elisha, Jesus performed many deeds of remarkable power, particularly healings. The **gospels** refer to these as 'deeds of power', 'signs', 'marvels' or 'paradoxes'. Our word 'miracle' tends to imply that God, normally 'outside' the closed system of the world, sometimes 'intervenes'; miracles have then frequently been denied by sceptics as a matter of principle. However, in the Bible, God is always present, however strangely, and 'deeds of power' are seen as *special* acts of a *present* God rather than *intrusive* acts of an *absent* one. Jesus' own 'mighty works' are seen particularly, following prophecy, as evidence of his messiahship.

Mishnah

The main codification of Jewish law (**Torah**) by the **rabbis,** produced in about AD 200, reducing to writing the 'oral Torah', which in Jesus' day ran parallel to the 'written Torah'. The Mishnah is itself the basis of the much larger collections of traditions in the two Talmuds (roughly AD 400).

parables

From the Old Testament onwards, prophets and other teachers used various story-telling devices as vehicles for their challenge to Israel (e.g. 2 Samuel 12.1–7). Sometimes they appeared as visions with interpretations (e.g. Daniel 7). Similar techniques were used by the **rabbis.** Jesus made his own creative adaptation of these traditions, in order to break open the worldview of his contemporaries and to invite them to share his vision of God's **kingdom** instead. His stories portrayed this as something that was *happening*, not just a timeless truth, and enabled his hearers to step inside the story and make it their own. As with some Old Testament visions, some of Jesus' parables have their own interpretations (e.g. the sower, Mark 4); others are thinly disguised retellings of the prophetic story of Israel (e.g. the wicked tenants, Mark 12).

Pharisees, rabbis

The Pharisees were an unofficial but powerful Jewish pressure group through most of the first centuries BC and AD. Largely lay-led, though including some of the **priests,** their aim was to purify Israel through intensified observance of the Jewish law (**Torah**), developing their own traditions about the precise meaning and application of scripture, their own patterns of prayer and other devotion, and their own calculations of the national hope. Though not all legal experts were Pharisees, most Pharisees were legal experts.

They effected a democratization of Israel's life, since for them the study and practice of Torah was equivalent to worshipping in the **Temple** – though they were adamant in pressing their own rules for the Temple liturgy on an unwilling (and often **Sadducean**) priesthood. This enabled them to survive AD 70 and, merging in to the early rabbinic movement, to develop new ways forward. Politically, they stood up for ancestral traditions, and were at the forefront of various movements of revolt against both pagan overlordship and compromised Jewish leaders. By Jesus' day there were two distinct schools, the stricter one of Shammai, more inclined towards armed revolt, and the more lenient one of Hillel, more ready to live and let live.

Jesus' debates with the Pharisees are at least as much a matter of agenda and policy (Jesus strongly opposed their separatist nationalism) as about details of theology and piety. Saul of Tarsus was a fervent right-wing Pharisee, presumably a Shammaite, until his conversion.

After the disastrous war of AD 66–70, these schools of Hillel and Shammai continued bitter debate on appropriate policy. Following the further disaster of AD 135 (the failed Bar-Kochba revolt against Rome) their traditions were carried on by the rabbis, who, though looking to the earlier Pharisees for inspiration, developed a Torah-piety in which personal holiness and purity took the place of political agendas.

present age, age to come, eternal life

By the time of Jesus many Jewish thinkers divided history into two periods: 'the present age' and 'the age to come' – the latter being the time when YHWH would at last act decisively to judge evil, to rescue Israel, and to create a new world of justice and peace. The early Christians believed that, though the full blessings of the coming age lay still in the future, it had already begun with Jesus, particularly with his death and **resurrection**, and that by **faith** and **baptism** they were able to enter it already. 'Eternal life' does not mean simply 'existence continuing without end', but 'the life of the age to come'.

priests, high priest

Aaron, the older brother of Moses, was appointed Israel's first high priest (Exodus 28—29), and in theory his descendants were Israel's priests thereafter. Other members of his tribe (Levi) were 'Levites', performing other liturgical duties but not sacrificing. Priests lived among the people all around the country, having a local teaching role (Leviticus 10.11; Malachi 2.7), and going to Jerusalem by rotation to perform the **Temple** liturgy (e.g. Luke 2.8).

David appointed Zadok (whose Aaronic ancestry is sometimes questioned) as high priest, and his family remained thereafter the senior priests in Jerusalem, probably the ancestors of the **Sadducees**. One explanation of the origin of the Qumran **Essenes** is that they were a dissident group who believed themselves to be the rightful chief priests.

rabbis, *see* **Pharisees**

redemption
Literally, 'redemption' means 'buying-back', and was often used in the ancient world of slaves buying their freedom, or having it bought for them. The great 'redemption' in the Bible, which coloured the way the word was heard ever afterwards, was when God 'bought' his people Israel from slavery in Egypt to give them freedom in the promised land. When, later, the Jews were exiled in Babylon (and even after they returned to their land), they described themselves as undergoing a new slavery and hence being in need of a new redemption. Jesus, and the early Christians, interpreted this continuing slavery in its most radical terms, as slavery to sin and death, and understood 'redemption' likewise in terms of the rescue from this multiple and tyrannous slavery, which God provided through the death of Jesus (Romans 3.24).

repentance
Literally, this means 'turning back'. It is widely used in Old Testament and subsequent Jewish literature to indicate both a personal turning away from sin and Israel's corporate turning away from idolatry and back to YHWH. Through both meanings, it is linked to the idea of 'return from exile'; if Israel is to 'return' in all senses, it must 'return' to YHWH. This is at the heart of the summons of both **John the Baptist** and Jesus. In Paul's writings it is mostly used for **Gentiles** turning away from idols to serve the true God; also for sinning Christians who need to return to Jesus.

resurrection
In most biblical thought, human bodies matter and are not merely disposable prisons for the soul. When ancient Israelites wrestled

with the goodness and justice of YHWH, the creator, they ultimately came to insist that he must raise the dead (Isaiah 26.19; Daniel 12.2–3) – a suggestion firmly resisted by classical pagan thought. The longed-for return from exile was also spoken of in terms of YHWH raising dry bones to new life (Ezekiel 37.1–14). These ideas were developed in the second-Temple period, not least at times of martyrdom (e.g. 2 Maccabees 7). Resurrection was not just 'life after death', but a newly embodied life *after* 'life after death'; those at present dead were either 'asleep' or seen as 'souls', 'angels' or 'spirits', awaiting new embodiment.

sacrifice

Like all ancient people, the Israelites offered animal and vegetable sacrifices to their God. Unlike others, they possessed a highly detailed written code (mostly in Leviticus) for what to offer and how to offer it; this in turn was developed in the Mishnah (*c.* AD 200). The Old Testament specifies that sacrifices can only be offered in the Jerusalem Temple; after this was destroyed in AD 70, sacrifices ceased, and Judaism developed further the idea, already present in some teachings, of prayer, fasting and almsgiving as alternative forms of sacrifice. The early Christians used the language of sacrifice in connection with such things as holiness, evangelism and the eucharist.

Sadducees

By Jesus' day, the Sadducees were the aristocracy of Judaism, possibly tracing their origins to the family of Zadok, David's high priest. Based in Jerusalem, and including most of the leading priestly families, they had their own traditions and attempted to resist the pressure of the Pharisees to conform to theirs. They claimed to rely only on the Pentateuch (the first five books of the Old Testament), and denied any doctrine of a future life, particularly of the resurrection and other ideas associated with it, presumably because of the encouragement such beliefs gave to revolutionary movements. No writings from the Sadducees have survived, unless the apocryphal book of Ben-Sirach (Ecclesiasticus) comes from them. The Sadducees themselves did not survive the destruction of Jerusalem and the Temple in AD 70.

salvation

Salvation means 'rescue', and the meanings of the word have depended on what people thought needed rescuing, and from what. Thus, where people have imagined that the human plight was best seen in terms of an immortal **soul** being trapped in a mortal and corrupt body, 'salvation' was seen in terms of the rescue of this soul from such a prison. But for most Jews, and all early Christians, it was death itself, the ending of God-given bodily **life**, that was the real enemy, so that 'salvation' was bound to mean being rescued from death itself – in other words, the **resurrection** of the body for those who had died, and the transformation of the body for those still alive at the Lord's return (e.g. 1 Corinthians 15.50–57). For Paul and others, this 'salvation' was extended to the whole of creation (Romans 8.18–26). But if 'salvation' refers to this ultimate rescue of God's created order, and our created bodies, from all that distorts, defaces and destroys them (i.e. sin, sickness, corruption and death itself), we should expect to find, and do in fact find, that often in the New Testament 'salvation' (and phrases like 'being saved') refers, not simply to people coming to **faith** and so being assured of **eternal life**, but to bodily healing and to rescue from awful plights (e.g. Acts 16.30–31; 27.44). Jesus' resurrection remains the foundation for a biblical view of salvation for the whole person and the whole creation, a salvation which, though to be completed in the future, has already begun with the mission and achievement of Jesus.

satan, the, 'the accuser', demons, devil

The Bible is never very precise about the identity of the figure known as 'the satan'. The Hebrew word means 'the accuser', and at times the satan seems to be a member of YHWH's heavenly council, with special responsibility as director of prosecutions (1 Chronicles 21.1; Job 1—2; Zechariah 3.1f.). However, it becomes identified variously with the serpent of the garden of Eden (Genesis 3.1–15) and with the rebellious daystar cast out of **heaven** (Isaiah 14.12–15), and was seen by many Jews as the quasi-personal source of evil standing behind both human wickedness and large-scale injustice, sometimes operating through semi-independent 'demons'. By Jesus' time, various words were used to denote this figure, including Beelzebul/b (lit. 'Lord of the flies') and simply 'the evil one'; Jesus warned his followers against the deceits this figure could perpetrate. His opponents accused him of being in league with the satan, but the early Christians believed that Jesus in fact defeated it in his own struggles with temptation (Matthew 4; Luke 4), his exorcism of demons, and his death (1 Corinthians 2.8; Colossians 2.15). Final victory over this ultimate enemy is thus assured (Revelation 20), though the struggle can still be fierce for Christians (Ephesians 6.10–20).

scribes

In a world where many could not write, or not very well, a trained class of writers ('scribes') performed the important function of drawing up contracts for business, marriage, etc. Many scribes would thus be legal experts, and quite possibly **Pharisees**, though being a scribe was compatible with various political and religious standpoints. The work of Christian scribes was of initial importance in copying early Christian writings, particularly the stories about Jesus.

second coming

When God renews the whole creation, as he has promised, bringing together **heaven** and earth, Jesus himself will be at the centre of it all, personally present to and with his people and ruling his world fully and finally at last. The Christian hope picks up, and gives more explicit focus to, the ancient Jewish hope that YHWH would in the end return to his people to judge and to save. Since the **ascension** is often thought of in terms of Jesus 'going away', this final moment is often thought of in terms of his 'coming back again', hence the shorthand 'second coming'. However, since the ascension in fact means that Jesus, though now invisible, is not far away but rather closely present with us, it isn't surprising that some of the key New Testament passages speak not of his 'return' as though from a great distance, but of his 'appearing' (e.g. Colossians 3.4; 1 John 3.2). The early Christians expected this 'appearing' to take place not necessarily within a generation as is often thought (because of a misreading of Mark 13 and similar passages), but at *any* time – which could be immediate or delayed. This caused a problem for some early Christians (2 Peter 3.3–10), but not for many. For the early Christians, the really important event – the **resurrection** of Jesus – had already taken place, and his final 'appearing' would simply complete what had then been decisively begun.

son of David

An alternative, and infrequently used, title for **Messiah**. The messianic promises of the Old Testament often focus specifically on David's son, for example 2 Samuel 7.12–16; Psalm 89.19–37. Joseph, Mary's husband, is called 'son of David' by the angel in Matthew 1.20.

son of God

Originally a title for Israel (Exodus 4.22) and the Davidic king (Psalm 2.7); also used of ancient angelic figures (Genesis 6.2). By the New Testament period it was already used as a **messianic** title, for example, in the **Dead Sea Scrolls**. There, and when used of Jesus in the **gospels** (e.g. Matthew 16.16), it means, or reinforces, 'Messiah', without the later significance of 'divine'. However, already in Paul the transition to the fuller meaning (one who was already equal with God and was sent by him to become human and to become Messiah) is apparent, without loss of the meaning 'Messiah' itself (e.g. Galatians 4.4).

son of man

In Hebrew or Aramaic, this simply means 'mortal', or 'human being'; in later Judaism, it is sometimes used to mean 'I' or 'someone like me'. In the New Testament the phrase is frequently linked to Daniel 7.13, where 'one like a son of man' is brought on the clouds of **heaven** to the 'Ancient of Days', being vindicated after a period of suffering, and is given kingly power. Though Daniel 7 itself interprets this as code for 'the people of the saints of the Most High', by the first century some Jews understood it as a **messianic** promise. Jesus developed this in his own way in certain key sayings which are best understood as promises that God would vindicate him, and judge those who had opposed him, after his own suffering (e.g. Mark 14.62). Jesus was thus able to use the phrase as a cryptic self-designation, hinting at his coming suffering, his vindication and his God-given authority.

soul, *see* **life**

spirit, *see* **life, holy spirit**

Temple

The Temple in Jerusalem was planned by David (*c.* 1000 BC) and built by his son Solomon as the central sanctuary for all Israel. After reforms under Hezekiah and Josiah in the seventh century BC, it was destroyed by Babylon in 587 BC. Rebuilding by the returned **exiles** began in 538 BC, and was completed in 516 BC, initiating the 'second-Temple period'. Judas Maccabaeus cleansed it in 164 BC after its desecration by Antiochus Epiphanes (167 BC). Herod the Great began to rebuild and beautify it in 19 BC; the work was completed in AD 63. The Temple was destroyed by the Romans in AD 70. Many Jews believed it should and would be rebuilt; some still do. The Temple was not only the place of **sacrifice**; it was believed to be the unique dwelling of YHWH on earth, the place where **heaven** and earth met.

Torah, Jewish law

'Torah', narrowly conceived, consists of the first five books of the Old Testament, the 'five books of Moses' or 'Pentateuch'. (These contain much law, but also much narrative.) It can also be used for the whole Old Testament scriptures, though strictly these are the 'law, prophets and writings'. In a broader sense, it refers to the whole developing corpus of Jewish legal tradition, written and oral; the oral Torah was initially codified in the Mishnah around AD 200, with wider developments found in the two Talmuds, of Babylon and Jerusalem, codified around AD 400. Many Jews in the time of Jesus and Paul regarded the Torah as being so strongly God-given as to be almost itself, in some sense, divine; some (e.g. Ben-Sirach 24) identified it with the figure of 'Wisdom'. Doing what Torah said was not seen as a means of earning God's favour, but rather of expressing gratitude, and as a key badge of Jewish identity.

word, *see* **good news**